P7-DXY-056

60

FARRAR
STRAUS
GIROUX

SISTERS

Sisters

The Lives of America's Suffragists

Jean H. Baker

ⓜ Hill and Wang

A division of Farrar, Straus and Giroux

New York

Hill and Wang
A division of Farrar, Straus and Giroux
19 Union Square West, New York 10003

Distributed in Canada by Douglas & McIntyre Ltd.
Printed in the United States of America
Published in 2005 by Hill and Wang
First paperback edition, 2006

The Library of Congress has cataloged the hardcover edition as follows:
Baker, Jean H.
  Sisters : the lives of America's suffragists / by Jean H. Baker.— 1st ed.
    p. cm.
  Includes bibliographical references (p.   ) and index.
  ISBN-13: 978-0-8090-9528-5 (hardcover : alk. paper)
  ISBN-10: 0-8090-9528-9 (hardcover : alk. paper)
  1. Women—Suffrage—United States—History.   2. Feminists—United States—
Biography.   3. United States—Politics and government—1865–1933.   I. Title.

JK1896 .B35 2005
324.6′23′092273 B—dc22

                                                        2005005722

Paperback ISBN-13: 978-0-8090-8703-7
Paperback ISBN-10: 0-8090-8703-0

Designed by Jonathan D. Lippincott

www.fsgbooks.com

1 2 3 4 5 6 7 8 9 10

For my children:
Susan, Scott, Rob, and Jenny

Contents

SISTERS

Introduction

The leaders of the American suffrage movement have lost their private lives. Of course we remember their public ones, at least fleetingly in awkwardly inserted paragraphs in textbooks or as brief episodes in the reform movements of the 1840s and the 1890s. We recall as well their final success in 1920 when the Nineteenth Amendment delivering the vote to women was ratified. Certainly monographs recount the strategies of the suffrage organizations in depictions of the headquarters history of this second American revolution for freedom. There are as well impressive biographies, often by relatives, describing the individual experiences of suffrage women, though in the more benighted versions these women emerge as dehumanized saints. With such a past it is no wonder that when the suffrage leaders are remembered at all, they are homogenized into stiff icons of feminized democracy. We conflate them into one middle-class overweight white woman with a severe look, hair unflatteringly pulled behind her ears, dressed in a high-necked black dress with a lace collar and cameo pin for decoration.

There are none of the lifelike paintings by Gilbert Stuart or Rembrandt Peale that breathe patriotism into the faces of the founding brothers and that have so enhanced modern-day remembrances of Washington, Hamilton, Franklin, and Jefferson. To be sure, the founding sisters had neither the time nor the money nor the ego to sit for their portraits. Later generations of activists, more cognizant of the uses of publicity, sought to place physical remembrances of the suffragists in public places such as the U.S. Capitol so that they might become part of the nation's historical imagination. Usually the results were unsuccessful. In 1921 when a statue of Lucretia Mott, Susan B. Anthony, and Elizabeth Cady Stanton was finally accepted by a bemused Congress, the women were indistinguishable. Congress promptly dubbed the statue "three women in a tub" and consigned it for a half century to the basement. Even the unsuccessful effort to have a suffrage sister permanently join the founders on that most popular of all material objects—the currency of the nation—foundered. Sacagawea, a Native American woman available to represent two inequalities, has now replaced Susan B. Anthony on the seldom used and manifestly clumsy gold dollar.

Heeding the call of modern feminists that the personal is the political, what follows is an attempt to retrieve the private lives of the suffrage leaders and to integrate their stories into their public work for women's rights, and especially the vote. The five women considered in *Sisters: The Lives of America's Suffragists*—Lucy Stone, Susan B. Anthony, Elizabeth Cady Stanton, Frances Willard, and Alice Paul— did not exist in a vacuum without family, friends, lovers, and companions. They had childhoods and parents as well as tempers and illnesses. In differences that emerged from their personal circumstances, they disagreed over many issues, just as their shared convictions and the hostility to their cause nurtured a sense of sisterhood.

What they shared as sisters, besides a support of suffrage, was their leadership, optimism, stamina, and remarkable longevity. Lucy Stone died in 1893 at seventy-five years of age; Elizabeth Cady Stanton in 1902 at eighty-seven; Susan B. Anthony in 1906 at eighty-six; Alice Paul in 1977 at ninety-two. Only Frances Willard died in her fifties, though a half-century's life span for her generation was hardly an abbreviated one. During most of their lives each ran with an iron hand the organizations that she had founded. Authoritarian and opinionated, as virtual oligarchs they created and retained authority, and while they appreciated the need for a "galaxy" of grassroots female supporters to fight for suffrage, they also understood the necessity of an unassailable hierarchy in the early stages of the women's movement.

There were other prominent suffrage leaders, but I have chosen these five because I believe them to be indispensable. Not only did they found and lead the national organizations that served as surrogate political parties for women before 1920, they also provided a network of leadership that shaped the goals of this first wave of American feminists. The excision of these women's private lives has often made it seem that the politics of organized suffrage summarized the entirety of their existence. For them the political seemingly became the personal. Indeed the fact that their private lives have so thoroughly leached into the fight for suffrage represents a muted, but continuing, stereotype about political women. Baldly stated, public women must be denied private lives.

I believe that one reason we so often overlook the suffrage crusade, beyond the general invisibility of all women's past, is that we have no sense of its leaders' personalities and temperaments, their love affairs and their sexuality, their homes and friendships. Americans easily recall the personalities of Washington and Jefferson, as well as their foibles even to dental problems and preferences in clothes. But they have no sense of the suffragists who suffered marital infidelities, battled to retain their femininity even as they were pelted by eggs during their speeches, worried about their children, and wondered, in the eternally unresolved battle for all working women, how to balance family responsibilities with time-consuming activism. To the extent that all history is biography, we need a collective profile of the suffrage leaders.

Certainly the cause these women served deserves more attention. The consent of the governed is the most important aspect of the history of American freedom, the latter an inheritance from England begotten in our national version during the Revolution and the subsequent writing of the American Constitution. The battle for votes for women became a struggle, albeit today largely uncelebrated, for the civil rights of half of the American population. In 1848 at Seneca Falls, New York, the first generation of suffrage sisters, amid their own fears as well as the ridicule and suspicion of their families and friends, moved from the privacy of their homes to engage in a public campaign for the vote. It was a struggle that lasted nearly three-quarters of a century—so long in fact that there is no one single suffrage generation as exists for the founding fathers. Instead historians of women's history must refer to decadal waves of feminism.

At the time votes for women was the most radical of their demands, but it was not their only one. They targeted injustices against women that ranged from overturning the automatic, court-imposed child custody rights bestowed on fathers to establishing equal educational opportunities for girls. They fought for dress reform at a time when conventional clothes imprisoned women, and they supported women's equal pay for equal, and even comparative, work.

Lucretia Mott, the quiet Quaker from Philadelphia, believed that the resolution at Seneca Falls in 1848 demanding the vote would make them seem foolish, although calls for controlling their wages as married women or a single sex standard evidently would not. Mott was right. In the nineteenth and early twentieth century, as the historian Ellen DuBois reminds us, giving women the vote threatened men because it overturned their control not just in public arenas where exclusion from the electoral process testified to female inferiority, but in their homes where husbands and fathers continued to rule. In the nineteenth century voting enacted the process of personal sovereignty. It established virtue and linked men to the primordial national value of a government based on the consent of the governed. Today voting hardly seems a radical enterprise, but it is only in the late twentieth and early twenty-first century that women's struggle for the essential democratic transaction can be seen as a chimera.

To make their claims for freedom in the public sphere, these women employed a language and vocabulary well known in their times—that of the American Revolution and especially of the Declaration of Independence. In the conventions that followed Seneca Falls and that for decades represented their collective voice, they resolved, in language first used by Elizabeth Cady Stanton, that in a government that denied women the vote "all laws which place [woman] in a position inferior to that of man are contrary to the great precept of nature and therefore of no force or authority." This was Stanton's addition to the convictions of the founders: liberty was a natural right for all humans, the Constitution's first phrase, "We the people," included women, suffrage was inseparable from freedom, and taxation without representation was cause for rebellion.

Stepchildren of the Enlightenment, the sisters of suffrage were also the half children (having been excluded from any participation in its councils) of organized religion. Especially Anthony and Paul drew on the imbedded sensibilities that Quakerism inspired—resistance to conformity and assertion of the power that the internal light of God's grace provided to those who challenged custom and habit. Methodism, meanwhile, instructed Willard in the useful pursuit of conversions and the discipline of missionary work, the latter ever so slow and full of obstacles. All of these women, except Paul, were also schooled in the antislavery campaigns of the 1840s where they first discovered each other along with a compelling example of their nation's oppressions. When as sisters in the cause, they began crusading for their own freedom, their task was nothing less than converting the entire United States to what most Americans thought a repellent, unnecessary purpose.

By the 1860s their efforts had congealed into a battle for the vote, which is not to say that they ever abandoned their crusades for other civil rights. But like all radicals, the women of suffrage and the strategies they employed were grounded in their times and their place. They suspended their suffrage work during the Civil War for patriotic reasons, and after the war, the emancipation of slaves and the efforts by Congress during Reconstruction to amend the Constitution in order to protect black males influenced their approach. In what they called "a new departure," suffrage leaders claimed the ballot as an entitlement of the explicit citizenship clause granted in the Fourteenth Amendment. Accordingly they tried to vote. In fact Susan B. Anthony actually cast a ballot in the presidential election of 1872, though it led to her prosecution for a felony.

In another legal case, the 1873 Supreme Court decision in *Minor v. Happersett*, a ruling as important to women's rights as the Dred Scott decision was to those of blacks, voting was decoupled from citizenship. According to the Court, the Constitution did not confer suffrage on women. The United States had no voters; the right to extend or withhold the ballot rested entirely with the states. Females might be citizens of a special variety, but that did not mean they held political citizenship and could vote. For Stanton and Anthony such a ruling returned the United States to its pre–Civil War past when the states were sovereign. "We really have no right as yet to call ourselves a nation, as the Supreme Court decision is in direct conflict with the idea of national unity," Stanton chided a Senate committee in 1878. Yet the implications of the ruling meant that suffragists must continue the tedious effort of securing the vote state-by-state.

In the last decades of the nineteenth century, while they never surrendered the conviction that voting was their natural right as Americans, suffrage leaders moved to another position: the vote was an instrument to change women's lives and simultaneously to improve America. With the vote, women could end barriers at state universities; revise the marriage, child custody, and divorce laws that Susan B. Anthony and Elizabeth Cady Stanton believed enslaved them; and in the process clean up the neighborhoods and party politics of the United States. If the suffrage as a natural right argument implied women's equality with men, the instrumentalist approach was freighted with the sensibility that women were different. This difference was usually developed in the context of women's superior moral development. "Woman," said Susan B. Anthony in 1876, "needs the ballot as a protection to herself; it is a means and not an end. Until she gets it she will not be satisfied, nor will she be protected."

By the 1870s suffragists had developed two national suffrage organizations run by women—the American Woman Suffrage Association founded and led by Lucy Stone and the National Woman Suffrage Association founded and led by Elizabeth Cady Stanton and Susan B. Anthony. Two decades later these two associations merged into the National American Women Suffrage Association. But until Alice Paul's National Woman's Party in the twentieth century, both employed only the feeble weapons of outsiders denied the essential political tool in a democracy. Having no votes, they used their voices, pens, legs, and minds to petition, lecture, write pamphlets and articles, and increasingly lobby both state and congressional committees. They organized newspapers, most notably Stone's *Woman's Journal*, and they held the movement together through the friendships that turned them into sisters with a cause.

The suffragists fought against an opposition that at first paid them no attention. Gradually when the logic and justice of their cause moved through a previously closed door of opinion into the vestibule of acceptance, their opponents took notice and began to circumvent their efforts by legal and constitutional maneuvers. In time success led to an organized opposition of men and women, and suffrage became one of the few reforms ever rejected by some of those whose lives it would improve. To the chagrin of Stone, Stanton, Anthony, and Willard, critics made the case that women did not want the vote. Therefore, went this easy dismissal, why give it to them?

By 1900 only four states—all in the West and all accepting women's suffrage because of special circumstances that had little to do with its justice or usefulness for women—gave women the right to vote. Another nineteen states had limited suffrage, permitting female voting only in elections for school boards and city officers. Given the attractions of this restricted ballot, it became an open question within the ranks—with Anthony always opposed—as to whether to accept the partial ballot or demand complete suffrage. No matter what the opportunity, during the nadir of the movement from 1885 to 1910, the suffragists traveled ceaselessly across the United States to increase the number of states where women could vote. Often they failed, but in the process they publicized their cause.

The federal nature of the U.S. government and the tangled jurisdictions over state and national authority complicated this endeavor. Suffragists had to engage the issue wherever it appeared—in South Dakota and Wyoming in 1890; in New York and Kansas in 1894; and back to both in the twentieth century. Ever optimistic, suffrage leaders always believed that suffrage was just over the horizon and if they lost in California as they did in a hotly contested referendum in 1896, then they would win somewhere, sometime. From 1896 to 1910 during the Progressive period when more acceptance might be assumed, they won no new suffrage states. Of six state referenda, all lost. It was indeed a time to try the patience of patriots' souls, but the sisters reminded themselves that if suffrage did not come in their lifetime, it would come in that of their daughters and nieces.

Carrie Catt, one of the movement's leaders, testified to the human exertion of this solely female crusade:

To get the word male out of the Constitution [required] fifty-six campaigns of referenda . . . 480 campaigns to get legislatures to submit suffrage amendments to voters; forty seven campaigns to get state constitutional conventions to write woman suffrage into state constitutions, 277 campaigns to get state party conventions to include woman suffrage planks, thirty campaigns to get presidential party conventions to adopt woman suffrage planks in party platforms and 19 campaigns with 19 successive congresses.

In every case, at least until a few Western states granted women the right to vote, they necessarily appealed to an all-male electorate. And after 1883 when Frances Willard pushed the Woman's Christian Temperance Union (WCTU) to support suffrage, suffragists faced the powerful liquor lobby.

The difficulty of a state-by-state strategy encouraged support of a federal amendment. Introduced in 1878 and first debated on the floor of Congress in 1887, the Susan B. Anthony Amendment gradually became their cynosure, though Lucy Stone and her daughter Alice Stone Blackwell continued to focus on states. As Anthony had written in what she hoped would become the Sixteenth Amendment, but which, there being other national priorities, became the Nineteenth Amendment, "the right of citizens of the United States to vote shall not be denied or abridged by the United States or by any state on account of sex." A notable weakness for the success of the amendment was the fact that suffragists had no core of supporters inside the halls of government. Both propertyless males in the early decades of the nineteenth century before universal white male voting was achieved by 1824 and male slaves in the 1860s had advocates in the halls of public power who shaped the opinions of others. For years women had only themselves and a stray senator or two.

It took a new generation of suffrage sisters to complete the work of what had begun in 1848. Alice Paul, a demure Quaker who learned her militancy in England as a student, with her friend Lucy Burns formed the National Woman's Party (NWP) in 1915. Employing an array of confrontational tactics, she embarrassed Woodrow Wilson's government during World War I when the president, in his idealistic fashion, held the banner of democracy aloft as a rallying point for postwar European governments as well as the explanation for American involvement. But as members of the NWP pointed out, Wilson was doing nothing to promote democracy in the United States. The comparison was a compelling one. Unlike her English counterparts, Paul did not throw stones or burn golf courses. But she did picket the White House and after being arrested and force-fed, she provided the suffrage movement with a galvanizing episode of heroism. In 1919, after Wilson capitulated and gave his support to the Anthony Amendment, it passed Congress. By August 1920 it had been ratified by three-quarters of the states. Approximately twenty-six million American women were enfranchised in time for the presidential election of 1920.

What follows is the private and public story of five women—Lucy Stone, Susan B. Anthony, Elizabeth Cady Stanton, Frances Willard, and Alice Paul. The intention is not to engage in hero worship, but rather to recover the lost lives of these sisters of suffrage and through that recovery to understand why the suffrage movement developed when and how it did. Surely if we know these women better, they will deservedly become part of the American political tradition.

1

The Martyr and the Missionary:
Lucy Stone and Henry Blackwell

By 1855 Lucy Stone had resisted the pleading of her suitor, Henry Blackwell, for three years. Ever since their chance meeting in Cincinnati when she had tried to cash a payment voucher from one of her lectures at his hardware store, he had pursued her—by letter, by attendance at the annual women's conventions (where Lucy, in her lover's eyes, always delivered the best speech), and once by arriving, unannounced, at her family's farm in western Massachusetts, where he waited several days reading Emerson before she returned from a lecture tour. "Let me be your friend and write to you occasionally," Blackwell implored, sending her long, engaging letters addressed to "Miss Lucy." "Love me if you can," he reiterated, adopting patient adoration as his courting strategy. "You may forget me if you will. I shall not forget you."[1]

By the 1850s Lucy Stone was one of the most famous women in the United States. Success as an antislavery lecturer in the late 1840s had reinforced her personal commitment to what she capitalized as "The Cause." At first Lucy had meant by that the abolitionist efforts of the American Antislavery Association to create a "thorough discontent" among Americans about slavery and the circumstances of "millions of slaves sighing for freedom." But to the chagrin of antislavery leaders like Frederick Douglass and Samuel May, Lucy increasingly inserted stories about the woman's plight in her speeches until she was told that during her lecture tours she must stick to antislaveryism on the weekends and save women's issues for her less well-attended lectures on weeknights. In 1854, on the front page of his newspaper, Douglass accused her of being willing "to say to her antislavery principles, stand aside while I deal out truth less offensive." By no means intimidated by such censure, Lucy responded that she was a woman before she was an abolitionist.[2]

"My life," she informed Henry Blackwell in a letter that might have chilled a less ardent suitor's passion, will be "an associative life . . . For myself I see no choice but constant conflict . . . made necessary by the horrid wrongs of society, by circumstances which it will be impossible to change until long after the grave has laid its cold colors over those who now live." It was the martyr's stance—her own suffering increased her identification with those whom she would free— and it became Lucy's lifelong reform habit. "The objects I seek to attain will not be attained until long after my body has gone to ashes." And like all martyrs, Lucy Stone's ideals were imbedded in personal history.[3]

Born in 1818, on her father's farm in the Massachusetts Berkshires—the eighth of nine children—she had nowhere observed the pleasant intimacies of a loving marriage, or the joys of parents in shaping their children's futures, or even the domestic security of the middle-class home that, romanticized as the female's separate sphere, served as the essential enterprise for American women. Instead this third daughter remembered her mother's plaintive and oft-repeated wish that Lucy and her younger sister, Sarah, had been boys. "A woman's lot is so hard," repeated Hannah Stone. Lucy had come to agree, as she watched her mother suffer from a drunken husband's abuse, the birth of nine children followed by the death of four, and the incessant domestic drudgery of women's work on an isolated farm. She had seen her mother beg for pin money, not for herself, but rather to buy a ribbon for Lucy or material for her older sister Rhoda's school dress. "I wish your life could have been happier," Lucy once wrote her mother, as she remembered how "ugly" her father had been about giving money to the women of the household.[4]

By the age of twelve, Lucy had absorbed a sense of duty that obliged her to run the Stone household when her mother's health failed—to milk the eight cows that were her mother's responsibility, to do Monday's washing, Tuesday's ironing, Wednesday's butter making, Thursday's cleaning, Friday's weaving, and Saturday's baking in the routinized cycle that ended only in Sunday's brief respite. It was, as she later acknowledged, "a perverse childhood."

Lucy's father, Francis Stone, was a hard man—as durable (he outlived his wife by four years) and impenetrable as his last name. On the nights when he and his friends drank rum and hard cider in the family parlor, Lucy and her sisters learned to avoid "his laying on the slaps," especially when he ordered them down to the cellar to bring up yet another bottle of liquor.[5] And later when Stone turned to the church to stop his drinking, he refused to pray with Lucy. In this family there would be no joyful conversion of the kind popularized across the United States during the religious revivals of the Great Awakening. "He told me he would not pray, that he felt like the lions when Daniel was in the den, his mouth was shut . . . and when I asked him if he thought it was the angel of the Lord that shut his mouth, he did not know what it was." Never would the proud Francis Stone bare his soul to the daughter who challenged his beliefs on the position of women.[6]

While Hannah Stone and her daughters had no context for any improvement in their circumstances, Francis Stone did, in the way of fathers whose ancestors had fought in the French and Indian Wars, the American Revolution, and in Stone's case, Shays' Rebellion. He was ambitious for his sons and sought for them something beyond his own life of relentless toil, first in a tannery and later on the farm outside of West Brookfield where he kept chickens, cows, and pigs and raised alfalfa and oats. Although he had little formal schooling himself, he paid for his sons' education in Maine and later their college tuitions at Amherst; he subscribed to the *Massachusetts Spy* and the *Antislavery Standard* so that they might envision the world beyond the rocky promontory of Coy's Hill. There his 145-acre property ended, though neither the view nor his expectations for his sons did. In his will he left his land and money disproportionately to his sons, for he expected his daughters to be supported by their husbands. Sarah, his youngest daughter, was outraged by this favoritism, but by 1864, when her father died, Lucy did not expect otherwise.[7]

For years the rebellious Lucy clashed with her father, even as she tried to gain his attention by good works, serving as a surrogate house-keeper, doing well in school, and even helping to repair his home-made shoes. "There was only one will in my family and it was my father's," Lucy Stone remembered, and it was a will enforced by insults and physical force. For a lifetime she blushed at the memory of his cruel comparison of her round face in its heaviness, rough texture, and shape to a blacksmith's apron. It would light no sparks, he said, wondering aloud whether his daughter with the large mole above her upper lip, unlike her pretty sister Sarah, would ever find a husband among the local boys who were the only ones she knew.[8]

Lucy retaliated. When the congregation of the West Brookfield Congregational Church debated the issue of whether women should speak in public as the South Carolina–born abolitionists Angelina and Sarah Grimké were doing in their lecture tours, Lucy embarrassed her father by insisting on voting, as no other woman did. Again and again she raised her hand for the affirmative, until the pastor finally rebuked her. Women might be church members, Deacon Henshaw instructed, but they were not voting members. In the end the congregation voted to accept the pastoral letter written by the leaders of the Congregational Church that condemned Angelina Grimké's lecturing. Women violated biblical edict if they spoke in public. The reason given was that the character of any woman who spoke in public became unnatural—too independent and "overshadowing of the elm." Later when Lucy lectured in the West Brookfield meeting hall, her father, humiliated that any daughter of his would speak in public and even more heretically on the rights of women, buried his face in his hands. Still it pleased Lucy that a father who once called her a slut had come at all.[9]

When Lucy proposed to her parents that she attend Oberlin College in faraway Ohio, Francis Stone refused to help. So she began a campaign to pay her own way, teaching in the district school for sixteen dollars a month, selling chestnuts and berries, and sewing shoes in the piecework household economy that still prevailed in western Massachusetts. Sometimes she took one of her mother's homemade cheeses to market and bargained for the highest price. It took nine years to save the necessary seventy dollars for the first year's room and tuition at Oberlin, but the process educated Lucy Stone in the uses of patience and determination. Having arrived at college in the summer of 1843 after a lonely five-hundred-mile journey by railroad to Buffalo, and then by steamer across Lake Erie to Cleveland (where she slept on deck), and finally by coach to the small town of Oberlin, Ohio, twenty-five-year-old Lucy proudly reported that, "in the words of Father I passed muster."[10]

But the battle was not over; indeed, for Lucy Stone, the struggle never ended. Now she must find the means to pay her tuition and board for her remaining years at Oberlin, though her crowded daily schedule required that she rise at four in the morning, attend recitations of Latin, Greek, and algebra after breakfast, write compositions in the afternoon, and study in the evening. Her father was so impressed with her hard work that he agreed to a fifteen-dollar loan the next year, with the stipulation that it must be promptly repaid after Lucy graduated. With this in mind, on Saturdays Lucy cleaned homes for three cents an hour and taught reading and writing to a class of African American men, some former slaves, for twelve and a half cents an hour. Her students, at first, were outraged that their teacher was a woman.[11]

Since its founding in 1833 Oberlin College had pioneered interracial coeducation, awarding degrees to both white women (three had graduated before Lucy's arrival) and African American men. The arrival in 1835 of a group of refugee students and faculty protesting the stifling of antislavery views at the Lane Seminary in Cincinnati reinforced the institution's commitment to abolitionism. Its faculty promoted the views of perfectionists who believed that man's sins could be atoned for by conversion experiences inspired by Christ's death on the cross. They also promoted the view that Oberlin students must dedicate themselves to the hard duty of improving self and society.[12] As Lucy wrote her sister, "you never heard such scorching, plain, personal, political preaching as we get there. Individuals are called out by name." The effect was to inculcate an approach to reform based on changing the minds of individuals who would be converted in public meetings by listening to inspired orators and prophets foretelling a better world. Thereafter the wayward would read propaganda and follow the example of ministers and reformers. Such were the means Lucy used for the rest of her life.[13]

Soon Lucy was known as a radical even among radicals. Before her arrival at Oberlin her future sister-in-law Antoinette (Nette) Brown was warned to beware the eccentric Lucy Stone, who not only read William Lloyd Garrison's abolitionist newspaper the *Liberator* but who also talked about how to end women's oppression. She deserved her reputation. Prevented from debating with the male students after reading assignments in Porter's *Rhetorical Reader* and Whately's *Logic and Rhetoric*, she organized a club for female students off-campus. Because wearing a hat in church induced the migraine headaches she suffered from throughout her life, she fought against the requirement and won the partial concession that hatless she might sit in the back of the church. For inspiration she hung in her tiny room a lithograph of Garrison, who had been jailed in Baltimore for challenging the U.S. Constitution, in its allowance of slavery, as an agreement with the Devil and a covenant with hell.[14]

There were limits to Oberlin's tolerance. Chosen by her classmates to present an essay at graduation, Lucy Stone was forbidden to read it before an audience of men and women—a so-called promiscuous gathering—although she could, as other seniors did, read it to the Lady Board of Managers and the other female students. Or she could have another graduate—necessarily a man—read her paper. Lucy acknowledged her agony, for she had worked tirelessly to place among the top students and deserved the honor. But in the end principle won and she refused to write, much less read, any essay to a gender-segregated audience. Already disposed to her lifelong habit of martyrdom, she would never, she wrote her mother, surrender her principles for some worldly honor.[15]

When she graduated in 1847, Lucy Stone was nearly thirty years old. Along with her college degree, she had absorbed essential training in the efficacy of self-help. But rather than a cause for celebrating obstacles overcome, her struggles and unremitting labor at Oberlin reinforced an earlier tendency toward the inspiration of tormented sacrifice. Disappointment became her talisman. In 1855, to a large audience in Cincinnati, she acknowledged as much: "From the first years to which my memory stretches, I have been a disappointed woman . . . In education, in marriage, in religion, in everything, disappointment is the lot of woman." She meant this as a generic comment about the fate of nineteenth-century women, but pessimism, a lifelong habit of mind, permeated her career as a reformer. Twenty years later these predispositions of temperament would drastically affect the suffrage movement.[16]

Unlike most of the women at Oberlin who expected no more than marriage and domesticity, by the time of her graduation Lucy had determined her future. She chose the controversial role of an itinerant lecturer. "I surely would not be a public speaker if I sought a life of ease for it will be a most laborious one; nor would I do it for the sake of honor for I know that I shall be disesteemed, may even be hated by some who are now friends." She would not teach school as her family hoped, but would labor for the freedom of the slave and the salvation of her sex. In biblical paraphrase, she believed that "while I hear the wild shriek of the slave mother or muffled groan of the daughter spoiled of her virtue and do not open my mouth, am I not guilty?" She sought "no life of ease or wealth . . . nor existence of ease or indolence which eats at the energy of the soul."[17]

Lucy's younger, now-married sister was astonished: "I don't hardly know what you mean by laboring for the restoration and salvation of our sex, but I conclude you mean a salvation from some thralldom imposed by men." Sarah, unlike her sister, did not feel "burdened by anything man has laid upon me, be sure I can't vote but what care I for that? I would not if I could." Besides their brothers and husbands would "as quick legislate for the interests of their wives and sisters as their own." Sarah ended with an unequivocal, "Father says you better come home and get a schoolhouse."[18]

Sarah was expressing two positions that by the end of the nineteenth century became the most popular arguments of suffrage opponents: women did not want the vote and in any case husbands, fathers, and brothers represented the public interests of women and children. For the rest of her life Lucy Stone contested such traditional thinking about the oppression of women and the insufferable ways females were treated in their homes. She had learned both in her own home.

Clearly the life of an itinerant antislavery agent and women's rights advocate precluded marriage. Years before her graduation from Ober-lin, Lucy had fathomed that marriage, like all institutions, from polit-ical parties to the church and colleges, favored men, giving women neither status nor protection. Yet for nearly all women, marriage was their entirety, with its incessant childbearing, running of the house, and deference to husbands for whom the fact of having a wife was merely an incident. For Lucy Stone a wedding meant a loss of iden-tity, the physical revulsion at marital sex, and intellectual suffocation in the prison of an isolated home. She knew that she would lose her name and the good money earned from her increasingly popular lec-ture tours. (In 1854 she earned nearly five thousand dollars.) But most of all she would lose the ability to serve the cause of women's rights that she once likened to raising a daughter with its opportunities for ceaseless attention and worry, but gratifying, purposeful hard work.[19]

Well before Nette Brown married Henry's brother, Samuel Black-well, she shared with Lucy the period's intimate female world of love and affection, with its kisses, embraces while watching sunsets, and long talks in bed. It was a world that had no need of men. "Well, Lucy," Nette agreed, "so you think more than ever you must not get married & there will be a lesson of truth to be learned from our very position which will be impressed deeply on the minds of the people as any we have to teach. Let us stand alone in the great moral battlefield with none but God for a supporter . . . Let them see that woman can take care of herself & act independently without the encouragement & sympathy of her 'lord & master' that she can think & talk as a moral agent is priveledged to. Oh no don't let us get married."[20]

The Marriage

But charming Henry Blackwell with his long black hair, sky-blue eyes, sparkling white teeth, and abolitionist sentiments persisted. Mar-riage, he told Lucy, did not have to involve the submission of wives. Certainly he sought no such arrangement and would in fact repudiate supremacy for a "true" marriage with an equal. She need not "feel as though *martyrdom* would demand *refraining* from marriage." Well aware of Lucy's penchant for sacrificial advocacy, Henry encouraged her lecture tours, and even offered to organize them. He would not impede what she called "a vagrant life," nailing her own posters to the trees, living in dirty boarding houses, riding from town to town in uncomfortable buckboard buggies, and everywhere suffering ridicule. With misgivings, he even accepted Lucy's adoption in the early 1850s of the controversial bloomers. Outraging men, Lucy, along with a handful of other women including Elizabeth Cady Stanton and Susan B. Anthony, briefly replaced their tight-laced corsets and inhibiting long dresses with more practical short skirts and comfortable trousers.[21]

By staying single, in Henry's view, she was punishing herself worse "than the Southerners treat their Negroes." "I don't think that either you or I should be less efficient together than separate. Above all I do not believe that we were created only for results ulterior to ourselves. We have a right to be happy in and for ourselves, if not what a stupid thing to make other people happy." Just as a doctor could treat smallpox without infecting himself, so, argued Henry, Lucy could reform marriage without denying herself its pleasant intimacies. "Will you permit the injustice of the world to enforce upon you a life of injustice?" As her husband he would dedicate himself to introducing Lucy to the love and affection of happy families like his own.[22]

While never offering the standard male promises of protection, which Lucy would not accept anyway, Henry intended to share her reform activities. And he would also tutor her in the "literary culture" about which she knew little—his first gift was a volume of Plato. As Henry Blackwell intended to bring freedom to slaves and women, so he would serve as a missionary to his wife. He would bring her the happiness and good humor of his sunny personality; he would sing and tell stories; and he would prove wrong her ideas about a husband's impediment to her life's work.

Still Lucy Stone resisted, explaining in the veiled language of the Victorian that sex revolted her, a natural enough concern given her mother's mental and physical deterioration following her repeated pregnancies. For Lucy sex inevitably diminished women's lives because it led to childbirth. When the ever acquiescent Henry delicately suggested that he would place few demands on her, she remembered her mother's advice that a young man's vows were quickly forgotten when women became wives.[23]

Soon Lucy offered other reasons to turn Henry away. Men, she argued, were more immature than women of the same age, and she was, given the conventions of the age, a shocking seven and a half years older than he. She felt even older than that: "Harry, excessive toil and excessive grief gave me a *premature* womanhood so that I expect a premature physical decay." When he protested that she overestimated "the natural defects of [her] being" as well as the consequences of the differences in their age, Lucy repeated her life's task: ". . . I do contemplate with proud satisfaction, my lone struggle with Destiny . . ."[24]

As Henry Blackwell worked to batter through this wall of objections, she held firm, believing, as her suitor did not, that the true reformer lived solely for external causes. "I have been all my life alone. I have shared thought, family and life with myself alone . . . all you are does not come near my ideal of what is necessary to make a marriage relation." Meanwhile Henry (now "Harry" to his "dearest Lucy" after a meeting in Niagara Falls in the fall of 1853) insisted that his idea of marriage was one that required no sacrifice of her public life. "I would not have my wife a drudge . . . I would not even consent that my wife should stay at home to rock the baby when she ought to be addressing a meeting or organizing a society. Perfect equality is the relationship . . . I would have . . ."[25]

In the end deeds, not words, changed Lucy Stone's mind and altered her future life as a reformer. In September 1854, as a member of the Western Antislavery Society, Henry Blackwell heard of a fugitive eight-year-old slave girl's forced return through Ohio to the slave state of Kentucky. It was a time of furious contention between Northerners and Southerners over the issue of slaves escaping north. With the comparison of the recent Jerry Burns Rescue in Boston fresh in his mind, Henry rushed to board the train carrying the young girl back to the South in Salem, Ohio. While her owners protested that the child was a slave and therefore their possession, he led the girl to freedom. But Ohio was not Massachusetts. In the incident's aftermath Henry Blackwell lost business, was harassed by proslavery factions in Kentucky and Tennessee that placed a ten-thousand-dollar bounty on his head, and was threatened with indictment for violating the recently passed Fugitive Slave Act of 1850, which made it illegal to help slaves find freedom in the North.

Now Lucy Stone was smitten. As other American women looked for a display of their intended's love—perhaps a piece of jewelry or a long chaste engagement—Lucy Stone fathomed Henry's commitment to her in his Salem rescue. "Many who are not capable of a noble action themselves do yet respect all the more those who are," she wrote. "What an exciting scene it must have been." A rescue was different from her persistent and routinized reform activities, which required long tedious trips. "How much of intense thought feeling and action were crowded in that little space of time. What a change in one human destiny!" The rescue was enough to secure her affection and to end what even Lucy now understood as "the barren desert of an unshared life." "I do so love you," she wrote shortly before their marriage. "My heart warms toward you all the time. I shall be so glad when it becomes possible for us to be ever together."[26]

They were married on May 1, 1855, at Lucy's home in West Brookfield. From its beginning until Lucy's death thirty-eight years later, the Stone-Blackwell marriage was unusual, but this day its external trappings, though not its substance, were conventional. The thirty-seven-year-old bride wore a silk dress the color of rose ash and cried like the country girl she once said she was. Her friend, the well-known abolitionist and ordained minister Thomas Higginson, arrived from Boston with flowers to preside over the service. For his part, Francis Stone grumbled that his daughter thought she was too good "for anyone in these parts." And the father of the bride predicted that all would not be sunshine in this, as it was not in any marriage. A hearty wedding breakfast of steaks, veal cutlet, and wedding cake followed the service, and then the bride and groom rushed for the train to New York and a honeymoon spent with various members of the Blackwell family.[27]

But as the ceremony began, its alterations of standard practice became obvious. First the groom read a long protest against marriage. The document rejected all the traditional marital iniquities giving husbands "the unnatural superiority" that Lucy emphasized in her lectures, and it made the Stone-Blackwell wedding one of the most unusual in nineteenth-century America. Henry also renounced all his exclusive legal rights as a husband and the word *obey* was omitted from the service. Henry gave up the custody of his wife's person; his "absolute" right to her money and property and their children; and he also delivered to Lucy the right to determine "when and how many children they would have," thus surrendering the sexual prerogatives over wives assumed by most American husbands in an era when marital rape was a contradiction in terms.[28]

Higginson, a veteran of antislavery and feminist crusades, placed the Blackwell protest in the *Worcester Spy*. Other newspapers copied it. Many responded with insulting doggerel about Lucy:

> *Hold your tongue you chatterbox*
> *Do let the men alone*
> *We sink beneath the stream of talk*
> *Rolled out by Miss Stone*
> *Ah would that Lucy Stone were married*
> *And had a house to care*
> *Will no one sacrifice himself*
> *To save us from despair*
> *Who with a wedding kiss*
> *Shuts up the mouth of Lucy Stone.*[29]

Like many American women and more than most, Lucy Stone suffered from marriage trauma. She knew nothing about sex, although there is a suggestion in her family history of sexual abuse by Francis Stone of his wife and daughters, and victims of sexual abuse are typically mistrustful of sex. What she had learned was imparted by her youthful observations of animal behavior on her father's farm and a limited physiology course at Oberlin that hardly mentioned human reproductive organs. True, on several occasions she had corresponded with her evidently chaste older brothers Luther and William Bowman Stone who urged the "use of the generative organs only for propagation," the necessity of marriage for all men to prevent fornication, and separate bedrooms so that men "ceased to look upon [their wives] to avoid lust." And she had read Henry Clarke Wright's *Marriage and Parentage: or the Reproductive Element in Man as a Means to His El-*

evation and Happiness, in which Wright argues that reproduction was not for sensual enjoyment. Rather sex, which must never be at the "mercy of blind reckless animal passion," was "an instrumentality through which human nature may be redeemed." This was not a recipe that inspired anticipation of a wedding night or, as promptly became the case for Lucy, any enjoyment of sexual relations.[30]

Arrived in New York, Lucy met Henry's famous older sister, Dr. Elizabeth Blackwell, who was the first formally educated and trained female doctor of medicine in the United States. Despite the refusal of four medical colleges to accept her because of her sex, Elizabeth had eventually graduated from Geneva Medical College, where the students, mostly as a joke, had voted to accept her as a fellow student. Like the other Blackwell sisters, Elizabeth had reservations about her new sister-in-law whom she knew, as she wrote Henry, only in the context "of the eccentricities and accidents of the American phase of this 19th century—in bloomerism, abolitionism, woman's rightism . . ." She had disapproved of Lucy and Henry's marriage protest as a "vulgar intrusion into a solemn event . . . dragging one's personal affairs into public notice." Elizabeth Blackwell had another reservation; neither she nor Lucy would make good wives because they were married to a cause—"something that commands our first loyalty."[31] She anticipated that Henry would be an unhappy husband.

The other English-born Blackwells were no more positive in their assessment of an American woman they thought less cultured than their distinguished, if temporarily impoverished, family. Writing from London, Anna Blackwell, who disliked "Yankee women," hoped that "your future wife passes in the qualifications essential to our respect and affection," which Lucy with her plain clothes and plebeian tastes did not. But it was Sam Blackwell who best explained the adoration of his younger brother. Lucy's independence and determination reminded Henry of his much-admired older sister Elizabeth.[32]

On their wedding night Elizabeth had arranged a reception in New York for the newlyweds. But Lucy had one of her headaches and went to bed for three days. The bride reported to her mother that Henry had let her sleep: "He is very kind and good to me and thoughtful." As for Henry, no matter what his sexual anticipations, he was pleased the wedding had taken place at all.[33]

By the time Lucy and Henry arrived in Cincinnati to visit his mother, the bride had decided to keep her birth name. Remaining Lucy Stone, she advised Nette Brown, was the symbolic solution to putting "Lucy Stone to death" through marriage. But Henry's commonsense sister Elizabeth grumbled that "it was absurd not to take the name of the man you had chosen in preference to a father you had not chosen." Others understood. Elizabeth Cady Stanton, whose marriage in 1840 had preceded her consciousness of women's issues, had taken her husband Henry Stanton's surname, as did most women in the early stages of the women's movement. But Elizabeth Cady Stanton immediately recognized the significance of keeping a birth name, even if it could not yet be a married woman's legal one: ". . . When the slave leaves his first act is to take to himself a name."[34]

Through her marriage to Henry Blackwell, Lucy joined a family that empowered her in a way that her own—and indeed most others—could not have. Her husband was a member of a free-thinking, reform-minded, closely knit group of religious and political dissidents who had emigrated from England to the United States in 1832. Seven years later Samuel Blackwell, the patriarch of the family, died, leaving his widow, Hannah, with five dollars and a brood of nine intelligent and energetic children who necessarily took up the task of supporting themselves and their mother. As Henry explained to Lucy, "My father died a stranger in a strange city, leaving a widow & nine children accustomed to comparative luxury and *entirely* destitute." While Henry aspired to be a full-time antislavery advocate "speaking and lecturing as a profession," he had no choice but to work in his hardware store until he could attain "*pecuniary independence.*" None of the five Blackwell daughters married; like Lucy they enjoyed their work and independence: Anna became a newspaper correspondent and a translator, Marian a poet and the stay-at-home child, Elizabeth and Emily doctors, and Ellen a writer and artist. Elizabeth explained the sisters' ethic: ". . . even the best husbands and children require some sacrifice and woman has to yield. But true work is perfect freedom and full satisfaction."[35]

While the Blackwell women provided Lucy with examples of competent, assertive, cultured, and aristocratic females to whom Lucy often felt inferior, the Blackwell men inverted the stereotype. They were compassionate, sensitive reformers who married independent women and supported women's rights. Eight months after Lucy and Henry married, Henry's older brother Sam married Nette Brown, who was an ordained minister. As Henry summarized the male Blackwells' view of marriage: "Equality is . . . a passion. I wish I could take the position of wife under the law and give you that of a husband. I would rather submit to the injustice than to submit you to it." To be sure, the family's reversal of nineteenth-century sex roles encouraged in the Blackwell sisters a feeling of superiority to their younger brothers. Such a childhood pattern attracted Henry to the older Lucy, who reminded him of his beloved bossy sisters. Often Lucy treated him as if he were a younger brother. "Oh, you naughty little boy," was a frequent salutation to her husband.[36]

The Blackwells had learned as children what Elizabeth called "habits of unconscious independence." As a member of such a clan, Lucy replaced her own flawed family, and organized her life and ideas around the personal experiences that had always been the principal source of her feminist convictions. Lucy might be a Stone forever in name, but in affiliation, she became a Blackwell. And it was through the Blackwells and especially her beloved "Harrykins" that she would eventually find the support necessary for her defection from the suffrage establishment.[37]

Motherhood and The Cause

The future patterns of their shared lives emerged this first summer of their marriage. Harry was often away, looking after his land speculations, selling books, running the hardware store, and searching, as he would for the rest of his life, for a stable, moneymaking activity. As he wrote his younger brother George, he wanted to make enough money "to get out of business and devote [myself] to the acquiring of knowledge and the culture of all my powers and affections." But financial success proved elusive and Henry remained an absentee husband—his boyish promises of a successful venture just around the corner or even of a prompt return home as often broken as fulfilled. Still he kept his pledge of marriage as a partnership. "I asked my husband now the honeymoon is over about going to a convention. He told me to first ask Lucy Stone. I can't get him to govern me at all," wrote a delighted Lucy to her friend Susan B. Anthony.[38]

Following her wedding, Lucy immediately returned to her career in the women' s movement, giving the powerful speeches that gained her a national reputation. Admirers commented on her remarkable voice—described as pure and beautiful—and her chaste, feminine appearance so at odds with the supposed masculinity of the castigated "she-men." She spoke extemporaneously, disdaining the prepared speeches of others. But like modern politicians she depended on a set speech. It was entitled "The Disappointment of American Women," and in various emanations, though with the same introduction, it focused on the social, political, economic, and educational disabilities of women. "From the years to which my memory stretches I have been a disappointed woman," she usually began. "There is disappointment in every woman's heart until she bows down no further."[39]

For evidence, she used her personal experiences and those of the American women she had observed in her six-year pilgrimage as an antislavery agent and freelance public speaker earning fifty to a hundred dollars a lecture. Lucy Stone's journeys took her from New England through the Midwest and even into the border states of the South. Reflecting her years as a schoolteacher, her approach was didactic; her evidence impressionistic and anecdotal. Never either ideological or abstract, rather the strength of her lectures lay in their specific tales of oppression, which were immediately understood by other women who had lived similar humiliations.

American women of another century would call this consciousness-raising. Lucy termed it "appeals to the sentiments of our sisters for the elevation of our sex." Such an approach led the few men who sympathized with women's reform to note that if women did nothing but talk, the process would take forever. But before the Civil War and the organized women's movement, Lucy's speeches attracted, and influenced, many listeners. Once in St. Louis she drew over two thousand men and women, and the New York papers commented that her audiences were as large as those of the fabulously popular singer Jenny Lind.[40]

At the time there was no organized women's movement and as

activists like Lucy recognized, the presence of women on public platforms disgusted most Americans—male and female. Leaders of this early generation of feminist outsiders shared ideas and reform intentions among themselves, but they resisted any effort to create the permanent structures that in their experience inevitably became hierarchical. After working with domineering men who invariably consigned them to inferior roles in abolitionist, temperance, and peace groups, they craved egalitarianism. Observing religious and political associations as prime agents of female oppression, women, according to Lucy, were "like a burnt child that dreads the fire."

Unlike women in the benevolent associations of the prewar period, Lucy and the leaders of the women's movement met only once a year in meetings they celebrated, dating from 1850, as anniversaries. In a bow to the popular concept of individual conversion, they used the singular: National *Woman's* Rights Convention. In these annual gatherings, they passed resolutions that urged not just suffrage, but educational and professional opportunities for American women. They sought from state legislatures "statistics on business opportunities for women, including wages paid to them as compared to men." But most Americans in this decade—North and South—were becoming preoccupied with the events that by the spring of 1861 led to the Civil War. Lucy was not. "I care less and less which triumphs—freedom or slavery. In either case all the women of the land are yet subjects ruled over by the white male population," she informed her family in the summer of 1856, that dreadnought year of the caning of Senator Charles Sumner, the Topeka convention, and President Buchanan's controversial ramming through Congress of the Lecompton constitution that supported slavery in the Kansas territory.[41]

In 1857 Lucy had reason to forget the women's movement. She had finally persuaded Henry to give up his Western land speculations and settle down in the East where the couple bought a home in Orange, New Jersey, to be near the tightly bonded Blackwells. She also was pregnant. Susan B. Anthony nonetheless insisted that Lucy arrange the details of the 1857 woman's convention, which included locating a convention hall, lining up speakers, and writing and sending "the call" to reformers, most of whom lived in New England and New York. Lucy declined, and so the convention did not take place. "I expect to be a mother and so will necessarily be absent," Lucy replied to Anthony's summons. "If you are ever in my situation, you will find that swollen feet and hands and general discomforts are not good assistants in our work . . ."[42]

Anthony was provoked. Given Lucy's status as the movement's star evangelist, "a Woman who *is* and *must* of necessity continue for the present at least, the representative woman, has no right to thus *disqualify herself* for such a *representative occasion*. I do feel it is so foolish for [Lucy] to put herself in the position of *maid of all work*, and *baby tender. What man* would dream of going before the public . . . tired and worn from such a multitude of engrossing cares."[43]

In the fall of 1857 thirty-nine-year-old Lucy Stone delivered her first child. Two years later she and Henry had a stillborn son, and though Lucy once had intended to have four children—they must be twins "to dispatch matters so as to gain time"—her daughter was her only surviving child. Lucy was attended at home by Henry's sister Emily, who now ran the New York Infirmary for Women and Children in Greenwich Village. Only after months of parental indecision was her daughter named Alice, significantly not a family name, though the baby's last name was easily derived. With Lucy assimilated into her husband's family, it was Stone Blackwell.[44]

After Alice's birth, Lucy, overcome by lassitude, retired from her strenuous speaking tours. With the help of the Blackwells she temporarily became a stay-at-home mother. Seven months after Alice's birth Lucy, suffering from boils as well as a postpartum depression, remained exhausted, and Harry, away again, wondered why. Lucy responded, ". . . but Harry, no one who takes care of a baby *can* rest. I have not felt rested for months—you may take care of a baby one day and you will understand it." Migraine headaches further immobilized her, and perhaps a sufferer from what Betty Friedan called the unspoken anxiety and crushing boredom of motherhood, she was chronically depressed with what she called the "blues."[45]

Henry, an increasingly absent husband, was away seven of the first eight months of Alice's life. At the time he was traveling in the Midwest, selling some of Lucy's land for a railroad project in Wisconsin that would make him rich. But the sale of property bought with his wife's hard-earned lecture fees broke the couple's prenuptial agreement that only Lucy could sell her land. Henry explained to his angry wife that he only intended to get her "affairs into a more productive shape." He was still her "darling Harrykins," but disappointed in the marriage she had resisted so long, Lucy felt betrayed. "Will you come home Harry dear?" she wondered in May 1858. But it was months before he returned to Orange.[46]

Rarely imperious, Harry now insisted that his wife delay her return to the lecture circuit until his mother and one of his sisters could help out. Lucy agreed. Only a week after Alice's birth she had boldly traveled into New York to deliver a speech to the Shirt Sewers and Seamstresses Union. It was intended to publicize women's issues to working women, a group often sought out by nineteenth-century feminists. Yet when she returned home, Alice was sick. "When I came home & looked in Alice's sleeping face and thought of the possible evil that might befall her if my guardian eye was turned away, I shrank like a snail into its shell & saw that for these years I can be only a mother— no trivial thing either."[47]

It was a difficult time. Lucy struggled with financial problems and her sense of failure as a wife, as well as the chagrin of abandoning her popular lecture tours. Henry's absences, as he traveled around the country engaged in a number of mostly failing enterprises, heightened her feelings of martyrdom. Nor did she provide what Henry began to call "a more normal life," by which he meant not only his presence at home but the sexual relations about which Lucy remained hesitantly prudish. Given her perfectionist ethic, Lucy tried to improve. "I am trying to be a good wife and mother. I have wanted to tell you how hard I am trying. But I have tried before and my miserable failures hitherto make me silent now. I hope to be more to you and better," she bleakly informed her husband.[48]

Some of the problem rested with her enforced retirement from the cause. Intermittent participation was a necessary strategy for married reformers. It was the reason that women's conventions met only once a year. Unlike the organizations of men, whose mobility made a formal structure easier to maintain, a national movement for women could only be accomplished, in its earliest phases, through letters and casual visits among the believers who were also mothers tending babies and running households. So Lucy stayed home with Alice, her

domesticity coinciding with the Civil War when the women's movement funneled its energies into ending slavery and restoring the
Union. But she suffered. "I don't believe I could live shut up with Alice in a suite of rooms all next winter," she wrote in 1864.[49]

Henry's sisters were not impressed with the Stone-Blackwell household and especially Lucy's domesticity. They believed that if women
wanted to be independent, they must remain single. Lucy and Henry,
wrote Marian to her sisters, "are so engrossed in woman's rights especially in its political bearings that they are busy, restless and preoccupied. There is no home atmosphere about them. There is never the
shadow of peace or domestic enjoyment."[50]

Lucy was available to preside over the first meeting of the
Women's Loyal National League organized by Anthony and Stanton
and held in 1863 in New York. There she supported a controversial
resolution that, linking slaveholders and "the aristocratic interest,"
connected to both a system of political oppression practiced on
"slaves, all citizens of African descent and all women who are placed
at the mercy of legislation in which they are not represented." But
Lucy had only limited time for the traditional women's work of seeking signatures for a petition urging black emancipation by means of
the proposed Thirteenth Amendment outlawing slavery. As a disenfranchised woman she also refused to pay her local taxes, and in the
family story, lost even Alice's cradle in the public auction of her property to settle the state's claim.[51]

Meanwhile most of the female Blackwells were engaged in the
Union cause that overshadowed women's issues. Lucy's sisters-in-law
Elizabeth and Emily organized a contingent of two hundred nurses
who served the Union army in Virginia and Hannah Blackwell
scraped lint for wounded soldiers' bandages. As for Lucy, "as I do all
the work—cook, wash, iron, sweep, dust *everything* and teach Alice an
hour a day, I get little time." She was biding her time until the re-
sumption of the battle for her rights.[52]

Postwar Strategies and Challenges

After the Civil War ended in 1865, Lucy Stone did not have to wait long. Pulled along in the trail of efforts to give black males citizenship, the women's movement narrowed its focus to issues of political freedom and specifically the vote. This new strategy did not mean that other efforts at legal equality were abandoned, but it did mean that women's suffrage became a priority. Sometime during 1865 Susan B. Anthony visited Lucy to map future plans. Then in 1866 Lucy and Henry rushed to Washington where Congress was debating the Fourteenth Amendment that would make black males citizens and extend to them due process and the equal protection of the law. Of particular concern for women reformers, the proposed amendment's second article introduced the word *male* for the first time into the previously sex-blind U.S. Constitution. The couple lobbied the renowned supporter of human rights, Massachusetts senator Charles Sumner, who offhandedly announced that he had been up all night trying to resolve the problem of women's citizenship, but could not find a way.

In the ensuing struggle over the ratification of the Fourteenth Amendment former allies deserted the women's movement. There was time and energy for only the efforts to achieve black male citizenship, went the argument, and so the antislavery coalition separated from the women's movement. This division spurred a period of national organization among women who now came together over the single issue of suffrage.[53]

The new focus of women during Reconstruction was a response to an activist national government's use of public policy to change the circumstances of former slaves. Women like Stone now appreciated the vote not only as a universal American entitlement, but as an instrument of political reform. Before the war enfranchising women had been one among several demands for women's equality; after the war the vote came to subsume other issues, like the cowbird that lays its eggs in other birds' nests. As popularized for black males, votes for women would be a key, unlocking the doors to other reforms. More palpable and concrete than amorphous discriminations such as unfair pay and more conservative than demands for equitable divorce laws and a single sex standard, universal voting seemed to this small band of sisters an American promise made by the Founding Fathers when they wrote the Declaration of Independence and the U.S. Constitution.

In the spring of 1867 Lucy and Henry began the trips that would take them throughout the United States. Filling their trunks with 250 pounds of documents and leaving ten-year-old Alice at home with her Blackwell aunts, they journeyed to Kansas where one of the first postwar state suffrage referendums took place in the fall. Once in Kansas, they traveled all day and lectured every night in churches, schoolhouses, and courthouses, "sometimes at noon too," everywhere passing out literature. So arduous was their schedule that it was in Kansas that Henry believed Lucy lost her beautiful voice. They kept their daughter well informed about a crusade that would be her inescapable legacy. As her father described, "We are trying to get little girls made as happy as little boys and we expect to succeed."[54]

But in Kansas strains in the prewar sisterhood increased. Before the war Stone had opposed Stanton over divorce reform, which Stone believed connected the women's agenda with free love, but which Stanton, in a less egalitarian marriage, considered essential. Stone also argued that marriage reform was not exclusively a women's issue and therefore required a separate organization. On one level these were disagreements of style. Stone was always more conservative than Stanton and Anthony on social issues. And when Stanton and Anthony also came to Kansas, traveling about the state with George Train, she was outraged. A railroad promoter and merchant who wore purple vests, Train race-baited at a level unacceptable to even nineteenth-century Americans. "Carry negro suffrage," Train told audiences in Kansas, where he spoke more often against blacks than for women, "and we shall see some white woman in a case of negro rape being tried by 12 negro jury men."[55]

Ever prudish, Lucy was offended by Train's crude racism. Her husband's version was more acceptable. In his pamphlet *What the South Can Do*, Blackwell argued that white Southern males should support women's right to vote because enfranchising white women would dilute black male suffrage. In what became a popular prosuffrage argument targeted at the South, Henry explained: "Your four millions of Southern white women will counterbalance your millions of negro men and women and thus the political supremacy of your white race will remain unchanged."[56]

The fissure between Stone and Stanton-Anthony deepened. While Stanton and Anthony remained nonpartisan, Lucy followed her husband in his support of the Republicans who could be identified, however tenuously, with support of black freedmen and so for Lucy, it was the Republicans who seemed a more promising affiliation as suffrage moved into the political arena. But Kansans were not swayed by party appeals. White male voters defeated both women's and black suffrage by three-to-one margins—with black suffrage receiving a thousand more affirmative votes (of thirty thousand cast) than women's suffrage.

During the months when Lucy was engaged in her increasingly divisive struggle with Stanton and Anthony, Henry was having an affair. The fracture in Lucy's marriage became the private backdrop for the split in the suffrage movement, a simultaneous fulfillment, in both her personal and public life, of her own suffering. In the late 1860s Henry had become involved with Abby Hutchinson Patton, the attractive wife of the wealthy financier and real estate broker Ludlow Patton. Abby Hutchinson Patton was famous in her own right. Eleven years younger and far more beautiful than Lucy, she was a member of the famous singing Hutchinsons, a family group that participated at antislavery and women's conventions. Stone, Blackwell, and the Pattons were friends in New Jersey, and Henry had briefly worked in Ludlow Patton's office on Wall Street.

Lucy's initial reaction to her husband's wandering into what was probably a sexual affair but may have been no more than a boyish romantic attachment is lost, though she did acknowledge in letters to her family "a terrible time." For a woman who detested any discussion of sex, who despised the contemporary symbol of sexual freedom, Victoria Woodhull, who believed her sister-in-law Elizabeth's writing on female sexuality impure and unnecessary, and who adamantly refused to include divorce in her reform agenda, Henry's cheating was a special humiliation.

Henry's relationship with Abby Patton was long lasting and obvious enough to draw a flurry of commentary. Lucy certainly knew about it, appealing to Henry's sister to "keep Harry away from [Patton's] office. It is not good for him to go there or take up the old snare. He is yet too near the old foils to escape if he lets himself come within their reach . . ." Of course she wished he would stay away—"but what will be will be . . ." concluded a resigned Lucy. Within the family the Blackwell sisters shared the news of Henry's philandering. Marian referred to Henry's "unhappiness." Emily wrote to Elizabeth, who was now living in England, that "Mrs. P. wants to terminate her relations with Harry." Elizabeth responded that she was grieved and disgusted. By late 1869 the news was better: "The relationship with Mrs. P. is dying out but he injuriously and foolishly keeps up Lucy's discomfort by refusing to terminate it." As the romance fizzled, Abby Patton publicly consoled herself with some lugubrious poetry, publishing *A Handful of Poems* in which she confessed to an anonymous love.[57]

News of Henry's probable adultery spread through the ranks of the reformers, some of whom were already aware of the tensions within the Stone-Blackwell marriage. While Henry had betrayed his wife, life with a woman to whom sex was a duty and marriage a sacrifice was often depressing. Given Lucy's style of martyrdom and sacrificial instinct and Henry's motive to demonstrate his financial acuity as well as his hope for some acknowledgment of his exceptional egalitarianism, perhaps his affair with a younger, more pliant and acquiescent woman was inevitable. But Henry was too important to Lucy to permanently disrupt this marriage. Her marriage might be flawed but to Lucy, all institutions were similarly marred. It was her job to improve them. Lucy's very sense of life as a painful duty, which had driven the two apart, now helped restore the marriage. And in time Lucy Stone and Henry Blackwell were again "Lucykins" and "my darling" to each other.

Later Lucy accepted her husband's physical, if not his sexual, restlessness. When he began another of his failed business projects, this time in beet sugar, she wrote as he left for an indeterminate stay in Santo Domingo in 1872: "You need to be free; You need change, variety, sunshine and birds in a larger sphere." Throughout their marriage Henry was an enthusiastic missionary not just for reform and his businesses, but for his status as a loving husband. In turn his absences and business failures rendered Lucy ever more the martyr.[58]

As solace Lucy directed her energies to the suffrage movement. In May 1869 she presided over a contentious American Equal Rights

Convention, the latter a postwar coalition of reformers who supported universal suffrage for blacks and women. At the time Congress was debating the Fifteenth Amendment, which would enfranchise only black males. A Stanton-Anthony resolution to oppose such an exclusive right led to a counterproposal when Lucy sought an impossible compromise: "We are lost if we turn away from the middle principle and argue for one class. Woman has an ocean of wrongs too deep for any plummet and the negro too has an ocean of wrongs that cannot be fathomed. There are two great oceans. In the one is the black man, in the other is the woman. But I thank God for the 15th Amendment and hope it will be adopted in every state." Her sense of martyrdom charted her course. "I will be thankful in my soul for anybody who can get out of the terrible pit."[59]

Voting to support a resolution in favor of the Fifteenth Amendment, Lucy accepted the argument that, in the words of Wendell Phillips and Frederick Douglass, "this is the Negro's hour." Douglass went further than Lucy, arguing that any concern for women's rights was a trick of the enemy "to assail and endanger the rights of black men." In this version of the similarities between an inferior gender and an inferior race, Douglass and some former allies of the women's cause held that black males needed suffrage for protection from white Southern males; women, less threatened and more controversial as voters, could wait. Stanton and Anthony, enraged by such a casual dismissal of women's need for security, promptly condemned the Fifteenth Amendment.[60]

Earlier Stone had agreed. She, Stanton, Anthony, and eleven other women had sent to Congress a petition demanding an "amendment of the Congress that shall prohibit the several states from disfranchising any of their citizens on the ground of sex"—a negative grant, to be sure, but one that preceded the Fourteenth and Fifteenth Amendments. As late as the winter of 1869, Lucy had opposed anything less than universal voting, noting the "strange blindness" that had overtaken those who previously supported female suffrage. She compared legislators who would not support women's suffrage to the men of the American Revolution who had promised to eradicate slavery, and for the sake of compromise during the writing of the Constitution, had continued it.[61]

Abruptly Lucy changed her mind. "Do not let us interfere with the real claim of our cause by allowing the enemy to suppose we are fighting the very principles we are seeking to establish." Still she felt "dreadfully hurt by this new load we have to carry, and there is no need of it." Lucy even forgave Sen. Charles Sumner for his decision not to help the women's cause. It was a blow, but "we should be grateful for what he has done directly for human rights . . . If Mr. Sumner doesn't want to be in this fight . . . in my heart I say God bless him. Our government is sure to come around and I can endure anything but recreancy to principle." But her opponents would make just this claim—that Lucy was being disloyal to the cause.[62]

In a burst of activity, in part to forget the agony of Henry's affair, Lucy Stone contacted her friends in the New England Suffrage Association, wrote supporters, convened the Massachusetts Suffrage Association, and encouraged the interested to come to a convention to be held in Cleveland that fall. Even as Stanton and Anthony organized their National Woman Suffrage Association (NWSA), Lucy marshaled her competing group—the American Woman Suffrage Association (AWSA). Henry, with all the restless exuberance he still commanded at forty-four, became a principal architect of this organization. It served as an avenue for his reconciliation with Lucy.

In 1870 Stone and Blackwell, well aware of the significance of a paper affiliated with their organization as *The Revolution* was with the Stanton-Anthony National Woman Suffrage Association, purchased Mary Livermore's *Advocate*. Renaming it the *Woman's Journal*, they transformed it into a more conservative paper than the short-lived *Revolution*. Ever enthusiastic, Henry rushed to New York to solicit subscriptions from old friends in the reform community like William Lloyd Garrison, Samuel May, and Theodore Weld. Selling some of their profitable properties in the West, Lucy and Henry purchased twenty shares at two hundred dollars apiece and five shares in Alice's name. Finally Henry had an occupation that would keep him at home and according to his sister Emily, "away from Mrs. P. . . ."[63]

After hiring female typesetters Lucy moved the press—and her family—to Boston, away from New York, the home of the rival National Woman Suffrage Association and far away from Abby Hutchinson Patton. At first Henry resisted. But soon he saw the matter differently, especially after his wife's ultimatum that she would move without him. When his sister Elizabeth wrote to ask him his progress in finding permanent work, he acknowledged he had made none, asserting "that I am less in earnest to find a field of activity of my own because the practical effect of doing so would be to separate us almost entirely." Like his wife and daughter, he labored on this journalistic family endeavor, raising money, soliciting advertisements, and writing articles for the weekly paper with Lucy doing most of the work.[64]

The continuity of the *Woman's Journal*, which was published from 1870 to 1917, its consistent coverage of the suffrage battles and other women's issues, and, for a time, its growing circulation were among Lucy Stone's significant accomplishments. But the paper had other uses. Nourishing Lucy's need for hard work and her associated sense of martyrdom, the *Woman's Journal* became, as Lucy once lamented, "a big baby always having to be fed and never growing up." For a woman so comfortable on a speaker's podium but so uncomfortable as a writer, it remained a perpetual punishment.[65]

Managing a weekly paper interfered with Lucy Stone's few recreations. It made impossible a first journey overseas for a Blackwell reunion in England in 1879. Henry, Alice, Sam, and Nette went anyway, and Henry could only commiserate with his wife's unimpeachable sense of duty. Summer trips to the Blackwell compound on Martha's Vineyard were often curtailed because someone, usually Lucy, had to remain in Boston to put out the paper. "Nearly everybody here has quartered for the summer by the sea and or in the mountains," Lucy wrote in the hot summer of 1876, "but if we left the *Journal* would stop." The "we" was an editorial one, for it was she alone who stayed in town.[66]

For over twenty years, when she was not on a suffrage trip, Lucy traveled daily on the train or horse cars from her home on Pope's Hill to her office on Tremont Street in downtown Boston, which also served as the headquarters of AWSA. An ineffable sense of duty learned years before prevented the kind of spontaneous glee and leisured amusements that her husband enjoyed. At an abolitionist reunion that took place in the late 1880s at her home, a stern Lucy, eyes averted from the camera, as was usually the case in her photographs, stared off to the side, lost in contemplation of that better future for women that had been the principal aim of her life. "Your father," she once told Alice, "should have married someone less grim."[67]

The paper also kept Henry at home, at least some of the time, in the family's fine new seventeen-room, twenty-thousand-dollar house overlooking Dorchester Bay, and to the west the blue-tinged hills past Milton. Here Lucy came to enjoy a domesticity that had eluded her mother. Henry raised vegetables and fruit and experimented with currant jelly. Lucy cultured her own yeast, canned her husband's produce, and presided over the cleaning and maintenance of a large establishment that included domestic servants as well as the long-staying adopted and natural children of the Blackwells. In the dining room was a long oaken table—itself a symbol of the size of this extended household. It accommodated a never-ending list of visitors—some family, others suffrage workers, still others workers from the paper. In a diary kept "to sift myself out and find what there is of me," Alice remembered her mother's conscientious "stewing, boiling, frying, baking, roasting, fricasseeing," as well as "mama's hard load—the *Journal* every week, the general supervision of the suffrage cause in Massachusetts, the care of this big place, and out planning what we are to eat three times a day, keeping an absent-minded daughter clothed and in running order . . ."[68]

Raising this bookish, wryly humorous daughter and instilling Alice with the ethic of hard work and dedication to women's issues was an essential part of Lucy's and Henry's life. Alice, who favored the Blackwells in looks, was separated from her schoolmates by her introspective personality and her parents' commitment to suffrage. In Alice's world her fellow students were divided into the few who supported suffrage, the some who did not care, and the many who were opposed. The latter, well aware of her famous mother, teased Alice for this difference. "I do wish I could have a little fun like the other girls," Alice once wrote even as she plaintively wondered why she was not invited "to things sometime."[69]

At her mother's insistence Alice attended coeducational schools. Both parents considered Boston's high school for girls an inferior institution that did not prepare its students for the college education they intended for Alice. At Boston's Chauncy Academy, fifteen-year-old Alice was one of fourteen girls among 250 boys—"a watermelon among peaches," she wrote. Later at Boston University, she was one of two women in a class of twenty-six. At stake in these choices was the quality of schooling and the competition, not the associations with boys. In fact Lucy's advice—"If you show boys any attention they immediately think you want to marry them"—directed Alice to be fearful of men.[70] So too did Lucy's public attitudes: her mother's campaign to force the dean at Boston University to remove salacious material from the required classics "that makes a modest girl blush and schoolboys giggle" and replace it with the kind of expurgated texts she had used at Oberlin, her outspoken contempt of Grover Cleveland (who acknowledged a daughter born out of wedlock) as a "male prostitute," and her distaste for Victoria Woodhull's ideas about sex.[71]

On these matters, as in few others, Henry Blackwell contradicted his wife, exhorting his daughter to break loose of the Blackwells and their tradition of not marrying. "Be on the lookout for a good fellow," Henry unsuccessfully encouraged Alice. With his five unmarried sisters in mind, Henry worried that Alice would pass into some "heritage of single blessedness which is so unnatural and unlovely as any other kind of convent and nunnery." But Alice would remain single, living at the end of her life with Kitty Barry, the unofficially adopted daughter of her aunt Elizabeth.[72]

Organizing for The Cause

The American Woman Suffrage Association that Stone founded in 1869 differed from its rival, the Stanton-Anthony–led National Woman Suffrage Association, in ways that revealed the differences between the two groups' leadership and strategies. At the same time there were tactical similarities that represented a common grounding in the women's movement of the 1850s. From its beginning in the fall of 1869 Lucy insisted that the AWSA be a federal organization based on auxiliary state organizations that elected delegates to an annual convention. Such an approach meant exhausting appeals in every state and territorial legislature and a movement at odds with efforts for a federal suffrage amendment. "Suffrage," wrote Henry in a signed article in the *Woman's Journal* in 1882, "is a question altogether outside of federal jurisdiction, expressly reserved to the legislatures and peoples of the respective states." The Fifteenth Amendment was, according to Henry, an exception adopted only as a result of the Civil War and carried with such extreme difficulty that it made the adoption of a women's suffrage amendment seem impossible.[73]

Lucy's organization reflected her ideals and personality. It would be what she was—dignified, conservative (even if in a radical cause), and single-minded. She required that delegates to her annual convention be dues-paying members, elected at the state level. No unofficial fellow-travelers like Victoria Woodhull, the Gilded Age's goddess of free love, would infiltrate the AWSA. The American, she promised, would not take positions on peripheral matters such as the notorious trials of women like Laura Train, who was accused of murdering her husband, or Hester Vaughan, who was prosecuted for infanticide. Her rivals, Elizabeth Cady Stanton and Susan B. Anthony, used the trials as illustrations of the legal injustice to women. For their part, Lucy and Henry declared, "We will keep our platform free from controverted theological and social types."[74]

But if its support of the Fifteenth Amendment, its inclusion of men (Henry Ward Beecher was its first president and Henry Blackwell was a member of its executive committee), and its base in Boston differentiated the American from its rival, the National, in its approach to getting the vote, the American depended on the same techniques. Outsiders often had trouble distinguishing between the two. Both organizations published tracts, documents, and other printed material for circulation to local societies, legislatures, and Congress. Lucy dubbed suffrage literature, which of course included the *Woman's Journal*, "the best little missionaries we have." Both the National and the American were overwhelmingly composed of middle-class white women, and as time went on, neither made an effort to appeal to black and working-class women. Both lobbied the legislative committees in state and territorial legislatures. Both organized public meetings, county conventions, and lectures; both held money-raising festivals and bazaars. And for twenty-two years both resisted a merger.[75]

Stone and Blackwell saw the division as salutary. "I hope you will see it as I do," Lucy wrote Susan B. Anthony in the fall of 1869, "that with two societies each in harmony with itself, each having the benefit of national names and each attracting those who naturally belong to it, we shall secure the hearty cooperation of all the friends of the cause, better than either could do alone." Disingenuously, she added, "So far as I have influence this society will never be the enemy of yours."[76]

Lucy was too optimistic. The division—for which Lucy was largely responsible—led to a duplication of energies in a movement that was numerically small and organizationally limited. A united suffrage effort would have led to cost-efficiencies in the running of a single newspaper, the writing, printing, and dissemination of pamphlets, and the centralized organization and recruitment of lecturers, especially in the West. Very few women were drawn into the suffrage movement because they believed the Stanton-Anthony National organization was too radical and found in Lucy's American an alternative. Arguably the competition between the National and the American inspired more (but not necessarily better) publicity and spurred the leaders of both to try to attract new members. Certainly newspapers did cover both groups. But usually this attention was trivialized, and marked by critical references to the "hens at war."

There were psychic costs to the division as well, although Stone denied that personal animosity had created the split. Still she told anyone who would listen that Anthony was selfish and egotistical and Stanton high-hat, though bright and witty. (Her daughter, Alice, was even more outspoken, describing Anthony as "tall, sharp, dictatorial, conceited, pugnacious and selfish—also plucky.") Armed with the searing anger of grudge holders, Lucy sought to keep her organization free from infection by "the dreaded incubus" of the Stanton-Anthony forces who believed Lucy too coldly sanctimonious to be a successful suffrage leader. Such judgments found their way into the newspapers and fueled the stereotype of women as gossiping backbiters. Even on the eve of a reconciliation in 1890 Lucy referred to the women of the National as her "late enemies. We don't know that they are our friends."[77]

Without the Blackwell family, it is doubtful that Lucy Stone could have challenged Stanton and Anthony. It was not just Henry's penitential service; it was also the inspiring lives of his sisters, who were

not so much prosuffrage as they were examples of independent
women. In fact only Henry and Sam, who were married to suffrage
advocates, supported women's rights. Expressing a judgment her intellectual sisters accepted, Elizabeth dismissed the suffrage movement as
having "energy and emotion, but no clear thought."[78]

The Blackwells—especially Anna, Elizabeth, Emily, and Sam's
wife, her sister-in-law Nette—exemplified what Lucy admired as useful lives spent "running upstream against wind and tide." For a
woman from a troubled family, these relatives provided inspiration
along with a practical and psychological sanctuary filled with resolute
women who took care of Alice, who shared their children and advice
on childraising, and who fostered the family celebrations necessary to
Lucy's sense of herself as fulfilling the traditional roles of wife and
mother.[79]

In time, Lucy and her supporters in the AWSA came to support restricted voting in school elections and municipal elections, and to
urge suffrage on the grounds of home protection—that is, suffrage as a
right that would help women participate in such matters as controlling the sale of liquor, choosing school officials, and challenging, at
the local level, legal discrimination against women. Meanwhile the
women of the National disdained any limited grants of the right to
vote such as municipal voting. Not Lucy. In 1879 she tried to cast her
first vote in a local election in Massachusetts where women could
vote for the school board, but registration officials, with neither statute
nor precedent on their side, insisted she sign the enrollment books as
Mrs. Henry Blackwell. Not even the attraction of casting a ballot
shook her commitment to her birth name.

For an activist, Lucy displayed a curious and no doubt comforting
acceptance of the dismal progress in women's rights, and this resignation separated her, in instinct, from the more impatient Stanton and
Anthony. "Woman will some day have the right of suffrage and we
must learn to wait as well. Round and round we run and every time
the right comes uppermost," Lucy wrote an uncomprehending Susan
B. Anthony who was more concerned with how soon the right would
come. "If it takes forty years to get out of the wilderness we must be
patient," Stone insisted. "Somewhere in the future equality reigns.

Your little girls and mine will reap the easy harvest which it costs so much to sow." Even in the 1880s a fatalistic Lucy signed herself "yours in the certainty that we are farther along in battle than we were."[80]

There was need for patience. In the postwar period suffrage referendums lost in the five states that held them. By 1869 only the territory of Wyoming had voted suffrage and when it came time for delegates to write a permanent state constitution in the late 1880s, the Wyoming convention nearly overturned the suffrage article. By 1892 only four western states—Wyoming, Idaho, Colorado, and Utah—had universal suffrage. For reasons of expediency (the specifics of which differed in each state) and not from arguments of moral or political justice for women, all had accepted a change the rest of the country rejected. In the face of such blows Lucy characteristically took the long view.[81]

The American Woman Suffrage Association achieved its greatest influence in the 1870s. But even then Stone's enthusiastic projects for Liberty Leagues to survey candidates' positions and suffrage clubs to lobby individual voters in each community had floundered. Of the twenty active state societies, only the one within reach of Lucy—the Massachusetts Suffrage Association—and that in Iowa did not lose members during the 1880s. "I don't think the American can continue much longer," Lucy admitted.[82]

Not only was the American Woman Suffrage Association too poor to keep more than one agent in the field, but in a rare statement of the degree to which the organization depended on her family, Lucy Stone acknowledged that "it was too much for Harry and me to lift it bodily as we have." With the circulation of the *Woman's Journal* declining, revenues from subscriptions no longer even covered expenses during this nadir of the entire suffrage movement, which had a special impact on the AWSA.

Lucy Stone did not give up. She had begun as an itinerant proselytizer and so she remained, working tirelessly on two fronts—first to sign up affiliate societies and then to get women's suffrage into state constitutions. Despite her arthritis and a chronic throat problem, she spoke to the increasingly numerous state legislative committees on suffrage—themselves a sign of glacial change—and to the Senate and

House Judiciary Committees in Washington. Alert to the importance of publicity, Stone depended on letters to the editor of other papers to convey her ideas.

She visited the state societies on which the American depended. She organized the annual conventions that took place in Western cities rather than, as the National had come to favor, in Washington. And especially in Massachusetts where she incorrectly anticipated general suffrage in her lifetime as opposed to school board or municipal voting, she spoke at women's clubs and lobbied individual state delegates, keeping careful count of the legislators' preferences. She used her traditional commonsense arguments with politicians, once reminding a state legislator that the Massachusetts legislature had brushed aside women's suffrage after a half-hour discussion, while it spent several hours debating the proper size of a cranberry barrel. Even when Alice began to take the family albatross of the *Woman's Journal* off her shoulders, Stone continued to write editorials and news reports for the paper.[83]

Well aware of her national reputation and its crucial role in the survival of her suffrage organization, Lucy Stone continued to rely on the slogans of American democracy which, after nearly a half-century's struggle for rights for women, had become tattered vestiges of her hopes. Characteristically she recalled her personal encounters with discrimination—the time when she had refused to pay her New Jersey taxes because she was taxed and voteless and the Orange County constable responded by ordering the sale of her furniture, including Alice's cradle, to pay the assessment; the time when she and her mother-in-law had marched to the polls in New Jersey only to have the official tear up their ballots; and the time when she had invested in some property and Henry had had to sign the deeds.[84]

Like all nineteenth-century American women Lucy Stone had accumulated a storehouse of personal examples of the discrimination practiced against women. Such episodes displayed the denial of what she had always considered the bedrock guarantee for all Americans—the consent of the governed. Without such a protection the whole panoply of oppression against women—in marriage, in the home, in jobs and professions, in the courts, and even in the church—would continue. For Lucy the ancient rationalization that men represented women was a fiction, writ large. Her sister Sarah's point, argued years before, that their brothers would never legislate against the interest of their wives and sisters was ridiculous, in Lucy's mind. Only women would protect the interests of women.[85]

A propagandist rather than a philosopher, Lucy never tried to unravel the implications of the doctrine of separate spheres that, in any case, she held subject to change and definition by each woman. She believed in natural rights, but she also expressed the contradictory conviction that women were the moral guardians of the nation. Nor did she ponder the relation of separate spheres to liberal assertions about the equality of individuals, although by the 1870s Lucy valued home and motherhood as central to every woman's life. As she told Alice before she died, "the truest place for women is in a home with a husband and with children and with large freedom, pecuniary freedom and personal freedom."[86]

Finessing such dilemmas, she hewed to the classic inspirations of the American Revolution. "I have no country and no hope of a country. Nowhere can I take my child and be protected in my God-given rights as a mother. I never hang up the flag as our object of veneration. I never bow down to it. I never sing 'My Country 'Tis of Thee.' " To prove the point, in 1876 she urged women not to participate in any centennial celebrations, organizing instead a women's Boston Tea Party. "The Declaration of Independence belongs to men. Let them have their masculine glory all themselves . . . let us get a church and toll the bell."[87]

While Lucy Stone avoided the angry racism of Stanton and Anthony, she nevertheless supported the nativist call for political restrictions on immigrants—the "wild Irishmen"—to whom she would deny suffrage until they had been in the United States for twenty-one years. Only in that length of time could these men learn American ways and the democratic values that native-born American women had learned in childhood.

Final Years

Sixty-one years old in 1879, "old, lame and blind and stiff" but still an activist, Stone never failed to answer the call, either to the American's annual conventions or increasingly in the late 1870s and 1880s to the West where the suffrage movement's best opportunities lay. She and Henry traveled to Colorado in 1877 where an amendment to the constitution was defeated. When she came home, she wrote a fellow suffragist: "I am so tired in body and soul it seems as though I shall never feel fresh again . . . [It is] the tired of a whole life." Nearly a decade later, with the "arthritis like a knife digging into my joints," she longed for "younger hands for personal release from the work. It is time to rest." But even as she suffered, Lucy Stone found sufficient energy to campaign in Michigan, Ohio, Indiana, New Jersey, Nebraska, Iowa, Rhode Island, and Washington State—and as well to resist any overtures to join with the National.[88]

So too did Henry. In the style of the Blackwells, he had become a missionary for the movement. He lobbied the Republicans at their state and national conventions for a votes-for-women pledge; he delivered his suffrage speeches throughout the United States; and he carried the word to aspiring politicians and office holders. In 1884 Henry obtained a pledge from the Massachusetts Republican Party to extend the vote on equal terms to all American citizens irrespective of sex. But when the same resolution was presented at the Republican National Convention, those who had earlier approved a women's suffrage plank voted against it. In its place the Republicans expressed only their "obligations" to women.[89]

More so than his wife because she was a natural-born pessimist, Henry Blackwell was often discouraged. From Washington State in 1889 during one of his extended trips came his report: "I am chafing under slow and tedious lobbying which I have to do single-handed and alone. If I leave all will collapse. If I stay, we may succeed." He stayed and won this battle, although like much of the work during the 1870s and 1880s this was a limited victory. For there was little chance that the state legislature, empowered with the right to make the addition to the constitution, would do so. As Lucy and Henry had learned, referendums were an even more difficult method of getting the vote than statutes passed in state legislatures. And as for a constitutional amendment, its support by the National was one of the tactical barriers separating the two organizations.[90]

From Montana in 1889 Henry Blackwell reported that "the women care nothing about the suffrage. It would be a good case for the remonstrants," referring to those who opposed suffrage on the basis that women did not, in fact, want the vote. From Olympia, Washington, came word of his "good speeches to very small and uncultivated audiences." In Kansas he fulfilled a lesser "mission" when that state's Woman Suffrage Association voted almost unanimously to affiliate with the American rather than the National.[91]

From everywhere he sent his love to the increasingly crippled Lucy, assuring her he thought "of his dearly beloved" every day. Often absent from Boston both as an indefatigable accredited ambassador from the AWSA and in pursuit of his fanciful business ventures, Henry had nevertheless kept his vows to be a full-time partner in his wife's crusade and to follow his wife's call "to be useful." Lucy praised him for this: ". . . for the abundant and unselfish work you have done for women . . . few men could have done it, leaving business, friends, pleasure for it."[92]

To be sure, as was the case with most members of his family, Henry Blackwell had always been a reformer who sought to convince others to free their slaves, give up marriage rights that enslaved wives, and especially after the creation of the AWSA, give women the vote. Still his suffrage exertions were also an act of contrition. "I know I have tried you in a thousand ways," he once wrote Lucy," but most of all by not being able to show you the sincere good will I have had. If it had been necessary I would have died for you at any time, but it is far harder to live so as not to wound and grieve the heart of the one that loves one. Neither you nor my mother can fail to have found in me much to forgive, but I can never forgive myself." It was an extraordinary confession from a man who was apologizing not only for his affair with Abby Hutchinson Patton, but for his absences and his failure to be what he had always promised—a successful businessman and dependable breadwinner.[93]

Over the years, the Stone-Blackwell relationship had mellowed. "It takes absence to make us know how much we love those who belong to us," wrote Lucy of her husband of twenty-two years. And two years later in 1879 on their twenty-fourth wedding anniversary, an occasion on which they were more often apart than together, Lucy remembered "how long we have jogged on pulling together. Well, the last part has been much the best for me." At the same time that she began to pamper her restless husband in a marital style her mother would have recognized, Henry became an admiring witness to her martyrdom: "You have overexerted yourself all your life. You have missed meals when in the city, broken up the good and settled habits of your life, and curtailed your sleep."[94]

Even as the American Woman Suffrage Association declined, Lucy continued to resist any overtures for merger with the National, finding differences rather than commonalities. With an implacability learned years before as a disciple of William Lloyd Garrison, who believed in no union with evildoers, Lucy Stone refused to consort with enemies who, she thought, supported free love, lobbied polygamists, and had "lunatic friends" and "wild alliances" with the likes of Victoria Woodhull and George Train. She also refused to participate in the writing of a history of the suffrage movement initiated by Susan B. Anthony, Elizabeth Cady Stanton, and Matilda Joslyn Gage, the first volume of which appeared, it might seem prematurely, in 1881. With a sure sense of the importance of the historical record, Stanton had earlier written Stone—"my olden time friend"—requesting a biographical sketch as well as the history of her American Woman Suffrage Association. Lucy acidly responded in a letter addressed to Mrs. Stanton: "The history of women's rights can't be written by anyone who is alive today. Your wing surely is not competent to write the history of our wing nor should we be competent to write the history of our wing even if we thought it best to take the time while the war goes on." Never did Lucy write the story of her organization or indeed of herself, and as a result both were slighted.[95]

It was Alice who finally convinced her mother that the time had come for reconciliation. "The younger ones want to unite and the old ones who remember the causes of division will soon be gone," admitted Lucy in 1890. And it was Lucy's emissaries—her husband, Henry, and her daughter, Alice—who over a three-year period negotiated the compromise constitution that brought the two wings of the suffrage movement together in the last decade of the nineteenth century. Lucy was too ill to attend the first meeting of the combined National American Woman Suffrage Association (NAWSA) in Washington in 1890, but Henry and Alice, who was elected corresponding secretary, served as delegates.[96]

In these last years of her life, Lucy glanced backward and by comparing the past with the present perceived the gains of forty years. Such was her topic for the fortieth anniversary of the first National Woman's Rights Convention held in Worcester in 1890 and her last important speech. Within her lifetime, Stone informed her audience, she had seen some progress. She and other women of her generation could recall ducking stools for disobedient wives, churches preventing female members (she herself) from voting, voting privileges denied women even in school elections where twenty-two states now extended that limited form of suffrage to women, the refusal of state legislatures to protect married women's property rights, every woman's legal existence obliterated by courts and statutes, and most higher educational and professional schools closed to women.

She remembered as well the denial of free speech to women who spoke in public by those, her father included, who condemned such women as "sluts." She recalled sticks and stones and once a hymnal hurled at her back. She had seen a woman forced to sleep in an outhouse after bearing three daughters to a husband who wanted a son. Impelled by instincts of sacrifice and glad to "have lived at a time when I could serve," Stone described a lifetime journey along the pathways of the women's rights movement from its tentative beginnings among the itinerant public speakers who began to include messages to women in their antislavery speeches in the late 1840s to its mature expression in the national organizations that had developed after the Civil War. "We first had to prove that a woman had any rights before we could specify the distinctive one of the ballot," she concluded.[97]

In 1893, after a summer of anorexia and vomiting, seventy-five-year-old Lucy Stone died of stomach cancer. She refused the iron pills and quinine capsules recommended by her sister-in-law Edith, correctly suspicious that they would in any way improve what she knew to be a terminal illness. "I am not going to be cured. I don't want to be cured. The kindest thing you can do is to let me pass on." Her friends

came to pay their final visits, though Lucy had always believed, with
the sanctimoniousness of which she was capable, that "a high consciousness of right has been more to me than friends." When Julia
Ward Howe, the author of the "Battle Hymn of the Republic" and
Lucy's convert and subsequent lieutenant in the American, brought
the inaccurate report that Elizabeth Cady Stanton was also dying,
Lucy mischievously added, "Perhaps of apoplexy." And Lucy pondered the irony of her longtime enemy being "the first human being I
met on the other side."[98]

Typically, Henry was away during some of this last summer of her
life, though he was home when his wife died in October, proclaiming
her "a lion in the face of death." Earlier he had advised a new medicine that Lucy refused to take. Rather than therapies, she wanted to
straighten out their often tangled financial accounts. And so she insisted when Henry came back from his suffrage work in Kentucky that
he return the rent money from her real estate to her bank. "It is the
right way," wrote a woman whose will specified that Henry's inheritance depended on his returning the six thousand dollars in stocks
to her estate before he received his inheritance of their Dorchester
home, sixteen acres in New Jersey, and two thousand dollars. Lucy
Stone left her daughter—besides the material assets of real estate in
New Jersey, Iowa, and Wisconsin, and government bonds—a daunt-
ing familial legacy. "My brave daughter. You will go on with the work
just the same!" Her final words to Alice—"make the world better"—
were worthy of her tombstone.[99]

Yet ever an iconoclast, Lucy Stone had no tombstone. But her
death was international news. Over a thousand mourners filled
Boston's Church of the Disciples for her memorial service, although
she had never attended and was, in Alice's description, "a theist."
Henry read their famous Marriage Protest at the service after which,
in a final statement of her anticlericalism, Lucy Stone was cremated.
Making the world for women better was the secular legacy she intended. She had spent most of her lifetime campaigning for women's
rights and shaping one of the first national organizations devoted to
votes for women. Conservative in her institutional approach to suffrage, Lucy Stone nevertheless revealed radical instincts throughout
her life. She had gone to college, kept her birth name after her mar-

riage, lectured in public, and in 1869 created a suffrage organization that became the principal occupation of her immediate family. And besides her personal contributions to the suffrage movement, she left two human legacies—her husband, Henry Blackwell, who died in 1909, and her daughter, Alice. Both worked tirelessly as officers of the National American Woman Suffrage Association for the rest of their lives.

2

In the Blessed Company of Faithful Women:
Susan B. Anthony and the Sisters

In May 1852 when Susan B. Anthony, clad in what its advocates were calling the New Dress, rose to speak to the World's Temperance Convention on the evils of drink, the audience gasped. Earlier Amelia Bloomer had described a revolutionary new outfit for women in her newspaper *The Lily*, but for six months Anthony had resisted shortening her long dresses into a tunic worn over homemade trousers. But the more she traveled and lectured, the more her skirts collected mud, dragged in puddles, ripped on carriage steps, and everywhere restricted movement. So she joined the handful of antislavery and temperance reformers who had seized upon "short" dress as both a convenience and a symbol.

Not that Susan B. Anthony ever objected to dress reform. In fact she believed clothes to be just another illustration of the subjection of women. Put a woman in boys' clothes and men acknowledge her equality at work. But "array her in woman's dress and . . . her presence becomes a sensuous thrill—due to the knowledge of the difference of the sex." As she informed her friend Lucy Stone, "Women can never compete successfully with men in various industrial vocations in long skirts." Lucy agreed in theory, but she insisted that she spoke "the truth in a short or a long dress." Still both women found themselves the object of ridicule in their new bloomers. But mockery was only part of a larger problem.[1]

Every one of the handful of dress reformers in the early 1850s knew that the female uniform of ten pounds of muslin petticoats, starched shirtwaists, and tight corsets made of unyielding whale bones had hazards beyond the medical effects of strained stomach muscles, bruised ribs, and compressed organs. As Elizabeth Cady Stanton observed, "Take a man and pin three or four large tablecloths about him, fastened back with elastic and looped up with ribbons; drag all his own hair to the middle of his head and tie it tight, and hair pin on about five pounds of other hair with a bow of ribbon . . . pinch his waist into a corset and give him gloves a size too small and shoes ditto, and a hat that will not stay on without a torturing elastic and frill to tickle his chin and little lace veil to bend his eyes whenever he goes out to walk and he will know what woman's dress is."[2]

Still, reform dress brought its own dilemmas. Men whistled, stared, and taunted, "Here comes my Bloomer." Most American women associated Turkish trousers with harems and prostitutes, and adolescent boys threw eggs and rocks along with their ridicule at women who wore trousers. Commitment to the new dress began to falter when Stanton warned Anthony that "the cup of ridicule is greater than you can bear. It is not wise Susan to use up too much energy and feeling that way." But as she would in all her endeavors, the dogged Susan, who had waited months to adopt the trousers, now persisted longer than her friends. After Stanton and Stone lengthened their skirts, Anthony continued to appear at temperance, women's rights, and abolitionist conventions in the bloomer outfit. She was convinced that the humiliation of such a "mental crucifixion" was good training for those intending to dedicate their lives to ending the oppression of women.[3]

Angrily she protested desertions. "If Lucy Stone, with all her reputation, her powers of eloquence, her loveliness of character . . . cannot bear the martyrdom of the dress, who, I ask, can?" "Everyone who *drops* the dress, makes the task a harder one for the few left." Finally, the price of Susan B. Anthony's public embarrassment outweighed the private benefits of what Stanton called "two-legged dress." Exchanging physical freedom for the conformity of silk dresses with lace collars and uncomfortable undergarments, Susan, after a year and a half, was also "dragging around with long skirts." Attired for the rest of her life in demure long dresses of black or gray enlivened in her later years only by more expensive fabrics, a famous red shawl, and eventually a garnet-colored dress—all the donations of suffrage supporters—Anthony forever remembered the freedom of short skirts and their service, like a uniform, as a unifying badge of the sisterhood.[4]

By the mid-1850s Susan B. Anthony had become an important member of this sisterhood of American reformers who sought, as she explained, nothing less than "Human Rights. We need not confine ourselves to the evil that woman suffers alone, but enlarge our borders as the truth shall be revealed." She was part of the sweeping reform movements that during the 1840s and 1850s emerged everywhere in America, but mostly in the Northeast. The leaders of these humanitarian crusades, whose views were often nurtured in their churches, shared the vision that if circumstances changed, so too would the behavior of human beings and the well-being of the nation. In myriad associations they struggled to liberalize prisons and mental asylums, overturn legislation imprisoning debtors, improve schools, establish utopian societies, and care for the downtrodden. They struggled to prohibit drinking, to prevent war, and in the largest mote they would remove from their fellow Americans' eyes, to end slavery.

At first, like many reform advocates, Susan had taken on a variety of causes, all linked to women—whether temperance, which sought protection of women and children from drunken, abusive husbands and fathers; or antislavery, which worked to end the sexual oppression of black women to white masters, or women's rights, which advanced their specific agenda of issues relating to wives such as fighting for married women's property acts and automatic guardianship rights for mothers over their children.[5]

Anthony had entered the movement in March 1849 when she made her first speech to the Daughters of Temperance in the small town of Canajoharie, New York, where she was a schoolteacher. Through temperance, she became acquainted with other pioneers of the women's movement, meeting Elizabeth Cady Stanton in an epic encounter on a street corner in Seneca Falls, New York, in 1851. As Stanton recalled, "There she stood, with her good earnest face, and

genial smile, dressed in gray delaine, hat and all the same color relieved with pale-blue ribbons, the perfection of neatness and sobriety.
I liked her thoroughly from the beginning."[6]

With the unshakable optimism that she always carried along with
her battered traveling bag and knitting, Anthony became a paid agent
of the American Antislavery Society lecturing throughout New York
State. Like widening ripples in a pond, her circle of friends soon extended to other pioneers of the women's movement—Paulina Wright
Davis, Lucy Stone, Ernestine Rose, Nette Brown, and the legendary
Lucretia Mott. She met as well the men who controlled the antislavery societies—William Lloyd Garrison, William Channing, and
Thomas Higginson. As an agent Anthony, like Lucy Stone, soon
found herself spontaneously including in her antislavery talks grim
tales of "the beautiful slave girls [who are] the unwilling victims of
licentious brutal tyrants" as well as examples of northern white
women's "grievances without number." These latter included "northern girls who are betrayed into so-called marriages with polygamists
and adulterers."[7]

Susan B. Anthony had become conscious of these grievances as a
teacher in the district schools of New York. Though fully as competent, well-trained, and hardworking as her male colleagues, she
earned only two-thirds of their pay. When she audaciously rose to
protest this inequity at the annual New York Teachers' Convention in
1853 and to ask that women serve as officers of the organization, a humiliating debate arose over whether she should be heard at all. Amid
shouts of "who is that creature," she was ruled out of order. With an
instinctive understanding of the persuasive uses of the histrionic gesture, throughout the discussion Anthony had remained standing:
erect, stoical, and determined.

Years later she was still employing dramatic action in order to
bring attention to her cause. Standing in the audience at the 1876
centennial celebration of the World's Fair in Philadelphia's Independence Hall, she refused to take her seat after the reading of the Declaration of Independence. Instead, with the dignity of those blessed with
good posture, she left her seat, climbed up the stairs, and strode across
the stage to present to the stunned presiding officer, Sen. Thomas
Ferry of Michigan, the woman's version of the Declaration of Inde-

pendence. Then amid cries of "Sit Down!" "Sit Down!" "Order!" "Order!," Susan B. Anthony calmly walked back down the stairs, handing out her manifesto as she went. Outside on a bandstand erected for musicians, sheltered by an umbrella for protection from the broiling sun, Anthony and other women took turns reading their declaration with its call for civil disobedience: "We declare ourselves no longer bound to obey the laws in whose making we have had no voice."[8]

Beginnings

Susan B. Anthony had learned about injustice at home, but in a different way from Lucy Stone and Elizabeth Cady Stanton, whose fathers had spurred their daughters to rebel when they treated their sons preferentially. Susan was treated with exemplary fairness. In the Anthony household Daniel Anthony's authority was modulated by his Quaker religion, his instinctive humanitarianism, and his practical need to depend for a time on his wife's relatives for financial support. He sent his three older daughters to expensive Quaker boarding schools in far-off Pennsylvania when he could afford the expense, and he made his home into a hospitable mecca for fugitive slaves and abolitionists including Frederick Douglass. There his six children—male and female—learned firsthand the brutality of slavery. Indeed he argued so heatedly against slavery and the slave trade that his children complained that they "never saw a man so wrapped up in a nigger as Father is in Douglass." When in a letter from school, Susan worried about the fragility of life, her father responded that she should not think of death or be so deeply "afflicted about that which we cannot help." Instead she must concentrate "on doing what we can to relieve the miseries of the afflicted and improve in every way possible the condition of man."[9]

Ever an iconoclast, Daniel Anthony was twice nearly expelled from Quaker meetings for transgressions of his inherited faith. He had married a non-Quaker, sold liquor, and worn a fancy cape to meeting. Left bankrupt and debt-ridden by the depression of 1837 after years as a prosperous factory owner, with the optimism and stamina he bestowed on his daughter, Daniel Anthony moved to Rochester to try to restore his fortune as a farmer and later as an insurance agent. But no matter how hard-pressed financially, he always managed to send money to his daughter when she, on the road for the cause of slaves and women, needed it for food and board. In turn, she contributed to the family finances from her teacher's salary of two dollars a week. With duty to her family a lifetime priority, Susan B. Anthony intended to be, and always was, "a worthy daughter."[10]

Susan's mother, Lucy, taught her daughter different lessons. Lucy Read Anthony's constant childbearing—eight pregnancies and seven babies in sixteen years—and her subsequent depressions and ill health made the costs of maternity obvious to her daughter. Homebound in the fog of domesticity that required she run a boarding house and feed her husband's mill workers in the aptly named village of Hard Scrabble, New York (later renamed Center Falls), Lucy Anthony raised her children. Remembered as sad and given to unremitting toil, she nevertheless shared her husband's views on public matters, collecting food and clothes for the poor. When the women of New York organized a convention in Rochester in the fall of 1848 and passed a resolution calling on the state legislature to give women the vote, Lucy and her daughter Mary, the youngest of the four sisters, were in the audience.[11]

Later Susan B. Anthony believed that she and her brothers and sisters had neglected their retiring, self-effacing mother for their outspoken, compelling father who died suddenly in 1862. When eighty-six-year-old Lucy Anthony died in 1880 two years after a stroke had paralyzed her, Susan was devastated. "But what is a home without a mother?" she consoled a friend. "My sister . . . used to say it will always be a home as long as mother sits here in her rocking chair. It will always be home as long as dear mother lies here in her bed. For two years she was almost helpless, never fed herself, but you know and I know what an aching 'no mother' makes in our heart, glad as we may be that she is beyond suffering."[12]

Even years later after their deaths, she remembered both her parents on their birthdays and the anniversary of their death. In a diary crowded with notes on her travels for suffrage, Anthony always took time to acknowledge both with some sentimental remembrance. As her mother had become old and feeble, she worried about her absences from home. But duty overrode guilt. "I know my high regard for her and my father and sisters gone before will be best shown by my best and noblest doing." She saw her responsibility as helping the living. To a friend she gave the same earnest appreciation of the practical uses of her personal losses: "but soon I saw that the best way to reverence my father's memory was to do more and better work than ever before, and . . . those of us who remain must live and do for those who are still on this side."[13]

From the closely connected triumvirate of older sisters born within three years of each other—Guelma, named after William Penn's wife; Susan, who carried her maternal grandmother's name; and Hannah, named after her paternal grandmother—Susan B. Anthony first learned about female intimacy. Distracted by constant childbearing, nursing, and housekeeping, her mother had little time for companionship with her daughters. Instead it was Susan's sisters who consoled her when she was homesick at boarding school; it was her older sisters who linked arms with her during their neighborhood walks, made quilts with her, and shared stories of relatives and increasingly of boyfriends. And when Guelma and Hannah decided to marry, they delayed their marriages so that Susan, who was teaching miles away, could return home in time to witness their weddings. Deprived of her sisters' primary attachment—Hannah had even stopped writing when she became engaged—Susan was never certain that her future brothers-in-law, Aaron McLean and Eugene Mosher, were worthy husbands for her beloved sisters.[14]

In family lore Susan also had several gentleman callers. Throughout her life insistent reporters, even before they had inquired about the suffrage movement, always asked if she had ever been in love or, more to the point in an age in which men could not comprehend what Anthony called "single blessedness," whether she had ever had a marriage proposal. That she had rejected several offers to enter what she considered "man-marriage" did not change her stock answer: "I would not object to marriage if it were not that women throw away every plan and purpose of their own life, to conform to the plans and purposes of a man's life." No Henry Blackwell, that rare breed of man who sought equality within marriage, had ever asked her to be his life-long companion. But she had no regrets about her status, calculating that "no man could have made me happier than I have been."[15]

Her independence, intensity, and early self-consciousness about a mildly crossed eye as well as her size—she was a giant among women at nearly five feet seven inches and 165 pounds—no doubt discouraged some suitors who sought a smaller and more submissive wife. Susan did not care. "These old bachelors are nothing but a nuisance to a society, but an old maid is the cleverest creature I ever saw." And so she joined the 10 to 14 percent of the New England female population of her generation who remained spinsters. The affection and love she would never bestow on a husband and children would be reserved for her blood relatives and for her sisters in the suffrage movement. And the latter, she came to believe, were blessed companions more faithful than any husband could be.[16]

Ahead of her times, Anthony articulated the radical position that marriage must not define the female existence. In a lecture written in 1877 entitled "Homes of Single Women," she connected the aspirations of single women to those of all Americans, taking as her premise that all human beings require the same things for their happiness. "The one thing alone of all others longed for, worked for, whether the humblest cottage or proudest palace [is] a home of one's own." Precisely because significant changes in the education and training of women had occurred, Anthony held that young women had to seek independence by "scorning to be mere helpers of men." "The logic of events," she declared to audiences as well as to the journalists who called her ideas "vile and disgusting," pointed to an "epoch of single women who will not be ruled," who will not accept the dependence of boarding or living with male relatives, and who could afford homes of their own. Along with young single women she included "deserted women, disappointed maidens, widowed mothers, fugitive wives and children," all of whom did not need to depend on "a spurious second-hand domesticity affected for the praise of some man."[17]

As evidence Anthony described the cheerful, comfortable havens of her single friends: Elizabeth Phelps, Lydia Mott, the Carey sisters in Philadelphia, and her physician and fellow suffrage supporter Dr. Clemence Lozier, now single after obtaining a legal separation from a drunken, gambling husband. After 1890 Anthony could have included the permanent home she had finally established with her sister Mary. On a quiet residential street in Rochester, New York, these two single women savored their three-story brick home, surrounded by the furniture, linen, and silverware donated by their brother, Daniel, and suffrage sisters. In a letter extolling her broiled steak, potatoes, sweet corn, tomatoes, and peach pudding, Susan exulted in her role as a homemaker: "I love to receive in my own home and at my own table."[18]

Causes

That pleasant repose was years off when, in 1850, thirty-year-old Susan B. Anthony left teaching and became a rare self-supporting member of "the lecturing corps." During her struggles for equal pay for male and female teachers she experienced an epiphany—a sudden rush of understanding that her life's purpose must be "to make things better." Yet life as an itinerant reformer preaching abolition and women's rights was sometimes perilous and often humiliating. There were the empty meeting halls that meant a slim financial return for the evening's effort. Just as often, there were the disruptions from the mostly male audiences—country women being largely confined to their homes except for church. Hissing and shouted interruptions sometimes degenerated into egg-throwing, and on at least three occasions she was hung in effigy. The clergy, citing St. Paul on the need for women to obey their husbands and in Susan's case, find one, refused to open their churches for her meetings. After the lecture there was the night's sleep in a dirty hotel or boardinghouse, and the next day's travel to yet more speaking engagements on the dusty trains and back-rattling horse-drawn carriages that were hours late, came at four in the morning and sometimes got stuck in the snow.[19]

Worst of all, there was the ridicule in newspapers. Anthony was derided as "an ungainly hermaphrodite, part male, part female with an ugly face and shrill voice"; she was a "reformatory Amazon," "a maiden philanthropist who spoke on the witches sabbath," and "a spinster who knows nothing of marriage and shouldn't talk about it."

Only the companionship of other women and the righteousness of the cause made such a life tolerable.[20]

Of special importance was the mutual intimacy of the sisterhood. "I love Lucy and Nette and Mrs. Stanton yes and Lydia Mott as no other women in the movement," wrote Anthony in a letter in the late 1850s. Susan and her female circle kept in touch through meetings and letters, the latter full of the romantic passion that women of this generation expressed so openly. But Susan's expressions of affection always included businesslike details often concerning the next of the annual conventions that connected these women to one another. The meetings had a larger purpose beyond their collegiality. By holding such conventions, the women linked their movement to the founders' practices, and their annual assemblies emerged as rituals connecting them to a larger political entity.

Usually it was Anthony who chose a city for the next formal gathering, who located an inexpensive meeting hall, who raised money, and who arranged for speakers, the latter no easy task at a time when few women spoke in public. Understanding the extent and nature of the struggle before them, the sisters of the movement adopted military language: they conducted campaigns, they marshaled their troops, and as needed they deployed their "biggest gun" who, most agreed, was Elizabeth Cady Stanton. But it was Susan B. Anthony whom they labeled their Napoleon.[21]

This platoon of militant women led by Anthony was maintained over long distances and separations of time, for they enjoyed none of the permanent buildings that housed and fostered numerous men's associations. Still the women of Anthony's circle kept their friendships alive through letters, visits to each other's homes, the yearly women's conventions in different communities that proliferated in the 1850s, and especially the national anniversary meetings that, as the years went by, heightened a sense of progress. They were endlessly optimistic about victory. To Lucy Stone, Susan wrote in 1854, "is not this a wonderful time—an era long to be remembered?"[22]

What Anthony called her "all-alone feeling" born of serving so unpopular a cause was diminished when she traveled in the company of other members of the sisterhood. Particularly after the Civil War, Anthony and her small band used these journeys to be together as they gathered signatures on petitions for legislative action, a process that promoted self-confidence and solidarity. As they walked from house to house, they met battered wives whose anguished stories became the counterpart to the abolitionists' narratives of cruelty to slaves in the South. For the disenfranchised, gathering petitions, those signatures of citizenship, was not just a matter of working together. It also served as their sole means of influencing lawmakers. Only in a few states did state judiciary committees permit women to present their case for voting or changes in common-law restrictions on a wife's control of her inherited property and her wages. And only in the 1870s did a woman appear before the U.S. Senate Judiciary Committee. To her friend Lucy Stone, a patient, but ever optimistic Anthony gave the advice that all these women followed, but none so completely as she: "Lucy, do lead a long life. There is a vast amount of work for you to do; therefore be prudent, that you may have strength to accomplish it."[23]

Being prudent required staying single for Susan B. Anthony. Already a wife and mother when Susan first met her, Elizabeth Cady Stanton could not be redeemed to "single-blessedness." But when younger intimates like Lucy Stone and Nette Brown married, Susan felt betrayed. Children, husbands, and home stole time and energy from the cause, and although the rarely self-scrutinizing Anthony never acknowledged as much, removed her from a central place in these women's affections. Just months before her marriage, Lucy had sworn a timeless devotion that Susan reciprocated: "You have not more confidence in my fidelity than I have in yours . . . no not more love than I have for your intimacy." But a year later in 1855 Lucy married Henry Blackwell and left the movement to have a baby. No longer did Susan sign her letters to Lucy "In Love, Susan," but more formally, "With best love, yours truly," or "Kind regards to your husband." In a signal of what she considered an abandonment, Susan continued to refer to Lucy as Mrs. Henry Blackwell until Lucy Stone complained.[24]

The next defector, Nette Brown, married Henry Blackwell's brother, Sam, in early 1856. That same year Elizabeth Cady Stanton announced that she had "got out the sixth edition of my admirable work, another female child [Harriot Eaton Stanton] . . ." Two years later Stanton was pregnant again, famously asking Susan to come and hold the baby and "make the puddings" so that she might have the time and peace to write a speech on women's rights. Disgusted that her friend had for the seventh time embarked "on the rolling sea" of morning sickness, Susan scolded that "for a *moments pleasure* to herself or her husband, she should thus increase the *load* of *cares* under which she already groans." And she ordered Nette *"not another baby* is my *peremptory command*—two will solve the *problem* whether *a woman can* be any thing *more* than a *wife and mother* . . ." In 1873 Nette no doubt irritated Susan when, as the mother of five, she contemplated "what the balance was between my immortal five and your eighteen years of going to and fro in the earth."[25] For Susan, the answer was obvious.

When married mothers like Lucy did return to lecturing, Susan found them ill prepared. "I am *provoked* at Lucy—just to think that she will attempt to speak in a Course with such [male] intellects . . . and then as her *special preparation* take upon herself in addition to *baby cares* . . . the entire work of her house . . . I do feel that it is so foolish for her to put herself in the position of *maid of all work*, and *baby tender*—*What man* would dream of going before the public on such an occasion as the one of tonight tired & worn from such a multitude of engrossing cares—It is not best to have too many *irons* in the *fire* at one time."[26]

The marriage of friends was more than an abandonment of personal loyalty and public commitment. It involved political principle as well. At the tenth annual Woman's Rights Convention held in 1860 in New York City, with Susan B. Anthony seated in what became her accustomed place on center stage, the convention divided over whether to consider marriage and divorce laws. Many activists believed that any discussion of divorce would contaminate with its radicalism attainable goals such as the guardianship of children, automatically assigned to fathers, as well as property rights for women. Even as they debated, the New York legislature, under intense lobbying by activist women, was voting to give married women rights over their property, along with limited powers to sue and to joint guardianship rights over their children, "with equal powers, rights and duties in regard to them, with the husband." Given such progress, more conservative delegates declined to rock their fragile boat.[27]

At this convention Anthony, rendering the personal into the political, provided a rebuttal. Her convictions emerged from her decision to remain single, at first made unconsciously but then raised to a matter of public policy. "Marriage has ever and always been a one-sided matter, resting most unequally upon the sexes. By it man gains all — woman loses all; tyrant law and lust reign supreme." Unequivocally likening women to slaves, Anthony argued that "by law, public sentiment, and religion . . . women have never been thought of other than as a piece of property." She saw the solution in the vote, which, once extended to women, would force changes in marriage laws.[28]

At the time Susan B. Anthony was assisting a fugitive wife, Phoebe Harris Phelps, in escaping from her abusive, philandering husband, Charles Abner Phelps. A wealthy, Harvard-trained physician and Massachusetts state senator, the prominent Phelps audaciously entertained his lady friends in his home on Boston's Beacon Hill. Confronted by his wife, who had intercepted love letters and once interrupted his sexual encounters, Phelps had her kidnapped and committed, on the basis of her supposed delusions, to the nearby McLean Lunatic Asylum. After seventeen months of confinement she escaped and came to Susan B. Anthony for help. On Christmas day 1860, playing the role Harriet Tubman had often taken with fugitive slaves, Anthony secretly rushed Phelps out of Massachusetts. Arriving at night in New York in the midst of a snowstorm, they discovered another of the civil penalties exacted upon women.[29]

Lacking the conventional male "protector" who dressed women with respectability in public places and could be counted on to pay the bills, the two women were turned away from hotel after hotel, as proprietors violated common-law requirements to take all comers. Finally Susan refused to leave, informing the hotel owner to call the police if he wished. And after an uneasy sleep the fugitive and her protector fled southward to Philadelphia and temporary safety from a husband who, owning his wife's "person," could legally enforce her return to his home. Aiding a fugitive wife was dangerous business, but Susan's father approved: "You are legally wrong, but morally right." Such a sentiment confirmed what Susan already knew. Had she not helped Phelps, "I should have scorned myself. I remembered only that I was a human being." The Phelps rescue deepened a conviction earlier spelled out to her brother Daniel: "I would like to have the good will of all, but I wish to have right on my side in the endeavor to obtain it."[30]

A few months later the Civil War suspended the women's movement that Anthony and Stanton had nurtured during the 1850s. There had been successes; New York had changed some of its property laws discriminating against married women, though some of these advances were repealed in its 1860 session. Activists like Anthony, Stone, and Stanton had also learned how to use the nineteenth century's persuaders—oratory and speechmaking, writing and pamphleteering, personal solicitation, and petition gathering—to promote their cause. Women had begun to lobby elected officials and to understand the importance of converting opinion makers, whether editors of newspapers or public figures. Anthony especially had become an adept fund-raiser. And she had learned how to train younger women to speak briefly and loudly and wear simple solid colors on the podium so as not to distract the audience from their message.

But mostly the results were imperceptible in public policies. Still the speeches of Stanton, Anthony, and Stone along with their visits to women in their homes had shifted the views of some wives and daughters, who had never before considered their degraded status as anything but natural. A growing number of women were beginning to see that custom, religious precept, and law were in fact man-made and therefore reversible.

When the boys of the Union, including Susan's two younger brothers, Daniel and Merritt, marched off to war in 1861, the women of the republic, "ready to pledge our time, our means, our talents, and our lives," temporarily surrendered their agenda to work for abolition. In a sharp disagreement with her friend Elizabeth Cady Stanton, Susan stubbornly but unsuccessfully insisted that women's conventions should continue. Her Quaker and later Unitarian religion underwrote her conviction, which she made more explicit thirty-seven years later during the Spanish-American War, that "women [should] hold themselves aloof until they have a country that recognizes them as responsible members thereof and a flag that protects them in their rights." Even during wartime, when women were called upon for special service to the nation under the claim of patriotism, she was reluctant to lose a single day in her work for women's causes.[31]

Most of the faithful core of the sisterhood, however, agreed with Stanton and disapproved of Anthony's pacifism during the Civil War. Gradually Susan gave way, recognizing that the rights of blacks and women could be linked in a common cause. To concentrate on the emancipation of slaves was to advance the equality of women, for both were oppressed. Even as male supporters dropped women's issues and focused exclusively on the rights of slaves, Anthony, too committed to sulk or even rest, organized wartime "emancipation tours" made up of a corps of speakers — one white man and one black man and the "best lecturers" from the women's movement. In Auburn, New York, as one of those antislavery lecturers, she was, for the third time in her career, threatened by a mob, burned in effigy, and pictured in lewd sexual poses on placards.[32]

In the spring of 1863 in New York City Susan B. Anthony and Elizabeth Cady Stanton founded the wartime successor to the women's conventions, the Women's Loyal National League. In their convention call they proclaimed the South's secession and war on the North an effort "to found an empire on the negro in slavery, and shame on us if we make it not a war to establish the negro in freedom." Their focus, as they organized the first national women's organization with a permanent headquarters, was on liberating slaves. Still the war also presented an opportunity for women. According to Anthony: "The hour is fully come when woman shall no longer be the passive recipient of whatever the morals and religion, the trade and politics of the nation may decree . . . Women of the North, I ask you to rise up with earnest, honest purpose . . . Forget what the world will say . . . I ask you to forget that you are women, and go forward in the way of right, fearlessly, as independent human beings . . ."[33]

Anthony moved beyond the traditional view of women as guardians of superior character watching over the private morals of the nation in their homes and sacrificing personal autonomy for duty to family, and during the war, Union soldiers. Yet she refused to choose between what she held to be the false polarity of either seeking the liberal goal of individual female autonomy based on natural rights or of achieving a collective women's consciousness based on female solidarity. This generation referred to the latter as "the race of women" during a period in which the word *gender* remained a grammatical classification for French nouns and pronouns. Meanwhile, the word *feminism* as applied to the reforms Anthony demanded awaited the twentieth century. In her day when others dismissed Anthony's core belief that the status of women and slaves was the same, she saw the similarity of oppression and demanded equality as a human being. Such a bold position was contested even among the sisterhood.[34]

Just as controversial was Anthony's opposition to President Lincoln, whose "milk and water policies" included an Emancipation Proclamation that left slavery untouched in the border states and areas not under the control of the Union army. To Anthony's thinking, Lincoln, whose final proclamation came in January 1863, nearly two years after the war had begun, had taken too much care to keep "the negro and slavery out of sight and hearing." His delay in accepting blacks as soldiers was also "a sin." She and the sisterhood wanted nothing less than a war "made for the Negro," followed by a peace made for both blacks and women.[35]

By 1864 the five thousand members of the Women's Loyal National League, fighting a self-proclaimed "war of ideas, not bullets and bayonets," had gathered a hundred thousand signatures on petitions presented to Congress by Massachusetts senator Charles Sumner during the debate on the Thirteenth Amendment outlawing slavery. By that summer even more petitions—long lists of signatures on bulky rolls, one for each state—cluttered Sumner's office. In all, one out of every twenty-four Northerners—over four hundred thousand in all—signed resolutions calling for emancipation in what Anthony believed was a first installment in a new freedom that would include women—white and black.[36]

After the war, in the tumultuous battles over Reconstruction policy during Andrew Johnson's presidency, the Fourteenth Amendment established citizenship rights, due process, and equal protection before the law, all seemingly advancing the potential for women's rights. But the ranks of reformers wavered and broke over the application to women of these constitutional changes. William Garrison's Antislav-

ery Society disbanded, and by the late 1860s, despite another exhausting petition campaign, Anthony and Stanton could not keep the exclusive designation "male" out of the second article of the Fourteenth
Amendment. What some called a notable advancement in democracy
because black males were made citizens Anthony labeled "an outrage
against women." By 1869 the Republicans were moving to ensure
their voting through another amendment to the Constitution. The
newly formed National Woman Suffrage Association, with Stanton
as its president and Anthony as its vice president, failed to persuade
Congress to include "sex" along with race in the Fifteenth Amendment's prohibited disenfranchisements. And as Anthony predicted,
the grants in the Constitution proved insufficient protection for
Southern black males.

To an audience in Missouri in 1867, Anthony made her case in
the comparative terms that later Americans labeled racist: "When you
propose to elevate the lowest and most degraded classes of men to an
even platform with white men . . . it is certainly time for you to begin
to think at least whether it might not be proper to lift the wives,
daughters, and mothers of your State to an even pedestal." It was a
harsh judgment on black men, but unlike the also-racist fathers of the
early republic who had placed slavery in the Constitution, Anthony
wanted to use black men as an inclusive, comparative reference point
to gain women the vote.[37]

In 1869 Lucy Stone and Henry Blackwell seceded from the
Anthony-Stanton women's movement, organizing their Boston-based
wing in a separation that shattered the cherished unanimity of these
first-generation feminist sisters—and forever wrecked the friendship of
Susan and Lucy. In Susan's mind Lucy had for the second time violated the rules of the sisterhood. First after promising fidelity to the
principle of remaining single, she had married. Now, according to Anthony, she was splitting the sisterhood because of her pride and "nar-
row pigheadedness." Henceforth Susan, who dismissed gossip as a
waste of energy and who rarely made personal comments about even
her enemies, disparaged Lucy—"Saint Lucy," as she ridiculed her rival. Lucy was lazy (she had rarely worked as a petition gatherer); she
had failed as a speaker (in the free-market world of lecturing her audiences were now small); and she was selfish (Lucy had divided the suf-

frage movement because she feared Anthony's competition). In the most unfair of her criticisms she even accused Lucy of not being legally married, which brought a prompt rejoinder from Thomas Higginson, who had presided at the Stone-Blackwell wedding.[38]

There were tactical and ideological differences between Stone's American and Anthony and Stanton's National Woman Suffrage Association. The former included men, while Susan held to her conviction that "women can get nowhere in an organization with men except to surrender our reason and instinct to them in the work and that I will not do." Unlike Lucy's organization, Susan and her National Association refused to support the Fifteenth Amendment—"not for what it is, but for what it is not. Not because it enfranchises black men, but because it does not enfranchise all women, black and white . . ." Giving black males the vote without enfranchising all women would only increase the numbers and power of what Anthony and Stanton were now calling the "aristocracy of sex."[39]

In the calculus of even the most liberal Republicans and male activists, there must be only one reform question at a time—"One idea for a generation to come up in the order of their importance. First negro suffrage, then temperance, then the eight-hour movement, then woman suffrage." "Put women's suffrage in a separate bottle . . . It is the Negro's hour," replied turncoat friends like Wendell Phillips and Frederick Douglass. But Anthony protested: "I cannot forgive nor forget the listless do nothingness of the men we had always believed our best friends—but no matter. We will still work on, even with greater vigor than ever . . . Now is the accepted time."[40]

Deserted by former friends, rivaled by Lucy Stone's American Woman Suffrage Association and its successful newspaper the Woman's Journal, unrecognized by political parties, Anthony and Stanton borrowed money in 1868 to start their own newspaper. They called it The Revolution. Committed to an editorial policy supporting "Men Their Rights and Nothing More; Women Their Rights and Nothing Less," the newspaper printed, as Stanton punned, "weekly, not weakly." For some time the two friends had recognized that in the battle for public opinion they needed a paper. The Revolution lived up to its name, suggesting the distance that the women's movement had come since the delicately labeled earlier newspapers—*The Una*, *The Lily*, *The Rosebud*, and *Sybil*.[41]

Above all, though briefly and erratically financed by the eccentric George Train, *The Revolution* was a woman's business. Female operated and staffed with female printers, and publishing the writing of mostly female writers, the work was entirely overseen by its soon debt-ridden proprietor, Anthony, who, as a single woman, could sign contracts as the married Stanton could not. For the last time before the battle for women's rights shrank to a nearly exclusive focus on suffrage, *The Revolution* proclaimed a progressive agenda. In editorials mostly written by Stanton, the paper called for an eight-hour day, inflationary greenbacks as legal currency, "an equal right before the law in those relations which grow out of the marriage state," a single sex standard, as well as suffrage and equal pay for equal work for women wage earners. Always interested in attracting every woman to the suffrage movement, Susan organized a Working Woman's Association in her office in the Woman's Bureau—next door to the editorial offices of *The Revolution* on Park Row in lower Manhattan.[42]

Nellie Hutchinson, a correspondent for the *Cincinnati Commercial*, expected grim surroundings and militant women after she walked up three flights for an interview in Susan's office. Instead she found smiling apple-cheeked female printers in "an atmosphere of womanly purity and delicacy." A pleasant Susan B. Anthony, whose "fascinating voice with a faint alto vibration," set "the tone of power. Her smile is very sweet and genial [but] lights up the pale worn face rarely."[43]

There were reasons for Anthony's pale worn face besides the growing debt of the short-lived *Revolution*. Daniel Anthony, her beloved father, had died on November 25, 1862, a date Anthony forever mourned with a sentimentalism she often disguised in her public appearances, reserving her tender, sometimes maudlin expressions for her diary. Nearly thirteen years after her father's death she described to a suffrage sister her feelings: "It seemed to me the world and everybody in it must stop. It was months before I recovered," a recovery only accomplished "through more and better work for Humanity." When Guelma's daughter—Susan's niece Ann Eliza McLean—died in 1864, followed by her younger brother Thomas King McLean in 1870, Susan's lamentations filled her diary. Even more disturbing, both of Anthony's sisters, Guelma and Hannah, were displaying the early signs—the coughing, flushes, and weight loss—of the tuberculosis that killed both in the 1870s. In order to nurse her dying sisters, Anthony took months off from pressing suffrage work, fulfilling a female role that her public commitments never superceded.[44]

Loving the Sisters

In this season of personal discontents, the Civil War had stanched the flow of new recruits into the women's convention movement. Now Anthony must search for young unmarried energetic women with strong voices loud enough for lecture halls and self-esteem impervious to humiliation. In her view only the strong-willed could avoid becoming entangled in domesticity; only the single-minded could provide the persistent, not just episodic, devotion to the crusade for women's rights. These latter would be the new women whose lives would be lived independently, on their own terms, and with the vote.

During the war Anthony had discovered, as had others in the North, a candidate in the golden-voiced, new star of the abolitionist movement and the Republican party, Anna Dickinson. Those who heard Anna Dickinson lecture never forgot her combination of authenticity and magnetism, as well as her spontaneous interchanges with audiences. All drew Republicans into her lecture halls until she became a national phenomenon.[45]

Anthony took a motherly approach in her first negotiations with the popular twenty-year-old Dickinson, whom she wanted to sign up for her informal lecture bureau. She was solicitous about Anna's health, especially the sore throat that was so threatening to her new friend's speechmaking. But Anthony was insistent, at a moment when slavery was ending and rights for women might share the national stage along with those for blacks, that Anna receive "the new baptism" [of women's rights] and incorporate their agenda into her lectures. "Anna, Anna, tell me if you will speak."[46]

Soon Anna Dickinson became more than just another of Anthony's speakers. In 1866, when Dickinson was twenty-four and Anthony forty-six, the passionate feelings of romantic attraction—at least on Anthony's part—temporarily replaced the business of reform. "Darling Dicky, Dicky"; "Chick-a-Dee-: I hope to snuggle you darling closer than ever"; "Well Anna I do wish I could take you in these strong arms of mine"; "I have a double bed and big and good enough to take you in." "I should like to have you smooth my face and fondle me a little. Meanwhile I love you." Susan B. Anthony sought the younger woman's company on her journeys to Kansas where an unsuccessful referendum on women's suffrage took place in November 1867, at Fourth of July picnics, and in Martha's Vineyard for a rare Anthony holiday. From her fourth-floor room in Mrs. Stanton's home in New York and later from her "plain quarters" in a boardinghouse on Bond Street, Anthony implored Dickinson to share a bed big enough for snuggling, whispering, and pinching ears.[47]

Foreign to today's penchant for sexualizing such behavior, Susan's understanding of sisterhood led her into a female world inhabited by many nineteenth-century American women. Excluded from the public world where men developed single-sex camaraderie based on mutual interests and extensions of their professional lives into personal associations, women established romantic friendships with other women marked by courting, flirting, pet nicknames, and baby talk, and when apart, rhetorical sighs of attachment and devotion. In their female world of love and ritual, women of the nineteenth century engaged in petting, kissing, and hand holding without outsiders paying much attention. Women, in the conventional wisdom of the day, were considered asexual and passionless. With society's negligent blessing they could engage in emotionally and sexually gratifying relationships as kindred spirits who, beyond the prying eyes of family or friends, may or may not have been involved in the homoerotic genital contact that forms today's definition of lesbianism.[48]

Immersed throughout her life in an intimate circle of loving women, the unmarried Susan B. Anthony was a perfect candidate for the intense relationship that she sustained for several years with Anna Dickinson. Yet she was too active and peripatetic to settle into a long-term monogamous Boston marriage. She never established a home in one place with another unmarried woman who was not a relative as did other American couples, most famously, Jane Addams and Ellen Starr, Willa Cather and Edith Lewis, and even her niece Lucy Anthony and suffrage leader Anna Howard Shaw.

In her fifty-six years of activism Susan B. Anthony probably traveled more than any other American, save railroad employees and possibly Frances Willard of the WCTU. In 1871, for example, Anthony calculated that she had journeyed thirteen thousand miles and delivered 171 lectures, and she was on the road another thirty-four years. Only in 1890 did she establish a permanent home in Rochester with her youngest sister, Mary, the unmarried stay-at-home daughter of Daniel and Lucy Anthony. But Susan was not too busy to have a love affair with Dickinson that was marked by trysts, hurried meetings, and affectionate letters. If lesbianism has as its minimal standard a loving relationship with another woman in which each confides in the other, seeks the other's company in an exclusive arrangement, engages in affectionate frication or rubbing together of bodies as an expression of love, and finds, as Susan B. Anthony did in Anna Dickinson's gray eyes, a soul mate, then Susan B. Anthony had several lesbian relationships.

The love affair with Anna Dickinson was the most passionate, though it was short lived and seemingly one sided. Exalted in her lover's words as the "world's evangel" and the "world's child," the younger woman was adored by many others—male and female. Less exuberantly romantic than Susan, Dickinson hoped after a lecture tour in 1869 that Susan might meet her on Cortland Street "and then sinner and saint will have the afternoon together and that seems too good to be true." But by the early 1870s Susan was deploring their distance—no doubt physical and emotional as well as geographic. "Dear Heart—Shall we never get close to you again as in days gone by and talk and listen [our] way into the wee hours of the night." By 1872 Anthony sensed Dickinson's coldness—"not the old time greeting"—and noted various "misunderstandings" in her diary. Given the twenty-two-year difference in these two women's ages and Dickinson's refusal to become a suffrage advocate, Anthony eventually reframed the relationship, but again in women's terms.[49]

This time she became a motherly counselor. Such a role was typical during a time when the eroticism of women's relationships blended with maternal postures of protection and instruction. As any mother might, Anthony now advised Anna Dickinson, at a time when the younger woman was being ardently courted by several men, not to marry. Instead, Anthony warned, at a time when mothers were anything but straightforward in sexual advice to their daughters, "there is a point beyond which nature will not cannot endure temptation." Gradually, rather than their passionate trysts, the wealthy ever-single Dickinson, who earned as much as a thousand dollars a lecture, was sending Anthony presents—an expensive gray silk dress as a fiftieth birthday present in 1870, and the next year jewelry and a shawl. In response Anthony offered her philosophy for a happy life: "Oh, Anna, I am so glad of it all because it [Anthony's life as a never married woman] will teach the young girls that to be true to principle [and] live an unpopular idea and live single without a man's name may be honorable."[50]

Anna Dickinson never joined the circle of women's activists—the sisters in the household of faith—who narrowed their postwar agenda to suffrage. In that sense she represents the defectors—male and female—who abandoned the feminist mission as it changed from addressing a broad-based coalition of women's issues into its concentration, for the next fifty years, on votes for women. Soon Dickinson and Anthony grew apart. Dickinson became a modestly successful actor and playwright, while Anthony spent a third to two-thirds of nearly every year from 1874 until her death in 1906 on the road, a messenger for suffrage.

In 1895 a bankrupt Dickinson wrote Anthony for money. In response the aging suffragist warmly recalled the different ways in which she had loved Anna, remembering "my elderly sister's love; my motherly love for Anna." There were, in Anthony's understanding, many ways in which women could love women, and these different bonds emotionally sustained her. But by the end of the nineteenth century same-sex passion in the United States had lost its innocence; no longer an acceptable form of affection for women, it was considered perverted. Never intimidated by the dictates of society, Anthony still recalled the passionate centrality of her relationship with Dickinson during a difficult time in her life thirty years before: "I have had several lovely Anna girls," she told Dickinson, "nieces they call themselves nowadays since my *first Anna*, but none of them has or ever can fill the niche in my heart that you did."[51]

There were other women in Anthony's intimate sisterhood, some of whom, like Rachel Foster, earned sobriquets such as "my darling," "my precious," and "my beloved." And because for Anthony all personal relationships must include a connection to the suffrage movement—"I am not fit to deal with anyone who is not terribly in earnest"—the hardworking Foster soon became "my dear little boss" and "my best girl." A wealthy Philadelphian who was thirty-nine years younger than Anthony and whose parents, like Susan's, were Quaker abolitionists and reformers, Foster represented a new generation of activists who were university trained. Soon this suffragist-by-inheritance was on the road with Anthony in endless state campaigns such as those in Nebraska in 1882 and Kansas in 1887.[52]

Not easily impressed given her high standards, Anthony admired Foster's stamina: "You understand just how to make agitation & that's the secret of successful work." Eventually Foster, by 1890 the corresponding secretary of NWSA, became Anthony's lieutenant in charge of arrangements for annual meetings—what everyone in the movement recognized as the "drudgery of the association." Anthony promised never to interfere, but for a woman who found it difficult to delegate authority, the temptation often proved too much. In the months before the annual meeting every February, Rachel always received a drumbeat of instructions on how to write a call to the convention without repetition, how to get the most favorable terms from hotels and meeting places, and how to edit the increasingly lengthy published report of the annual meetings.[53]

But Foster was more than just an efficient collaborator. Playing a significant role in Anthony's emotional life, she became a member of the older woman's fictive kin, a family circle drawn together not by the bonds of blood but through collaboration in a common cause. The two women traveled together in Europe during Anthony's first visit overseas in 1883, during which they slept in the same bed and shared their reactions to the great monuments of Europe, though characteristically Anthony was less interested in statues and museums than she was in current conditions for women. In 1904 when the eighty-four-year-old Anthony insisted on traveling to Berlin for the meeting of the

International Council of Women, an organization that she and Stanton had founded, she visited Foster in Switzerland where the latter was living with her children. In return for her privileged relationship with Aunt Susan, Rachel Foster responded with the solicitude of a relative. She, more than anyone in the suffrage movement, understood Anthony's perpetual poverty as a volunteer and acted to end it by raising enough money from the suffrage sisters to provide Susan with an eight-hundred-dollar annuity. And Rachel almost single-handedly promoted into a ritual observance the celebration of Anthony's February 15 birthday that often fell during the annual national meetings.[54]

Committed to attracting younger women to keep the suffrage movement alive in its doldrum years, Anthony shaped ever-changing relationships with Foster and her other "best girls." To older women she became "beloved sister Susan." To younger recruits she was "Aunt Susan," a name that Rachel initiated, believing Miss Anthony too formal and Susan too disrespectful. To this third generation of young admirers who sometimes found themselves crushed by her long powerful arms in bone-rattling embraces, she was deified as "Saint Susan," a term of respect different from the label of saint disparagingly applied by Stanton and Anthony to the assumed holiness of their rival Lucy Stone.[55]

In 1888 Rachel Foster married Cyrus Miller Avery, the son of a Chicago suffragist and himself a supporter of votes for women who had gallantly sat in the galleries for hours watching his future wife run suffrage conventions. Their courtship pleased Elizabeth Cady Stanton, who now had evidence that women's meetings, criticized in the press as routine and dull, were not without romance. But Susan, remembering all the other married women who had drifted away from the work of suffrage, was disappointed.[56]

Ten years later, when Anthony began to plan for her self-scheduled resignation as the president of NAWSA, Rachel, now the mother of three daughters, promised to remain as corresponding secretary for the duration of her administration. But family problems intervened, and Rachel advised Aunt Susan that because of a "desire to do the best for my children," she must resign immediately. In her diary Susan confessed that Rachel's priorities made "me almost ill." Again she felt deserted; again she remembered the episodic commitments of married women who were forever being drawn away from the essential work of getting the vote.[57]

Anthony's company of women also included her blood nieces— brother Merritt's daughter Lucy Anthony who, along with Lucy Stone's daughter, Alice Stone Blackwell, negotiated the merging of the two wings of the suffrage movement into the National American Woman Suffrage Association in 1890; brother Daniel's daughter, namesake Susan B. Anthony, who drowned in 1889 but who "showed great promise" through her interest in the suffrage movement; and sister Hannah Mosher's daughter Helen, whose education Susan oversaw. With a determination that often intruded on parental decisions, Aunt Susan expected all her female nieces at least to delay their marriages until they were properly educated, which meant going to college and establishing themselves in an occupation. And she expected her intimate circle—the sisters in the household of suffrage—to serve in the capacity of relatives, listening, talking, writing, sharing, caring, and loving. "Were it not for the loving sympathy and confidence of the little handful of ever faithful as you," she wrote to one of these women, "my spirit I fear would have fainted long ago."[58]

The New Departure

As her passionate relationship with Anna Dickinson faded in the 1870s and before Rachel Foster emerged as a surrogate niece, Susan B. Anthony depended on a group of Rochester women when she embraced a new suffrage strategy. On November 2, 1872, she led her three sisters, a cousin, and ten other female friends to the polls located in her ward in a barber's shop in Rochester's Eighth Congressional District. In the custom of the day, the women handed their paper ballots to the election officials who after checking their registration rolls accepted the votes.[59]

Afterward, Anthony exulted to Elizabeth Cady Stanton: "Well, I have been and gone and done it, positively voted the Republican ticket strait this morning at seven o'clock and swore my vote in at that . . . Now if all our suffrage women would work to this end of enforcing the constitutional supremacy of National over State law, what strides we might make from now on . . ."[60]

In adopting this new departure of the suffrage movement, Susan joined other American women who, rather than deploring the Fourteenth and Fifteenth Amendments as postwar additions to the U.S. Constitution exclusively guaranteeing rights to black men, used them to justify their right to vote. Two years earlier Victoria Woodhull, the first woman invited to speak to Congress, had made the case before a skeptical House Judiciary Committee (with Anthony seated behind her) that women as "persons born or naturalized in the United States" already had the right to vote and needed no further acknowledgment of their entitlement. Observing that the American system of government depended on popular sovereignty, that voting was a federal privilege, and that women were granted national citizenship with its inherent right to vote guaranteed by the Fourteenth Amendment, Woodhull shifted the responsibility for granting suffrage from the states to the federal government. And because the Fifteenth Amendment granted to Congress the power of enforcement, women had an established avenue for the protection of their voting rights.[61]

In Anthony's view citizenship was a political category that conveyed membership in the body politic and was not a specific term referring to only male citizens. How could it be otherwise given the fact that the only other recognized legal categories of persons were those of minors, idiots, aliens, and felons? The 1870 Enforcement Act, intended to protect former male slaves' political rights in the South by granting access to federal courts, now offered women a similar protection. They too could sue local election officials who interfered with their right to vote.[62]

Along with the Rochester Anthonys, hundreds of American women—in Vineland, New Jersey, in St. Louis, in the territory of Washington, and throughout the United States—took to the streets on this presidential election day in 1872 to place their paper ballots in election boxes singing, in their patriotic gloss on a Civil War song, "We are Coming, Uncle Sam, with 15 million more." Like the blood-connected Rochester sisters—Susan, Guelma, Hannah, Mary, and cousin Lottie Anthony—other members of the sisterhood marched to claim their right as Americans. Some were successful in having their votes counted; others saw their ballots torn up by election judges. Still others, like Elizabeth Cady Stanton, who stayed at home, claimed the right rhetorically. But only Susan B. Anthony was arrested.

Ironically she had voted for the Republican Ulysses S. Grant, no supporter of women's suffrage, rather than the reform, more liberal candidate Horace Greeley, a former Republican endorsed by the Democratic Party who was just as opposed to women's suffrage as Grant. But unlike Lucy Stone and "the Bostons," Susan had little faith in any particular politician or political party. Like Stanton she despised politicians who exploited women by using them "to fill up their empty seats, to wave our handkerchiefs, and clap our hands when they say smart things, but when we ask to be allowed to help them in any substantive way by helping them choose the best men for our lawmakers and rulers, they push us aside and tell us not to bother them." Anthony's intention was to claim the right to vote, no matter what Democrats and Republicans did, and she meant to bring action against any election official who might interfere. Instead, as she wrote a friend, "Uncle Sam waxed wroth with holy indignation."[63]

Two weeks after the election a federal marshal arrived at the Anthony home on elm-shaded Madison Street in Rochester. Alert to the propaganda possibilities inherent in her arrest, she had earlier refused to go to the courthouse. Declining to use handcuffs on his prisoner, although she stretched out her arms for him to do so, the marshal took fifty-two-year-old Anthony to the Madison County Courthouse where she was arraigned and indicted for the federal offense of illegal voting. In the initial arraignment the U.S. District Attorney concentrated on proving that she was a woman, asking Anthony how she had been dressed at the time she cast her vote. To this line of questioning her counsel objected. She had not tried to fool the election inspectors, who were themselves indicted, tried, convicted, and jailed for accepting her vote. That was hardly the point. Of course she was a woman. In her prim, high-necked, long dress and shawl, who could have thought otherwise?

As she told the magistrate, she had cast her ballot not as a woman but as a citizen. And if women were not citizens, what were they?

Some congressmen, faced with this conundrum, were arguing that they were not persons. Then, responded Anthony, they must be subjects or serfs, for adult females were not minors, nor aliens, nor idiots, nor felons. And slavery had been outlawed after the Civil War. But this was no legal defense and Anthony was indicted; bail was set, and though she preferred jail, her attorney posted the four-hundred-dollar bond.[64]

The trial that followed six months later displayed the support of her sisters along with the ominous intentions of American officials. Before the trial her friend Matilda Joslyn Gage had joined her, lecturing throughout Madison County on "The United States on Trial, Not Susan B. Anthony." In the towns and villages that Gage missed, the defendant delivered her lecture "Is It a Crime for a United States Citizen to Vote?" to audiences containing the potential pool from which her jurors would come. Of course, as she made clear, jurors could not be her peers, for they were all male.

The authorities believed that the indefatigable Anthony's local canvassing was so thorough that she might influence public opinion. To take no chances, the case was remanded to the neighboring county of Canandaigua to a courtroom where the all-male jury would not be influenced by her speeches. In fact the jury played little role in the extraordinary trial of the *United States v. Susan B. Anthony*.[65]

Rather than a possibly sympathetic local district judge, Ward Hunt, recently appointed to the U.S. Supreme Court and in Susan's mind a man who took his orders from antisuffrage New York Republicans like Sen. Roscoe Conkling, presided. As she sat at a plain wooden table facing the judge, behind her were the sisters—her own, those other female Rochester voters, and even some of her suffrage sisters from out of state who had come to exhibit the solidarity of a virtual household. After testimony from her counsel and the district attorney, the judge announced that there was no question of fact for the jury to decide. She was a woman and she had illegally voted. Directing the jury to find guilty the defendant who had not been permitted to testify and refusing a requested poll of the jury, the judge preempted a defense motion to appeal. Abruptly the clerk entered a judgment and assessed a fine of one hundred dollars and court costs that

Susan B. Anthony announced she could not pay. In the cause of women's suffrage, Susan B. Anthony was now a convicted felon subject to six months' imprisonment.

She intended to appeal to the Supreme Court, so that her case might provide the women's movement with a judicial target similar to the infamous Dred Scott decision of 1857. But "the aristocracy of sex"—Anthony's analogue to the plutocracy of class and the supremacy of race—wanted no more publicity. The court did not require her to pay her fine and issued no bench warrant for her arrest. Hence she had no grounds for appeal.

Still, she had her day in court. Before her sentence Justice Hunt, as required, asked if she had anything to say as to why sentence should not be pronounced. With the judge telling her to sit down six times before she finally did, an erect Susan B. Anthony made her case:

> May it please the Court, your denial of my citizen's right to vote is the denial of my right of consent as one of the governed, the denial of my right of representation as one of the taxed, the denial of my right to trial by jury of my peers as an offender against the law, therefore, the denial of my sacred rights to life, liberty, property . . . May it please the Court to remember that since the day of my arrest, this is the first time that either myself or any person of my disfranchised class has been allowed a word of defense before judge or jury . . .[66]

By the 1870s Susan B. Anthony had accumulated enough personal insults and mistreatment to animate any abstraction about the need for justice to women. The evidence began with her unequal pay as a schoolteacher, followed by harassment on the lecture tour, the denial of hotel rooms and carriage cars, and the refusal of male allies to further the women's cause after the war. Now she had another, the arrest for voting by the federal government for an alleged violation of a state privilege. With the donations from her loyal suffrage sisters, Anthony printed ten thousand copies of the proceedings of her trial and circulated them throughout the United States. Thereafter Susan B. Anthony personified the suffrage crusade: "I stand before you as a convicted criminal" became the riveting opening line of speeches delivered by this dignified, bespectacled, gray-haired matron who hardly seemed a threat to the Republic.[67]

Two years later, in 1875, the Supreme Court disposed of the new departure. In *Minor v. Happersett*, a case brought in 1872 by suffragist Virginia Minor when she was not allowed to register in St. Louis, the Court ruled that states defined certain privileges and immunities of their inhabitants, including voting rights. "The United States has no voters of its own creation," declared Chief Justice Morrison Waite, and women were excluded from suffrage in nearly all states. In fact, ruled the Court, women were a special category of person—"members of the state"—whose inability to vote did not mean that they were not citizens. Nor did their nonvoting status mean that the United States was not a republic. In response Anthony and others pointed out that the United States did have voters. The evidence existed in its delivery of the vote to black males in the Fifteenth Amendment, Congress's enactment of suffrage for some Indians, and its removal of the suffrage from women in polygamous Utah. Other classes of voters had been enfranchised by federal law, and so too under federal law, went Anthony's argument, should women be.[68]

Ever the tactician rather than the philosopher, Anthony concluded that there were three possible avenues toward obtaining the vote—the first now closed off through the denial of the "taking our rights under the Constitution as it is, on the principle that all persons are citizens and all citizens are voters"; the second through the slow process of persuading state legislatures to change their constitutions by referendums or in constitutional conventions, a never-abandoned but rarely successful process that took Anthony, like the ancient mariner, on endless journeys into every state of the forty-eight states and territories except three. The third avenue was through the cumbersome process of amending the U.S. Constitution, and this was the strategy to which she turned. "Washington is the point of attack." Anthony referred to this method as the process of getting what she numbered as the Sixteenth Amendment passed by Congress and ratified by three-quarters of the states. Her young followers promptly named it the Susan B. Anthony amendment, but such a title was much too prideful for a former Quaker and current Unitarian to accept. In any case it took so long to accomplish that it became the Nineteenth Amendment.[69]

During a period that represented the lowest ebb of the suffrage movement, Anthony kept the faith with her undaunted optimism. At times disheartened, she acknowledged that "the way seems blocked," but never for long. Only a founding mother of the movement could exult, after losing a referendum in Kansas in 1867, that "never was defeat so glorious a victory." Only a determined activist could write to a young disciple in 1900, when after a half century of vigorous reform effort only four states permitted full suffrage, "Buckle on your armor, do not be discouraged and go ahead holding meetings, organizing societies and scattering literature. Work on, work on . . . Ever try, try again in the name of justice and equality to women."[70]

Eclectic in her arguments for suffrage, Anthony never depended on just one reason. Throughout her life she used the natural-rights argument that in a democracy voting was the primary transaction whereby the people delegated authority to their representatives. But she combined this with practical instrumentalist arguments that enfranchisement would protect women, would guarantee them better wages, and would promote a sense of autonomy beneficial for all society. There was little of the essentialist thinking that women had special qualities and virtues that would bring morality into politics. By the end of the century her best-known speeches—"Women Want Bread, Not the Ballot" and "The Necessity of Woman Suffrage" mixed these different approaches, in keeping with Anthony's view that the NAWSA must include different kinds of women from members of the popular but more conservative Woman's Christian Temperance Union to members of labor unions, farm labor parties and freethinkers.[71]

When reporters asked about the stalled suffrage movement, Susan was ready with statistics on the number of communities with municipal voting and expectations of winning a future statewide referendum. When they countered that women did not want to vote, but preferred to let their husbands deal with public affairs, she noted that some women did not have husbands and even for those who did there were many obstacles—inside and outside the home—that diminished their will and interest in voting. Increasingly, but never as often or with as much vitriol as Elizabeth Cady Stanton, she noted the opposition of black males and the foreign-born to woman's suffrage, the latter having by her calculation furnished 75 percent of the vote against suffrage in the 1894 referendum in South Dakota.[72]

The Best Friend

Like that of any radical change—and women's suffrage, however unremarkable today, was a revolutionary goal—the undeniable righteousness of Anthony's cause and her own indomitable energy fostered an impressive enthusiasm. But she was sustained as well by the sisterhood, that growing circle of women that included her sister Mary, the leaders of the association who were her lieutenants, and especially her friend Elizabeth Cady Stanton, the woman she called "my special sister."[73]

Friends for over fifty years, these two shared their dogged commitment to, and leadership of, the suffrage movement. They first collaborated during the early women's conventions of the 1850s on speeches and at meetings when as Stanton described ". . . I forged the thunderbolts and she fired them." As a young woman Anthony carried the ideas of the homebound, child-enveloped Stanton throughout the United States. "I cant get up a decent document," implored Anthony to Stanton in 1856, "so for the love of me and for the saving of the *reputation* of *womanhood*, I beg of you with one baby on your knee and another at your feet and four boys whistling buzzing hallooing *Ma Ma* set your self about the work."[74]

Forever uncertain about her talent as a writer and ever appreciative of what she called Stanton's "big brain," Anthony came to depend on the older woman in a reciprocal interchange of talents. As Stanton explained, "In thought and sympathy we were as one, and in the division of labor we exactly complemented each other. In writing we did better work than either could alone. While she is slow and analytic in composition, I am rapid and synthetic. I am the better writer, she the better critic. She supplied the facts and statistics, I the philosophy and rhetoric . . ."[75]

In the 1860s the two friends organized the short-lived Women's Loyal National League. After the Civil War, again together, they created the National Woman Suffrage Association, with Elizabeth Cady Stanton annually installed as president and Anthony, before she became president in 1892, as vice president. For over thirty years they traveled from coast to coast, wherever a state convention might be considering a resolution calling a state constitutional convention or a referendum on suffrage. Then with every decade providing what Stanton called stronger "hooks of steel" for their friendship, during the 1880s Anthony and Stanton, later joined by Matilda Joslyn Gage, reinvigorated their friendship by writing the first volumes of their monumental, eventually six-volume *History of Woman Suffrage*.[76]

For years Anthony had kept an archive of letters, reports, and newspaper clippings, the latter sometimes pasted into scrapbooks by her mother and sister, though as often simply stuffed into the cubbyholes of Anthony's desk. They had always agreed on the importance of some sort of historical record. As they wrote in their advertisement for *History of Woman Suffrage*: "Men have been faithful in noting every heroic act of their half of the race, and now it should be the duty as well as the pleasure of women to make for future generations deeds of the other half." But Anthony had delayed, announcing that she "preferred to make history rather than to write it . . . That is my forte."[77]

But when the sedentary sixty-five-year-old Elizabeth Cady Stanton was no longer willing to travel or even to give the keynote addresses in the women's conventions and Anthony was sixty, the moment had come. For months at a time, from 1880 to 1885, in the Stanton home in Tenafly, New Jersey, and later in Stanton's childhood home of Johnstown, New York, Stanton wrote *History of Woman Suffrage*. Meanwhile a restless Anthony, who complained that she felt like a prisoner, solicited material, organized the records, negotiated with printers, and intending that every library and school have a copy, marketed the first three volumes of what eventually became six volumes and three thousand pages. Finished, it became the essential source for the women's movement.[78]

In 1890 at the Riggs Hotel in Washington following the annual NAWSA convention and on the occasion of Anthony's seventieth birthday, before an audience of over two hundred suffragists and Susan's brothers, sister Mary, and nieces, Stanton spoke on the "Friendships of Women." It was her birthday present to her best friend, but she also intended to refute the malevolent suspicion that females could not sustain the kind of profound relationships that men enjoyed. Characterizing their relationship as one of "hard work and self-denial," Stanton quoted Emerson's dictum that it was better to be a thorn in the side of friends than their echo. "She has kept me on the warpath at the point of the bayonet so long . . . that before I was summoned, [I hoped] that I might spend the sunset of my life in some quiet chimney corner . . . Well, I prefer a tyrant of my own sex, so I shall not deny the patent fact of my subjection."

In response the more prosaic Anthony noted that, alone, they would have accomplished far less. "If I ever had had a husband and children or opposition in my own home, I never could have done it. How much depends on the sympathy and co-operation of those about us." Of course Elizabeth Cady Stanton had been a part of that sympathetic collegiality. Expanding on the theme of female support, Anthony acknowledged her debt to her special friend as well as to her acolytes—the entire company of faithful women who had sustained her: "I wish they knew how much."[79]

Left unsaid was the degree to which Anthony and Stanton differed as human beings and the extent to which their friendship shaped the women's movement. Perhaps neither could have tolerated a duplicate, but their sisterly relations were marked by provocations and fissures, at the same time that they were bound together by the cause and a collaboration that blended their strengths. Stanton's daughter Harriot Stanton Blatch once observed that Susan was "action," her mother "thought." Even after their worst clashes, the friendship endured. "If your life depends on me, I will be your stay and staff to the end. No power in heaven or hell or earth can separate us for our hearts are eternally wedded together. Ever yours and I mean ever," wrote Stanton after one of their spats. The more emotionally reticent Anthony expressed her affection for her friend in letters signed "everlastingly yours."[80]

Physically they were as different as their approach to the suffrage movement, which Anthony stuck to as "the needle to the pole" and Stanton came to see as only one of many goals. Anthony was tall, angular, and as erect as any soldier on parade, with her straight hair drawn severely behind her ears in a bun. Serious, dutiful, hardworking, humorless, never did she call her snobby best friend anything but Mrs. Stanton. With her ill-fitting dental plates her greatest physical discomfort for years, Anthony's good health was legendary. It was part of the heroic image she fashioned for herself. "Susan wants to drop on the platform like John Quincy Adams on the floor of Congress," Stanton told her son.[81]

Whereas Stanton, who believed a good nap the essential precursor to hard thinking, was short, round, and rosy-cheeked with puffs of white curls that made her look like, though surely not think or behave like, a jolly Mrs. Santa Claus. In fact Stanton was so fat by middle age that, to the disgust of the ascetic Susan who considered strawberries and cream a banquet and good coffee a day's greatest pleasure, she entered the Danville Sanatorium to lose weight. By her sixties Stanton was experiencing the eye problems and arthritis that may have been the result of adult-onset diabetes complicated by her obesity.[82]

Sitting across the table in Stanton's various houses, writing convention calls and letters, discussing organization and appeals to the public, they frequently clashed. "You say women must be emancipated from their suppression before enfranchisement will be of any benefit. I say just the reverse," objected Anthony after one of their arguments. When Stanton began to campaign for "educated suffrage," a cue word for restricting suffrage "of the ignorant classes until the better element of society is fully recognized," Anthony was appalled at such a casual dismissal of the universal suffrage she believed their common mission. It was, she decided, another of her friend's "crazes."[83]

Yet they considered such disagreements private and continued to solicit from each other the intelligent criticism they did not always receive from others. According to Stanton, in a measure of the level of their intimacy, like any loving husband and wife, they disdained public arguments and chose instead to stand as one before the world. Not only did Stanton puckishly send Anthony valentines, a frivolous exercise in Anthony's view, but when Harriot Stanton was born in 1856, the mother proudly held the baby up and exclaimed that her second daughter looked just like Susan. And when some suffrage delegates grew tired of Stanton's presidency and encouraged Anthony as an alternative, the latter always made certain that delegates understood that if they had any love for her, "Don't vote for any human being but Mrs. Stanton."[84]

Never jealous of a friend whose brilliance she acknowledged and whom she fought hard to install as president of the National American Woman Suffrage Association when it was reconstituted in 1890, Anthony still wished that Stanton would just once stay and hear her deliver what was always the second speech.[85] Meanwhile Stanton generously celebrated, but sometimes patronized, Susan's "noble" characteristics. In a time of increasing consumerism Stanton counted only four times that her friend lapsed into any personal extravagance and then only to buy what most would hardly term luxuries—a watch, two brooches, and a pair of lace cuffs. Condescendingly she referred to "poor little Susan," the woman who in turn labeled her, in recognition of her haughtiness, "Queen Mother."[86]

In the final slight, when Stanton returned from Europe in 1890, Anthony hoped that they might share her home in Rochester and thus make their collaboration easier. "I could help you carry out the dream of my life—which is that you should take all your speeches and articles, carefully dissect them, and put them in a nice volume." But the idea simply exhausted Stanton. She chose instead to set up a new household with two of her children in Manhattan.[87]

In 1902 eighty-seven-year-old Elizabeth Cady Stanton died. Anthony was devastated. To the press she recalled "an unbroken friendship . . . If she had outlived me, she would have found fine words." Instead Anthony simply described their lives together—the rides in the Stanton phaeton when they got to talking so much that the old horse would simply stop, the campaign in Kansas in 1867, the trip to California when they were snowbound in the Rockies with nothing to do but talk in their stranded railroad car "as happy and cozy as lovers neither controlling the other," their travels in England in 1883, and the writing of *History of Woman Suffrage*. "It was," she acknowledged, "a great going out of my life."[88]

Four years later, on March 13, 1906, eighty-six-year-old Susan B. Anthony followed her friend, in the terminology she invariably used about death, "across the river." Earlier that year she had seemed to defy episodes of fainting, a small stroke, and shingles by traveling to Washington and meeting with the Republican president Theodore

Roosevelt to urge him to submit a suffrage amendment to Congress. In the midst of a harsh winter, she had traveled from Rochester to attend the annual NAWSA meeting in Washington where she was touched by the Chautauqua salute of suffragists waving their handkerchiefs. To the press she had denounced the president who had sent her a complimentary tribute, but no support of the amendment. Said an angry Anthony in her last message to the suffrage sisters: "When will men do something beyond extend congratulations? I would rather have President Roosevelt say one word to Congress in favor of amending the Constitution to give women the suffrage than to praise me endlessly." The exchange was only another instance of the ways in which politicians used women. Anthony ended with a characteristic nod to those, like herself, who had devoted their lives to the cause ". . . with such women consecrating their lives—Failure is impossible."[89]

Traveling home, Anthony developed pneumonia and died three weeks later in Rochester with her blood sister Mary and her suffrage sister Anna Howard Shaw at her bedside. As Shaw recalled the last afternoon of Anthony's life, "she suddenly began to utter the names of the women who had worked with her as if in a final roll call. Many of them had preceded her into the next world; others were still splendidly active in the work she was laying down. But young and old, living or dead, they all seemed to file past her dying eyes that day in an endless, shadowy review, and as they went by she spoke to each of them." And so the woman who had lived in the blessed company of faithful women died in their presence.[90]

3

Elizabeth Cady Stanton
and The Solitude of Self

In 1826, during a memorable encounter, Judge Daniel Cady told his eleven-year-old daughter, Elizabeth, that he wished she was a boy. Vividly she recalled the scene seventy years later in her autobiography—her father's anguish at the death of yet another of his sons, his unconsciousness of her presence in a darkened parlor as he wept beside the casket, her climbing onto his lap, and his deep sigh accompanied by the words, "Oh, my daughter, I wish you were a boy."[1]

The year before Elizabeth's birth in 1815, Margaret and Daniel Cady had watched two sons die, one eight years old and the other an infant, both named after their father. The arrival of yet another daughter, after the death in one year of two male namesakes, was an occasion for renewed anguish. Quite simply, their new child was the wrong sex. Four years before, another of their sons, five-month-old James, had died, and eleven years later, twenty-year-old Eleazar Livingston Cady, a promising honors graduate from Union College and "the pride of my father's heart," had suddenly succumbed to the croup, within twelve hours of its onset. Another son arrived this same year—named Eleazar after his dead brother and his paternal grandfather by parents who recycled family names in symbolic testimony to their conviction that sons represented not so much individuals of a new generation but rather dynastic replacements. Like his brothers, Eleazar never survived childhood. Instead five healthy daughters—

often attired in matching red dresses, hats, and coats—briefly carried on the Cady name, but none of their father's ambitions, until they surrendered it, each in turn, when they married.[2]

Judge Cady's preference for sons was not unusual. Most American women grew up knowing that both their parents favored boys. Mothers preferred boys not just because of their husbands' satisfaction, but because, like Lucy Stone's mother, they had experienced the female toil of unchecked childbearing and heavy routinized domestic work. Wanting the best for a child, they had concluded that life was easier for men. Fathers had different reasons. They expected a son to work on their farms or in their businesses, to carry on their names or, in wealthy families like the Cadys, to share a profession and conversation about intellectual and political matters, as few women could. "The death of my boy," said Cady, "has robbed me of a source of affection and a source of my anticipated happiness."[3]

The only son in a family that had settled in Columbia County, New York, in the seventeenth century, Daniel Cady felt a special need for male descendants. Apprenticed to a shoemaker, he had lost an eye in an accident. Evidently less able to see hooks and buttons than writing, he turned to schoolteaching and then the law. He hoped, as he explained in a letter to his cousin, that a son—perhaps Daniel or James but certainly Eleazar—would become a lawyer and "come into my office and [I would] try to make him eminent in his profession." To fathers like Judge Cady sons were living legacies and reincarnations. Some shone as bright as Eleazar Cady, others duller, and a few brought "disgrace and . . . shame," but all were part of a constellation mirroring their father.[4]

Enveloped in his losses, Judge Cady overlooked Elizabeth, the third eldest of his surviving daughters, until neglect became impossible. He was, after all, a busy lawyer and public official, and she was at first unremarkable, located within his family as neither the eldest nor the youngest nor the prettiest of his offspring. Certainly she was never the most obedient or ladylike. Nor did his ever-pregnant wife, the regal, well-born Margaret Livingston Cady, have much time for Elizabeth. Her constant childbearing and mourning—she delivered eleven children in twenty-six years beginning when she was barely seventeen and ending only when she was a menopausal forty-four years old—

left her depressed, distracted, and withdrawn. In the Cady household, there were servants, free blacks from the surrounding counties, and nurses from Scotland, to extend care and affection to the children and to become the emotional center of the young daughters' worlds.

The year Elizabeth was born Judge Cady was elected to Congress as a Federalist and spent months in Washington. Earlier he had served in a number of public offices in his hometown of Canaan, New York, and later in Johnstown, where he moved in 1798. A persistent public man, he served in the New York legislature, meanwhile establishing a profitable practice as a real estate and equities lawyer. Later he was appointed a circuit court judge, an honor that took him frequently to Albany. And when he returned to his white frame house (later replaced by a grander brick one) on the corner of Market and Main in the center of Johnstown, New York, a town of one thousand in the foothills of the Adirondacks forty miles northwest of Albany, he was forever reminded of his five dead sons.

Judge Cady's Presbyterian religion with its harsh providential theory of deserved punishment to sinners provided little solace. Although he believed in the Christian doctrine of the resurrection of the dead in Heaven, his religious convictions could never expunge the melancholy that made this formal, distant man accessible to his daughter Elizabeth only through his vulnerability and her unseemly interest in public matters.[5]

Most American girls accepted "their deficit of sex." Understanding that they could not be surrogates for dead brothers, most suffered little from the favoritism of family politics that assured their fathers' celebration of sons. But lively, intelligent Elizabeth Cady at first misunderstood the impossibility of her father's directive that she be a boy and throwing her arms around her father's neck, promised Daniel Cady that she would try to be all her brother had been. Only later could she acknowledge that "while my father was kind to us all, the one son filled a larger place in his affections and future plans than the five daughters together." For the time being, acting like a boy became the intention of her childhood.[6]

At first she succeeded, although her father hardly noticed. As a tomboy she set as her goals to ride faster, run harder, play chess better, learn more, and practice more mischief than any Cady son might have or for that matter any boy in the neighborhood did. When her sisters received Christmas stockings filled with candy, oranges, and raisins, Elizabeth, the organizer of her younger sisters' and cousins' escapades, found a long stick representing her parents' assessment of her behavior. Throughout she remained a gifted student of Greek and Latin, the disciplines that served as a college entrance exam for this generation of men and that, there being only two colleges in the United States in 1830 accepting females, were irrelevant curriculum for girls. She learned these classical languages in the local Johnstown academy and from a kindly neighbor, a Presbyterian minister who, inspired by affection and interest, tutored her. When she won the second prize in Greek at the public recitations of the school, she rushed home to her father. Unimpressed, Judge Cady promptly administered his own test and only then recognized his daughter's aptitude. Once again he sighed his impossible dream: "Ah, you should have been a boy."[7]

In 1830 sixteen-year-old Elizabeth Cady entered the most famous and fashionable girls school in America—the Troy Female Seminary, later renamed after its imposing head, the Emma Willard School. Founded in 1822, the school followed the directives of its founder to train teachers—a burgeoning occupation especially in the Northeast as communities began to fund public schools. Young women had emerged as acceptable, cheap teachers. With teaching a natural extension of a maternal role and therefore a respectable means of supporting themselves, Elizabeth's future compatriots Susan B. Anthony and Lucy Stone had also tried to enroll. But neither could afford the tuition, and neither merited a scholarship. For women from affluent families who did not have to support themselves before they married, a substantial education provided learning to be imparted to sons as well as domestic skills essential to the management of households. To this end, and as a mark of family affluence, three of the five Cady daughters attended Willard's school.[8]

Even in the most academic environment available to her generation of American girls, Elizabeth Cady learned not just the male subjects of math and classical languages, but also the feminized studies of music, French, dancing, and embroidery, which she had avoided in her early years as a tomboy. For the rest of her life she was "humiliated . . . whenever I see the daughters of our grand republic knitting, tatting, embroidering or occupied with any of the ten thousand digital absurdities that fill so large a place in the lives of Eve's daughters." She absorbed two other lessons. From Emma Willard's *Universal History* came Elizabeth Cady's never-forgotten examples of female heroism and activism, available to illustrate the point that society, not innate characteristics, enslaved women: Joan of Arc, Elizabeth of England, Catherine of Russia. From this single-sex school also came Elizabeth Cady's conviction that coeducation at every level was best for both sexes; separation into single-sex communities only magnified the weaknesses of both genders. But educated together, "girls acquire strength, courage and self-assertion and boys courtesy, refinement and self-control." Educated separately, "the isolation of the sexes breeds all this sickly sentimentality, romantic reveries, morbid appetites, listlessness and lassitude."[9]

Elizabeth Cady did not graduate from Willard's, although she was undeniably its most brilliant alumna. In 1831, during her second year, the evangelist minister Charles Finney came to Troy. He brought his doctrine of man as a moral free agent who chose evil, but who through prayer and confession could replace an eternity in hell with salvation, sanctification, and a new life. Sinners, having been instructed by Finney's fiery sermons, had only to repent and give their hearts to Jesus in a public display of conversion. In nearby Rochester hundreds had become "new" Christians, first rising before their fellow congregants to acknowledge their sins and then prostrating themselves on their knees to dedicate themselves to Jesus Christ in great public spectacles. Lyman Beecher, the celebrated Presbyterian clergyman, proclaimed the religious revival of 1831 the largest the world had ever seen. The year marked the beginning of a missionary crusade that swept through the susceptible "burned over district" of upstate New York during the Second Great Awakening.[10]

Her classmates were easily converted, but Elizabeth refused to give her heart to Jesus, even after a conversation with Charles Finney himself. As she reported: "I cannot understand what I am to do. If you should tell me to go to the top of the church steeple and jump off, I would readily do it, but I do not know how to go to Jesus . . ." To which, in her recollection, Finney replied, "Repent and believe. That is all you have to do to be happy here and hereafter." But her heart would not "melt," and rather than a convert, she became a casualty of "this terrifier of human souls." Leaving Willard's after troubling dreams of hell and damnation, Elizabeth Cady required rehabilitation through a soothing family trip to Niagara Falls, with religion a forbidden topic during the journey. As an incident of self-description similar to her desire to please her father by acting like a son, this rebellion against the ministry was another chapter in her ongoing construction of an autonomous, independent self.[11]

After Willard's Elizabeth Cady returned to the leisured indulgences of young women from rich families who had nothing to do except to "enjoy a period of irrepressible joy and freedom" and, of course, to find a suitable husband—the latter the necessary vehicle for the next stage of her life as wife and mother. Later she concluded that these were "the most pleasant years of my girlhood," and they were spent in the pleasurable vacuity of visiting friends, riding horseback through the Mohawk Valley, and joining her father's law clerks in discussions of constitutional law and the legal inequities practiced against women. Years later, she would not recommend such an empty existence for her own daughters, whom she hoped would not only avoid "the trap of matrimony" until they were thirty, but would spend their premarital years studying, traveling, and learning a profession. Under such a program when the time came they would produce "grander children . . . not sickly, snubbed ones" as do-nothing adolescent mothers did.[12]

For the first time her mother, mentioned only twice in her autobiography, emerged as something more than a bearer—and mourner—of children. As a teenager, Elizabeth would observe her mother's management of the Cady household; she learned the tricks of caring for babies and how to cook, talents she would proudly display in her own life. She also saw her mother's chronic depression over the deaths of six children and her inability to deliver a son who survived adolescence. For her mother's consequent guilt, she later held her father—and society—responsible. In her family, Elizabeth Cady, for whom "everything I liked and enjoyed was messy or injurious . . . everything I disliked was just the thing," was more a disruption than a source of maternal solace. In every way her sisters—Tryphena, Harriet, Margaret, and Catherine—more successfully filled Margaret Livingston Cady's expectations that her daughters be efficiently domestic and socially charming.[13]

Of course there were some maternal lessons to be learned. Elizabeth did not inherit her mother's imposing five-foot-nine stature; in fact at five-five, she favored the shorter Cadys in height and also in the roundness of her face and her large forehead. But she did imbibe, as transparent in her upbringing as the air she breathed, a sense of class prejudice. Margaret Livingston Cady's ancestors were Dutch aristocrats; her father—Col. James Livingston—had commanded a regiment at the revolutionary battles of Quebec and Saratoga and had been responsible for uncovering Benedict Arnold's treason. From such a heritage Elizabeth absorbed upper-class notions of superiority, as well as a fierce devotion to the principle of individual liberty for all Americans.

But there was little that Elizabeth Cady chose to remember about a mother who was not her essential parent. Although she often sent her own children to Johnstown for the summer where their grandmother impressed them with her diplomacy and social grace, Margaret Livingston Cady was something of a fugitive presence for Elizabeth. It was always her rejecting father whom she challenged, tested, and sought to impress, for it was his world that she must enter.

Courtship and Marriage

In 1839, after eight years of adolescent indulgence, twenty-four-year-old Elizabeth Cady met her future husband—handsome, firm-jawed, bearded Henry Brewster Stanton. At the time Stanton, a well-known abolitionist agent and lecturer, was visiting Elizabeth's favorite cousin, Gerrit Smith, at his home in Peterboro, a tiny town sixty miles from Johnstown. The wealthy Smiths ran a subversively radical household, with meals taken at a long table where fugitive slaves, Oneida Indians, women, reformers, even Millerites who expected the end of the world in 1844 sat as equals. Temperance was discussed; pacifism was entertained; support of abolishing slavery was expected.

At the time Henry Stanton was lecturing in nearby Madison

County, and his future wife became enthralled with what nearly all listeners to his antislavery rhetoric appreciated—the depths of his feeling against the South's "peculiar institution," and the power of oratory peppered with personal accounts of his courageous encounters with proslavery mobs. It was incorrectly rumored he was already engaged, so Elizabeth found herself discussing the barbarity of slavery not as a flirtatious young unmarried woman might with a potential suitor but as a fellow abolitionist. Like Lucy Stone's and Henry Blackwell's, this couple's mutual attraction flamed in serious discussions of public matters. Within weeks Henry Stanton and Elizabeth Cady were engaged. According to his future wife in an impersonal comment about her romance, after a horseback ride through the woods to a favored picnic spot, Henry Stanton made "one of those charming revelations of human feeling which brave knights have always found eloquent words to utter and to which fair ladies have always listened with mingled emotions of pleasure and astonishment."[14]

Now began another of Elizabeth Cady's struggles with her father. To the self-made Daniel Cady, Henry Stanton had no prospects at all. Itinerant lecturers earned meager—and often unpaid—salaries from the American Antislavery Society. Henry had no profession, and most important, Judge Cady despised the extremism of abolitionist zealots, of whom Henry was an outstanding example. In theory Cady believed that his daughters should pick their own husbands. "If a daughter disobliges an indulgent father and gets a bad husband, God knows she is sufficiently punished without one frown from her father," he wrote a friend. Tryphena, his eldest, had married Edward Bayard, one of his law clerks from a politically prominent Delaware family; Harriet a cousin; Margaret another of his law clerks; and Catherine a lawyer and journalist. But when Elizabeth informed him of her love for Henry Stanton, in a classic example of parental interference in mate choice, Daniel Cady forgot his principles and threatened to disinherit his daughter.[15]

While Henry made his case—that he had college training from Oberlin and the Lane Seminary, that he had been self-supporting for years after his father had gone bankrupt, that he had supported two younger brothers, that he "had never received a dollar's gratuitous aid from anyone," that as a Brewster he was from sound Yankee stock, and finally that he adored Elizabeth—she broke the engagement. Such a disruption was hardly unusual. Nearly a third of all engagements in the 1840s, and especially those undertaken as rapidly as Elizabeth's and Henry's and with as much opposition from the bride's family, floundered. But whipsawed between father and lover, in personal terms the break in the engagement indicated Elizabeth's dependence on the men in her family. She had not yet achieved autonomy.[16]

Elizabeth's authority over the courtship was not unusual, for American women of this period had veto power, though not freedom of selection, over their choice of a husband. So, four months after she broke her engagement, Elizabeth changed her mind again and "determined on May 10, 1840 to take the fateful step without the slightest preparation for a wedding or a voyage." Henry had been selected as an antislavery delegate to a London meeting, and "we did not want the ocean to roll between us."[17]

In the calculus of courtship love, a time when romantic sentiment reigns and before the power relationships of marriage are installed, Elizabeth Cady loved Henry Stanton for his looks, his attractiveness as a conversationalist and a dancer, his intelligence, his willingness to accept her as an intellectual equal, his commitment to something that was more important than dancing and needlework—and, perhaps as well, because her father opposed him as a husband. Ten years older than she, he came with the authority of experience and worldliness. His letters, peppered with second-rate sentimental poetry to "darling Lizzie," were full of adoration, although this was not a premarital pose. Throughout their marriage a supplicant Henry begged for news from home, apologized for any "coldness on my part," and sought his wife's admiration as he struggled to play the role of a breadwinner. In fact, throughout their marriage friends found this couple too similar in temperament and ambition, and too dissimilar in their views on issues such as women's rights. As the abolitionist reformer Sarah Grimké counseled in a letter to Elizabeth: "Henry greatly needs a humble, holy companion and thou needst the same."[18]

Thirty-four years old in 1839, Henry Stanton certainly needed a wife after years of lonely service as an antislavery lecturer and fundraiser. He had discovered in Elizabeth a lively humorous compatriot who shared his reform ideals. But his future wife also became a pri-

vate subject for improvement for a man who was never entirely liberated from his conviction that husbands were the rulers of the family.
He meant, as he wrote Gerrit Smith, to deliver Elizabeth from the
pointless life of "a giddy whirl of fashionable follies. It pains me to see
a person of so superior a mind and enlarged heart doing nothing for
the wicked world's salvation." In the early stage of their marriage he
contributed to his matrimonial intention, but soon this project spi-
raled well beyond his control.[19]

Marrying fifteen years before Lucy Stone, Elizabeth Cady and
Henry Stanton's hasty wedding in her home in Johnstown did not include any denunciation of the legal codes involving marriage. But the
word *obey* was omitted, to the consternation of the Presbyterian minister who, according to the bride, found his revenge in an extralong
prayer. They were married on the unlucky day of Friday because the
groom, on his way to Johnstown by boat on the North River, was
stranded for a day on a sand bar. Years later Elizabeth Cady Stanton
declared that her marriage proved that Friday was not a bad day for
weddings. She and Henry Stanton "lived together without more than
the usual matrimonial friction, for nearly half a century, had seven
children . . . [who] have been well sheltered, clothed and fed, enjoying sound minds in sound bodies . . ." Certainly not a robust endorse-
ment of a marriage that lasted forty-seven years and one in which
husband and wife lived apart more often than together, it was nevertheless an honest one.[20]

Elizabeth Cady did not keep her birth name, although she later
admired Lucy Stone's courage in doing so. On the other hand, she refused "the tyrant custom" of being Mrs. Henry Stanton, complaining
that women were individual persons, not extensions of their husbands.
"The custom of calling women Mrs. John This and Mrs. Tom That
and colored men Sambo and Zip Coon, is founded on the principle
that white men are lords of all." She also objected to the silly "pet
names" that trivialized women into Kittie, Fannie, and Mamie, while
boys rarely suffered such undignified nicknames. She was, and would
be for the rest of her life, Elizabeth Cady Stanton or as she sometimes
signed letters, E. Cady Stanton. Chiding her friend the abolitionist
Wendell Phillips about his letter addressed to Mrs. H. B. Stanton, she
explained that women and Negroes were beginning to repudiate the

names of their masters. As a symbol of their autonomy, both claimed the right to a lifelong name bestowed at birth. But like so many things that Elizabeth Cady Stanton pioneered, the transmission of this legacy to the next generation proved difficult. When her oldest daughter, Margaret, married, she became Mrs. Frank Lawrence. And a disappointed Susan B. Anthony confided to her diary: "If the daughter of Elizabeth Cady Stanton does not keep her name, then who will?"[21]

Nor was Elizabeth Cady Stanton deferential to her husband at a time when wives called their husbands mister, at least in public. Even after they had been married over a decade, she embarrassed her husband when the two years in which she wore bloomers coincided with his reelection campaign for the New York State Senate in 1852. In the minds of some voters a candidate whose wife wore trousers was henpecked and did not deserve their vote. As the doggerel went:

> Heigh ho! The carrion crow
> Mrs. Stanton's all the go:
> Twenty tailors take the stitches,
> Mrs. Stanton wears the britches.[22]

Within a week of their wedding the couple was on its way to England where Henry was a delegate to an antislavery convention. In London, surrounded by antislavery radicals, Elizabeth awoke to women's issues. Before, having only painful private experiences of discrimination from the men in her family, she lacked any historical consciousness or theoretical context. She would soon provide both in the Seneca Falls Declaration of Sentiments in 1848.

The honeymooning bride received a never-forgotten lesson in the public discrimination practiced by men when the elected American women delegates from the antislavery societies in the United States were refused seats and speaking privileges and, greatly humiliated, were forced to sit behind a screen in the visitors' gallery of London's Freemason Meeting Hall. Here the fiery American abolitionist William Lloyd Garrison joined them, for he would be true to his principles of equality for women and slaves. Henry Stanton did not, although he assured his wife that he supported the seating of women on the floor. But, in the first of their disagreements on public matters, he never spoke publicly to the issue, so the bride found her sympathies with Garrison. ". . . by marriage [I] was on the wrong side." Later it would become clear that while she embraced antislavery with her husband, he did not share women's rights with her. Throughout their marriage friends noted how "they differed in their notions of things," and marveled, according to one, "that they did not pick each other's eyes out."[23]

Among the delegates banished to the gallery was the Philadelphia Quaker Lucretia Coffin Mott, a "new revelation of womanhood" for Elizabeth Cady Stanton. Unlike Susan B. Anthony or Angelina Grimké Weld (the latter, to the disgust of the suffragists, retired from public life after the birth of her first child), Mott successfully combined family and public life. Cady Stanton often quoted Mott's epigram that marriage consisted of mutual dependence, equal independence, and reciprocal obligations between spouses, a high standard evidently attained by James and Lucretia Mott, but by few other partnerships and certainly not her own.[24]

There was much to admire. According to Cady Stanton in a eulogy delivered at Mott's memorial service in 1880, "this noble woman" raised "entirely" six children; she ran a frugal household "in which everything from garret to cellar passed under her supervision." Even though her husband was wealthy, she saved money by stitching rags into rugs, and managed a home where visitors enjoyed warm hospitality. But Mott was also an independent female who spoke out in public (she was the first woman that Cady Stanton ever heard give a lecture), challenging the male-controlled institutions of her time—church, government, slavery, and marriage. She was the perfect model. "As we walked home arm in arm commenting on the incidents of the day," wrote Cady Stanton in her autobiography after one of the sessions at the World Antislavery Conference that June of 1840, "we resolved to hold a convention as soon as we returned home, and form a society to advocate the rights of women." It would be, given the distractions of married life and childbearing and -raising, eight years before that convention took place.[25]

A trip through England, Scotland, Ireland, and France followed the antislavery conference, during which Henry spoke to large antislavery audiences, and Elizabeth continued her conversations with

Mott and met the radicals of the emerging British women's move-ment. A voracious reader, she now had intellectuals with whom to discuss the ideas of George Combe, the Scottish phrenologist, John Locke, the seventeenth-century natural rights advocate, and the femi-nist Mary Wollstonecraft, whose *Vindication of the Rights of Woman* was a familiar volume in early American libraries and as well at the Troy Seminary. At the end of the year, the Stantons returned home. By this time Henry believed that abolitionism could only be accom-plished through political organizations such as the Liberty and Free Soil parties. Ready to give up antislavery lecturing, he acknowledged defeat, not just living with the Cadys in Johnstown but reading law with the man who had opposed him as a son-in-law. With expecta-tions that were never realized in politics, the law, or later in journal-ism, Henry established a practice in Boston. His wife, who sometimes attended the debates in the Massachusetts State Senate, promptly be-came absorbed in the intellectual life of a liberal community that fur-thered her private inclinations to challenge public givens.[26]

Motherhood

In March 1842 Elizabeth Cady Stanton left Boston where her hus-band was preparing to be certified for the bar and returned to Johns-town to deliver the first of her seven children. Born nearly two years after his parents' marriage, Daniel Cady Stanton was followed by three more sons named Henry Brewster, Gerrit Smith, and Theodore Weld. Only intermittently at home and admittedly sometimes "cold and unkind" when he was, the absentee father was rarely present for his wife's deliveries, writing a month after Gerrit's birth in 1845 that he could hardly believe he had another son. Not present at his name-sake's birth eighteen months before, instead he complained about his wife's constancy as a correspondent, feeling "lonesome, cheerless and homeless, without you." And for the rest of his life his plaintive suppli-cations to dearest "Lizzie" to write more letters and share more details of domestic affairs and his wife's businesslike responses to "Dear Henry" displayed her emotional control over a relationship both she and Susan B. Anthony defined to the world as "male marriage."[27]

Within this all-male family until the birth of her first daughter in 1852, Cady Stanton developed her feminist agenda of reforming marriage, divorce, child custody, abuse of wives, and the raising of boys and girls. Her lifelong quest centered not on acquiring new rights, but rather on establishing equality for women within those grants already delivered to men. "We ask," she told a committee of the New York legislature in 1854, "no better laws than you want for yourselves." With different emphasis at different times, domestic subjects at first comprised her reform message, although she acknowledged that the vote—a public matter—was an essential hammer to destroy oppressive practices fixed in the concrete of habit. In 1871 Elizabeth Cady Stanton unraveled the implicit radicalism in her diverse program of interdependent reforms, arguing to the single-minded and more discreet Susan B. Anthony that "the men and women who are dabbling with the suffrage movement should be at once emphatically warned that what they mean logically if not consciously in all they say, is next social equality and next Freedom or in a word Free Love." The latter meant for Elizabeth not the kind of promiscuous adultery and fornication men engaged in, but the freedom for women, married and unmarried, to control their sexuality as men had always done.[28]

Clearly the Stantons controlled their fertility through the birth control methods that circulated throughout the United States in the 1840s and 1850s. Such devices included a range of contraceptive choices that account for the dramatic fall in the birthrates during the nineteenth century, especially among white middle-class native-born couples. From books like Robert Owen's *Moral Physiology*, her friend Mary Gove's *Lectures to Ladies on Anatomy and Physiology*, the anonymously authored *The Young Married Lady's Medical Guide and Marriage Friend*, and a variety of self-help manuals, couples like the Stantons learned about douches, vaginal sponges, spermicides, condoms, and the most reliable method of this generation's birth control, coitus interruptus. In the underground world of birth control—for the church, medical profession, and respectable opinion were all opposed—druggists and apothecaries as well as mail-order houses sold everything from condoms (sometimes advertised as "French male safes") to salves and the extracts from roots and herbs. Newspapers and pamphlets advertised such products as protections from syphilis, but they were available to anyone interested in family planning and its corollary, recreational sex. Entrepreneurs in cities peddled euphemistically labeled drugs like "Dr. Cameron's Patent Family Regulator" as well as pessaries and "prevention powders." Homeopathic doctors, including Elizabeth Cady Stanton's brother-in-law Edward Bayard, supported contraception as a private matter, but traditional doctors continued to oppose birth control as an interference with nature.[29]

To be sure, a couple with seven children hardly seem effective practitioners of birth control. But the spacing of the Stanton children suggests otherwise, as does Cady Stanton's interest—and pleasure—in sex, her desire to have a daughter, and the ease of her deliveries, at least until her last child's birth in 1859, the latter an unplanned menopausal child born when she was forty-four. An obviously fecund couple, Elizabeth and Henry Stanton waited nearly two years to have a child because they were in Europe. According to most modern studies, an overwhelming number of women in their twenties—close to 90 percent—become pregnant within three or four months if they do not use birth control. Returned to the United States, the Stantons' first three sons arrived in traditional intervals—"my biennial clumsiness," as Elizabeth called it, referring to the natural contraceptive effect on ovulation from nursing babies. Then, when Elizabeth Cady Stanton moved to Seneca Falls and became more active in the women's movement, there was a five-and-a-half-year gap, until a son and finally two daughters were born in 1851, 1852, and 1856, followed in 1859 by a final son.[30]

Elizabeth Cady Stanton acknowledged her desire for a daughter, and long after the birth of her eldest, Margaret, she admitted rejoicing "that no boy was sent in her stead." Her daughters gave her "fresh strength to work for women." While such partiality seemingly only reversed what she despised as her father's favoritism for boys, she simply wanted a family with both sons and daughters. Proud of the ease with which she accomplished motherhood, Elizabeth had no reason to dread pregnancy and childbirth. That is, until 1859 when the forty-four-year-old mother confessed, after twelve-and-a-half-pound Robert's difficult delivery, that she had "no vitality of body or soul. All I have & was has gone into the development of that boy."[31]

During this last pregnancy she canceled a prestigious lecture engagement in Boston, the first to be given by a woman to the Boston Lyceum. As she explained to Susan B. Anthony when she was five months pregnant, "My present experience differed from all its antecedents. I grew worse instead of better—sick, nervous, timid, and so short-breathed that it was impossible for me to read one page aloud." Committed to the proposition that "maternal difficulties" should never be used as an argument against women's public activities nor employed by them as an explanation in order to avoid public commitments, she fabricated an excuse to the lecture bureau. And after Robert's birth, no more Stantons were conceived under her program of "voluntary motherhood," by which she meant that women must not only control their sexuality, but its derivative, their childbearing.[32]

In a process that often destroyed any interest in public causes, other women suffered through months of discomfort, followed by an agonizing childbirth. Thereafter some resisted sex in order to prevent another pregnancy, but not Elizabeth Cady Stanton. Easy childbearing became another exhibit in her embodiment of good health established through ubiquitous naps ("I have a genius for sleep"), good eating habits (mostly vegetables, whole wheat, and a little fat), and exercise, at least until she became obese in later life. During her traveling days she presented the lessons from her personal experience to other women in a lecture entitled "Marriage and Maternity" that conveyed "all aspects of marriage" as well as her prescriptions for good health. In turn she learned from the households she visited across America the sacrificial service of women to their husbands and children. And during her visits to the homes of domineering men, when she was asked to give the grace before the meal, Stanton always thanked their wives and daughters, "the patient hands in weariness and toil that have made this meal."

Her childbearing was a remarkably easy process, especially in a period before numbing whiffs of chloroform diminished pain. As she described her third son Theodore's birth in 1851, "I was sick but a few hours, did not lie down [until] half an hour before he was born, but worked round as hard as I could all night to do up the last thing I had to do." And to Lucretia Mott, who was already impressed with "Elizabeth our hardy reformer," she wrote after Margaret's birth in 1852: "I am the happy mother of a daughter. Rejoice with me all Womankind . . . I laid on a lounge for about fifteen minutes, and alone with my nurse and female friend brought forth this noble girl. I sat up immediately, changed my own clothes, put on a wet bandage and after a few hours repose sat up again. When the child was twenty hours old I took a sponge bath, a sitz bath and then walked out on the piazza and the day being fine I took a drive on the plank road of three miles." As Henry was in Syracuse, Amelia Willard, her housekeeper, and a nurse—but no midwife or doctor—"officiated," and after her delivery, all three helped raise the family flag that celebrated the arrival of her babies.[33]

Nor was Elizabeth Cady Stanton a woman who fit the contemporary understanding that women did not like sex. Insulted by Walt Whitman's "speaking as if woman must be forced to the creative act," she understood "that a healthy woman has as much passion as a man, that she needs nothing stronger than the attraction to draw her to the male." Denying men the authority to appropriate sexual pleasure for themselves and consign to women the role of passionless, often nonconsensual subjects, she argued for androgynous satisfaction. Certainly her husband enjoyed what he called her special kisses. Like so many issues, the conditions she placed on sexuality emerged from her understanding of male misbehavior. Writing in Amelia Bloomer's paper, The Lily, in 1852, she described men as "having animal pleasures . . . but even animals spared their females the dangers of intercourse during pregnancy and lactation." What had been private—an unmentionable issue—now became public with Cady Stanton, who insisted that woman's most basic right was to control her body.[34]

Embracing homeopathy with its approval of sex and reproduction as natural processes, she argued that women, rather than dreading pregnancy, should celebrate voluntary motherhood. In this age of heroic medicine when doctors blistered, purged, and bled in harmful interventions, Elizabeth became a convert to the therapies of Dr. Samuel Hahnemann, who accepted birth control and recommended benign therapies such as cold water cures and diluted disease-carrying agents in a process similar to inoculation. She argued with nurses who did not understand the curative powers of fresh air and sun, and she challenged "the ignorance of doctors" who had established an authoritative masculine medical culture.

From the time of her first child's birth she served as doctor as well as nurse to her own children. In 1842 she ripped the tight, doctor-applied "severe" bandages off her three-month-old son Neil's shoulder, which had been dislocated during his delivery, replacing them with her own regime of rubbing, looser bandages, and hot compresses. "I turned surgeon myself," she proudly wrote her husband, who remained suspicious of his wife's doctoring. A few years later when Neil was feverish, coughing, and growing so weak that she wanted her husband home if his illness continued, she instituted her own methods, having no faith in regular medicine. With "my simple remedies . . . my quack remedies," her son gradually improved. Having grown up in a family where one-half of the children expired from some bacterial infection, her maternal record of seven surviving children became part of her self-conscious exceptionalism. When asked what she knew about babies, Elizabeth Cady Stanton replied, "that is a department of knowledge on which I especially pride myself." And with the self-confidence gained from her success, she tried to rouse listless, complaining, adult female neurasthenics from their rest cures and sanatoriums where, exhausted, they surrendered to more self-defeating bed rest.[35]

Clearly the number of her children distinguished Elizabeth Cady Stanton from other members of the suffrage movement, and indeed most women of her generation who had fewer children than she. Susan B. Anthony chided her about the number of her pregnancies, the result of "a moment's pleasure" but which eroded her time and energy for the cause. In fact most married activists had well below the national average number of children, and the movement attracted more single women than the roughly 10 percent in the general population. Of the presidents of the national suffrage associations during the nineteenth and twentieth centuries, Lucy Stone had only Alice, and of its second tier of leaders the median number was two; Carrie Catt, though three times married, had no children and Susan B. Anthony and Anna Howard Shaw never married. Pridefully as a complete woman, Elizabeth was making herself the hero of her own life.[36]

In 1847 the Stantons moved from Boston to the isolated village of Seneca Falls in the Finger Lakes region of New York. Their house, a few miles out of town on two acres overlooking the Seneca River, was purchased by Daniel Cady in his daughter's name. But Elizabeth knew only too well that she did not "own" the house in fee simple, for as a married woman, she had no power to convey it. Henry owned the property her father had bought, at least until the New York legislature passed a Married Woman's Property Act in 1848, which was further revised in 1860.

Henry had initiated the move from Boston to Seneca Falls. More often the victim of nervous anxieties than his vigorous wife, he was suffering from migraine headaches and lung problems in Boston. Seneca Falls was famous for its healthy air. And its politics were reform Whig. Such a partisan inclination was an added benefit to Henry, who intended to enter politics. But, as he informed his wife, his law practice and political career would now occupy all his time. She must take complete charge of both the parenting and housekeeping.[37]

Elizabeth Cady Stanton found the change from Boston depressing. Henry was frequently away; the boys required supervision and discipline when they teased their baby sisters, threw stones at the pigs and windows of their Irish neighbors, fell out of apple trees, and once experimented with their baby brother, Theodore, to see if, tied with corks, he would float in a tub. Untrained, usually Irish-born servants fueled nativist prejudice in a susceptible Stanton. Like many other middle-class women she complained about the ignorance of the "Hibernians," the laziness and departure to the factories for better-paying jobs of her Marys and Bridgets—that is until the efficient housekeeper Amelia Willard arrived in 1852 and stayed for thirty years. While others older women, single women, and women with fewer children— could leave their families and travel to the women's conventions in the 1850s, Cady Stanton continued to feel like a "caged lioness, longing to bring nursing and housekeeping cares to a close."[38]

By all accounts, Elizabeth Cady Stanton was an intentionally indulgent mother, determined that her children be the masters of their own fate, although, of course, she expected them to support women's rights. She had suffered under her father's regimen of stern masculine discipline and had grown "tired of that ever lasting no!no!no! At school, at home, everywhere it is *no!*" She intended to raise her children differently. From her expansive repertoire of activities for active children, she offered her specific ideas for child's play in humorous lectures that sometimes began with the anecdote of the man who, fearing an earthquake, sent his boys to stay with a friend until the danger passed, only to receive a telegram in a few days: "Please take the boys home and send the earthquake." She told mothers she often felt the same way; many laughed and clapped in a shared maternal experience.[39]

As the mother of five sons, she offered practical advice to all mothers. "Do not shut up and darken the best rooms in the house for company and give the boys no place where they can enjoy freedom with their books and games and household goods about them. Realize that boys must have some exciting amusements." But mothering boys brought an intellectual dilemma: "When I think of all the wrongs that have been heaped upon womankind, I am ashamed that I am not in a condition of chronic wrath . . . my lips overflowing with curses & my hand against every man & his brother. Oh! How I repent me of the male faces I have washed, the mittens I have knit, the pants mended, the cut fingers and broken toes I have bound up & then to multiply my labors for these white male popinjays by ten thousand more, and then to think of all these Lords & Lackeys strutting the deck of the old ship of state . . . & warning us to remain in our appropriate sphere! oh! dear it is too much."[40]

Raising girls required a different approach, not because they should be treated differently than boys but because "the tyrant custom" still barred them from sports and intensive academic programs. They required remedial efforts. Until the turn of the century America's most esteemed physiologists such as the Harvard Medical School's Dr. E. C. Clarke opposed higher education for women, or at least girls who would be mothers, which should be every one of them, believing that it transferred blood from their reproductive organs to their brains and consequently led to inferior children. Stanton condemned such male misunderstandings and sought for American girls including her own a "hearty and romping, free and unrestrained [childhood] developing alike the physical, mental and moral powers."[41]

During her years of domesticity Elizabeth Cady Stanton maintained the optimism about women's rights that was the essential temperament for all its leaders. One of her early pseudonyms was Sunflower, and Susan B. Anthony frequently noted her "bright and beaming face as usual." Her daughter Margaret remembered her mother as "sunny, cheerful, indulgent." Cady Stanton felt as she looked. She grew plumper, even on the Stanton diet of vegetables, whole wheat, no pork and beef, and little fat. And as her hair, fixed in unassailable waves of tight curls, turned white, she resembled a jolly squire. In the same spirit as religious millennialists who anticipated a perfect universe with the second coming of Christ, she expected the soon-to-be installation of women's rights to transform the world into a better place. Such a view was reason enough for a sanguine heart.[42]

Later Cady Stanton's study of Auguste Comte, Charles Darwin, and Herbert Spencer's evolutionary positivism provided her with the evidence of what she had intuitively known. But after three decades of domesticity her personal experience, like marrow flavoring the cooking, served as material for the movement. ". . . It is not in vain that in myself I feel all the wearisome care to which woman in her best estate is subject." And to Susan B. Anthony earlier, "But it may be well for me to understand all the trials of woman's lot, that I may more eloquently proclaim them when the time comes."[43]

Eventually that time came, but for nearly thirty years Elizabeth Cady Stanton suffered the timeless complaints of women trapped in domestic seclusion with small children, circumstances named by Betty Friedan, more than a century later, as the feminine mystique, the problem "that lay buried, unspoken—that has no name." Mostly Cady Stanton wanted to be alone. "Have you," she wrote to her cousin Elizabeth Smith Miller, "lived long enough to enjoy solitude, to look upon a few hours of uninterrupted quiet as a precious feast for the soul?" Until her children were older she dwelt in what she called "the externals," longing for "the inner, the higher life" of solitude. But for the time being, "I am bound hand & foot with two undeveloped Hibernians in my kitchen a baby in my arms & four boys all revolving around me as a common center . . . Woman must ever be sacrificed in the isolated household." And to Susan B. Anthony she acknowledged her desire "to be free from housekeeping and children so as to have some time to read, and think, and write." For the time being, however, her priorities were clear: "I will not deal with humanity's problems until I have finished nursing this baby," she exploded when asked for yet another letter to be read at a convention.[44]

Philosopher of the Cause

From this isolation came an act of creation—the organization of the Seneca Falls Convention, a founding moment in the history of American feminism. The story of the convention that took place on two hot days—July 19 and 20, 1848—is well known: the meeting of five mostly Quaker women, including Lucretia Mott, in Waterloo, New York, around a tea table with Cady Stanton "stirring [myself] and the rest of the party to do and dare anything"; the discussion of the agenda of their proposed meeting; Elizabeth Cady Stanton's application of the form and rhetoric of the Declaration of Independence with "man" replacing George III as the source of oppression; the placing of an advertisement for a women's convention in the *Seneca Falls County Courier*; the locked door at the Wesley Chapel the day of the meeting, and once inside, the women's reluctance to chair the meeting until James Mott called the first session to order. The unexpected size of the turnout and the importance of the issue inspired courage among a group of women who, as they considered how to go about setting up their meeting, were admittedly as "helpless as if [we] had to design a steam engine."[45]

By the end of the first day Elizabeth Cady Stanton had spoken twice. First she had read the Declaration of Sentiments that, like Thomas Jefferson with his committee of four in 1776, she had mostly written with her committee of four. Then in the afternoon she had offered a detailed rationale for the specific resolutions to be voted on the next day by over a hundred attendees. By the evening she had emerged as a natural leader, defending the eighteen accusations she had made against "the Lords of Creation."[46]

Cady Stanton's indictment rested on what she had learned from her relationship with men—the closure of nearly all colleges to women, the legal discriminations that made her "civilly dead," the exclusion of women from the professions, the "different code of morals for men and women," the usurping by the clergy of what "belongs to her conscience and her God," and finally what she had observed even among her Cady sisters and her mother—the destruction of women's self-respect and self-confidence. Only the structure of the Declaration of Independence was derivative. Of the thousand words in Cady Stanton's call for freedom only 152 appeared in Jefferson's declaration, but like Jefferson and his attacks on the monarchy, she challenged the institutions of her oppression, in this case religion and marriage.[47]

It was by comparison to men—to her brother Eleazar who was admitted to Union College; to the Scottish Presbyterian minister who encouraged girls to raise money selflessly in mite boxes to educate male clergymen instead of investing it in women's schools; to her lawyer father and brother-in-law who teased that after she married she could not own property; to her "ignorant and degraded" male neighbors in Seneca Falls who held rights she did not—that she understood the multifarious oppressions of her sex. Taking on the growing reality of middle-class women's lives, she held that "there is no such thing as a sphere for sex."[48]

By every account Elizabeth Cady Stanton offered the most controversial resolution—women's "inalienable right to the elective franchise." Lucretia Mott was shocked: "Why, Lizzie, thee will make us ridiculous." Both her father and her husband opposed votes for women. Daniel Cady again threatened disinheritance, and a few years later when his daughter spoke before a judiciary committee of the New York legislature, he questioned her sanity. "I passed through a terrible scourging when last at my father's," she wrote Susan B. Anthony. "I cannot tell you how deep the iron entered my soul . . . To think that all in me of which my father would have felt a proper pride had I been a man, is deeply mortifying to him because I am a woman."[49]

Henry Stanton, in the midst of his campaign for a seat in the New York State Legislature, helped with some resolutions, but he made good on his threat to leave town if voting was included in the Declaration of Sentiments. "Henry," she admitted, "sides with my friends who oppose me in all that is dearest in my heart." Neither her father nor her husband approved of her writing on women's issues, much less speaking in public on such a topic, and as Susan B. Anthony noted, of all the pioneer women suffragists Elizabeth Cady Stanton was the only one who stood "all alone, without Father, Mother, Sister, Brother or Husband." But opposition, rejection, and even desertion—for

surely she wanted her husband in attendance as that model husband
James Mott was—taught Elizabeth Cady Stanton what she encouraged for all women—self-reliance.[50]

Just months after the Seneca Falls Convention, Stanton argued for
the vote on the grounds of natural rights and protective expediency
before an audience that included the black abolitionist Frederick
Douglass. The vote was as essential in a representative government as
"air and motion are to life." It was the essential transaction in a
democracy of the self-governed. Certainly men knew "the advantages
of voting, for they all seem very tenacious about the right," she declared at a women's convention in Rochester two months after Seneca
Falls. "Think you if woman had a voice in this government, that all
those laws affecting her interests would so entirely violate every principle of right and justice?" Indeed if evidence about the radicalism of
suffrage was ever needed, it rests in the reaction of those at Seneca
Falls, their relatives, and the ensuing seventy-year struggle for the
vote.[51]

As Cady Stanton made clear, for men women's political equality
would cut into their households, endangering traditional, comfortable
domestic arrangements. Middle-class women were permitted limited
degrees of authority within their homes, but men were the established, not easily displaced sovereigns of the public domain. Yet most
American women accepted men's authority. "Women will not claim
their civil rights," she explained to Lucy Stone, who never thought in
such theoretical terms, "until they know their social wrongs." Therein
lay the challenge for the suffragists.[52]

For the rest of her life Elizabeth Cady Stanton worked for the
pledges she had made at Seneca Falls in 1848. What she had resolved
was nothing less than an effort to end the discriminations against
women both within their households and beyond. She spent little
time on what she considered the distractions of volunteering in political parties and benevolent associations, both of which exploited
women for men's interests. But Seneca Falls also made Cady Stanton
aware of her own talents—to speak spontaneously before an audience
and to run meetings efficiently. She could write with power; she could
summarize an agenda in logical, compelling prose, with the cadence
of her words in harmony with the meaning of her message. Like Jef-

ferson, her writing was felicitous and memorable; her verbs pungent, her images evocative. The nineteenth-century women's movement resonated with her shorthand labels of various insults of male oppression—"the aristocracy of sex," "the lords of creation," "male marriage," "satellites of the dinner-pot and cradle," and the devastating "spaniel wives."

But until her children were older, she had no time "to search books." Overwhelmed by "children, washing dishes, baking, sewing," it was infuriating "to not have a moment of quiet to read and write." Men, her husband among them, "can shut themselves up for days with their books and thoughts [and] know little of what difficulties a woman must surmount." Henry spent his days with adults; she spent hers with boisterous children, entertaining them, adjudicating their quarrels, shopping and mending their clothes, taking them to the dentist, and feeding them. "How rebellious it makes me feel when I see Henry going about where and how he pleases. He can walk at will through the whole wide world or shut himself up alone, if he pleases, within four walls. When I contrast his freedom with my bondage and feel that because of the false position of women I have been compelled to hold my noblest aspirations in abeyance in order to be a wife, a mother, a nurse, a cook, a household drudge, I am fired up anew and long to put forth from my experience the whole long story of women's wrongs." As all mothers knew, but especially those with a household of young children, she was rarely alone. When she signed her letters good night, it was not due to convention, but because night, with the rowdy Stanton boys finally asleep, was the only time she had the peace and quiet to write.

Instead Susan B. Anthony, with time and energy but less talent as a writer, "held the baby and made the puddings," sometimes spanking the Stantons harder, as Robert remembered, than their mother. Anthony also did the research and most of the lecturing. How many states had married-women's property laws, Elizabeth wanted to know in 1854 before she wrote her speech to the New York Judiciary committee. What were the divorce laws in Maryland? Did all states grant men automatic guardianship of their children? Stanton put Anthony's information to work in the fugitive women's newspapers of the 1850s as well as in her speeches. With the fluency of a natural writer, she

contributed the visionary language of the American women's movement, drafting calls for conventions, writing the resolutions discussed
at those meetings, and composing on half-sheets of paper in her hurried, sometimes illegible handwriting the speeches to be given by Susan B. Anthony. There was no pride of ownership between these two
women over the message.

As Cady Stanton moved from harassed mother of young children to a respected commentator—a public intellectual in today's
terms—on everything from suffrage in Great Britain, the Irish question, the need for policewomen, and how to raise boys, she emerged
as the voice of the women's movement—its Jefferson to Anthony's
Napoleon. Through the process of writing and its attendant solitude,
Cady Stanton developed her message. Women were individuals, not
just dependent daughters, sisters, wives, and mothers collected into a
family. They must be responsible for their own lives. Women, like
men, made "the voyage of life alone, and for safety in an emergency,
they must know something of the laws of navigation."

In her application of Enlightenment principles of individualism to
women, she argued in a speech Anthony thought her best for education, suffrage, and equality in civic and economic life. To women her
message was clear and unchanging: be self-reliant; to men it was a re-
monstrance—given "the inner being which we call ourself . . . who
dare take on himself their rights, the responsibilities of another human soul? Nothing strengthens the judgment and quickens the conscience like individual responsibility. Nothing adds such dignity to
character as the recognition of one's self-sovereignty . . ."[53]

One way to practice what she preached was the unique schooling
she organized for her children. When they were very young, Elizabeth Cady Stanton homeschooled them, correctly convinced that she
knew more than the ignorant teachers of most district schools. Later
she sent them to boarding schools. Setting a family tradition, the oldest boys attended the reformers' Angelina and Theodore Weld's Ea-
gleswood Academy near Raritan, New Jersey. Aged nine and eleven,
Neil and Kit were miserable and begged for a visit from their mother,
but not in bloomers. In the didactic style she adopted in letters to her
children—for in their lives as in hers experience became a parable of
learning—she replied that if she was free from petticoats she could

run from wild animals. Then came the lesson: "you must learn not to care what foolish people say." Later the boys attended Dr. Reid's progressive school in Geneva, New York. But during the 1870s when their younger sister Harriot went off to boarding school, she survived only two days at the Rockland County Female Academy until she rode her pony home to a sympathetic mother who found another school where the schoolmaster "understood human nature." The latter meant, for Cady Stanton, an appreciation that boys and girls should study and play together in coeducational settings.[54]

The importance of boarding schools was clear. They taught the self-reliance necessary for noncompliance and independence. For some upper-class parents they represented badges of privilege. Both Stantons intended that their children meet the right people, not for sociability but for economic and intellectual advantage. Cady Stanton intended her offspring to be, as she was, exceptional—"saints with strong bodies." It was a hard parental commission, given her own capabilities; not surprisingly, less-gifted colleagues in the women's movement complained of her arrogant superiority. That six Stantons finished college at a time when only sixty thousand Americans were even enrolled illustrated the importance of education to a woman who had never had the chance to go to college. Both Harriot and Margaret were among only eleven thousand American women to attend college at a time when, as their mother knew only too well, only 41 institutions out of 582 accepted women.[55]

Not only did six graduate, but all six received some postgraduate training, even if their mother had to join James Redpath's lecture bureau and travel around the United States to pay the tuitions. In 1878—a year in which she gave twenty-six lectures throughout the United States and earned two thousand dollars "above all expenses"—Kit and Gat graduated from Columbia Law School. She picked coeducational Cornell for her sons Robert and Theodore, hoping that her daughters could go there as well. But no dormitories existed for women at a time when conventional wisdom held that girls must remain at home, there to be nurtured by their natural maternal guardians. Although Elizabeth Cady Stanton proposed to rent a house in Ithaca where her daughters could live with her, instead they attended Vassar, the newly founded women's college in Poughkeepsie.

Aunt Harriet Cady Eaton, who paid the college tuitions of the Stanton daughters, opposed coeducation, and so dictated the choice of Vassar for her nieces.[56]

City Influences

In 1862 Elizabeth Cady Stanton moved to New York City, joining her husband who, the year before, had taken a much-sought patronage appointment as deputy collector of the Port of New York, and had promptly appointed his son Neil as his clerk. Three years before, Daniel Cady had died and because he never made good on his threat to disinherit Elizabeth, she used her inheritance, now under her control by state law, to buy a house and educate her children. Her father had been largely correct about Henry's limited abilities as a breadwinner. In another of those hard lessons learned at the hands of male relatives, Henry's feeble talents as a wage-earner (he earned the clerk's salary of twenty-five hundred dollars in his patronage job as a deputy collector), made evident the reasons why women must be financially self-sufficient. Writing and lecturing became her profession.[57]

At first the family rented in Brooklyn. Then they bought a four-story brownstone in Manhattan on West Forty-fifth Street. Uncertain whether she preferred the beauty of nature or the intellectual stimulation of cities, in 1868 Elizabeth Cady Stanton reached for both when she built a house in Tenafly, in northern New Jersey, near the railroad station on the Northern Railway Line. Only an hour's ride from New York, her home provided views of the distant spruce-laden, blue-toned hills of the Palisades. But Tenafly also afforded easy access to the largest city in the United States. Meanwhile, Henry rented an apartment in town, visiting Tenafly every other weekend in the couple's unorthodox cohabitation patterns. At the end of her life and after long visits to her married daughter, Harriot Stanton Blatch, in England, she returned to New York, sharing a fourth-floor apartment on West Sixty-first Street with her son Bob and daughter Maggie. But wherever she lived, even in Harriot's home outside the rural village of Basingstoke, England, Susan B. Anthony had a room of her own.[58]

In New York, a metropolitan center of over a million in 1870, Elizabeth Cady Stanton lived at the center of a diffuse women's movement. In the city she sought out the most radical men and women of her generation. Robert Dale Owen, the reformer and supporter of birth control, came to town; the sisters Victoria Woodhull and Tennessee Claflin ran their brokerage house and published their newspaper *Woodhull and Claflin's Weekly* nearby. During these same years Cady Stanton and Anthony were struggling to publish their weekly paper *The Revolution*. Homeopaths, such as her brother-in-law Edward Bayard, believers in hydropathy and the curative powers of water, spiritualists like Stephen Pearl Andrews, and phrenologists had businesses nearby. (One phrenologist, after examining the bumps on Elizabeth's head, declared her, as she knew herself to be, combative, strong, intelligent, and "with energy of character.") She dined with writers like Theodore Tilton of the *Independent* and Horace Greeley of the *Tribune*. Residence in a transportation hub with railroads, stagecoaches, and steamboats also accommodated her travels as a high-priced lecturer.

Elizabeth Cady Stanton now emerged as the unpaid leader of the suffrage movement, its spiritual and intellectual pilot as well as its most important propagandist. But there could be no solitude amid the demands of a growing organization like the National Woman Suffrage Association, although there was prestige and self-gratification. After the 1869 split in the suffrage movement, when Lucy Stone went off with her followers to Boston to set up the rival American Woman Suffrage Association, Elizabeth had wanted to write a book, study philosophy, and "be alone with my thoughts." Susan, she thought, could run the organization.[59]

In fact, it would be another twenty-four years before she was liberated from organizational affairs and by that time, in her late seventies, she would be a national figure with many claims on her time. In the meantime her coadjutor Susan B. Anthony served as an effective campaign manager, drumming up support in the conventions for the perennially nominated and elected Stanton, who was now dubbed "our Washington" by her followers. Despite her growing desire to give up her presidency, she still provided a vision of leadership. Admiring Emerson from her days as a young wife in Boston, she self-consciously tried to enact the New England philosopher's dictum that leaders provide "some promise or explanation." Promises and explanations she gave annually in her addresses to the assembled membership of NWSA.

Her tactics were straightforward. First there would be no more concessions like the ones women had made during the Civil War when they gave up their own work for the war effort and then in the postwar period surrendered their program for that of black males. Reformers who compromise have not yet "grasped the idea that truth is the only safe ground to stand upon." Stanton had no reservations about her ability to know that truth, and so extended the woman's agenda into divorce reform, women's rights in marriage to control their bodies, and at the end of her life, a reinterpretation of the Bible. Cady Stanton was never ingratiatingly representative or commonly average. Nor did she depend on the mutual sycophancy that infected the relations of other suffragists. On the contrary, she was authoritarian and imperious. Her grandchildren knew her as "Queen Mother," and some followers called her that too. She was increasingly elitist, racist, and nativist in her support of the educated vote, and in her opposition to immigrant and black male voting, the latter invariably demeaned as Sambo.

Conscious of the lack of education of newly enfranchised blacks, Elizabeth Cady Stanton reacted as a privileged daughter of the aristocracy, with the oppressions of class, but not of race or gender, obscure to her. She had begun her suffrage life as a proponent of universal voting, but by the 1880s Elizabeth Cady Stanton had descended into a restrictive agenda of educated suffrage for men and women, black and white, native and immigrant. The oppressors she fought were "ignorant" black and naturalized male voters who opposed suffrage and reinforced the "aristocracy of sex" already in existence against women. "If Saxon men have legislated thus for their own mothers and daughters, what can we hope for at the hands of Chinese, Indians and Africans?" she asked a friend. She noted how women were accused of prejudice against blacks if they supported "educated suffrage," while blacks, given a free ride, were never held accountable for their bias against women. What she intended was a suffrage and equal rights movement in which all educated women— whether black, native-born, or immigrant—would submerge their distinctions in their sex. In response to the popular argument that giving women the vote would increase the number of ignorant voters, she acknowledged that illiterate women, like males, should not vote.[60]

The essential requirement for voting must be intelligence as measured by literacy in English, not sex or race. In any case if the movement wanted her as president, they must take her with these views, along with her published comments about free love, divorce reform, and even what many considered her most outlandish act—her self-nomination and candidacy for New York's Eighth District congressional seat in 1866 when she received twenty-four votes and joked that she wanted to meet all her supporters.[61]

But as a celebrity no one better conveyed the message of her following to outsiders or more successfully mediated among fractious colleagues inside the movement or presided over large meetings with such dignity and authority, even if by the 1880s she sometimes napped on the platform. In a movement that sought respectability and a single issue, Elizabeth Cady Stanton was nevertheless an unlikely president of the wartime Women's Loyal National League from 1863 to 1865, an officer of the American Equal Rights Association from 1865 to 1868, the president of the National Woman Suffrage Association most years from 1869 to 1892, the president of the International Suffrage Association from 1889 to 1891, and in her late seventies, the reluctant president of the merged National American Woman Suffrage Association in 1892.

Shortly after the Stanton family moved to New York, a scandal descended on the family. Henry Stanton was accused of taking bribes during the Civil War. Certainly he had the opportunity to do so. In his patronage post as the deputy collector of the Port Authority of New York, he was in charge of the bonds shippers were required to post to prevent the shipment of wartime contraband to the Confederacy. But of the five thousand bonds processed by Stanton's office, some 150 had been tampered with or illegally removed from his office. Henry stood accused of theft, in the newspapers and in the view of his superiors, the chief collector of the port Hiram Barney and Secretary of the Treasury Salmon Chase. In October 1863 Henry was forced to resign. After a three-month investigation he was absolved of any criminal conduct, but his superiors remained critical of the way he and his son Neil had managed the department.

In fact, his twenty-two-year-old son—the eldest of the Stantons—had forged his father's signature, taken bribes, and returned a handful of bonds to the parties who had given them. His father forced him to make restitution and Neil was never charged with a crime. But the harm was done. "One weak boy and two wily scoundrels try to do their worst . . . ," lamented Henry, whose unrealistic hopes for a political career abruptly ended, to be replaced by intermittent work as a journalist. But he persuaded his wife that the charges were only insinuations and that he was the victim of an internal partisan struggle in the Lincoln administration. "Political necessity and personal malignity were at the bottom of it."[62]

Loyal to Henry, Elizabeth Cady Stanton used her influence—especially with the editor Horace Greeley and the New York political boss Thurlow Weed—to prevent any "humiliation" to her husband. Unlike most American women who had only social relationships with men who were not relatives, she had friendships with influential men. Still, for a woman who despised groveling, she was embarrassed when she begged Greeley to delay any coverage of the matter in the *Tribune* until Henry had time to present his side of the matter: "Will you my friend be careful in your *editorial statements* in reference to my husband? In this hour of the deepest sorrow of my life I ask not mercy but justice."[63]

In the way of mothers, she glossed over her son's dishonesty. As usual, her personal feelings remained veiled; she saved her passion for her public pronouncements. Whatever she felt about the most difficult of her children—a first son named for her father, who had been a chronic bedwetter, had lied, been unable to finish school, and was the only one of the Stantons not to attend college—she never disclosed. Soon the restless Neil moved to Louisiana where he served a term in the legislature and, during a time of unlimited opportunities for corruption in that state during Reconstruction, made money. For a brief time he lived in Tenafly with his mother, but then moved to Iowa, married, had a child, and divorced. When he died in 1889, the only Stanton child to predecease Elizabeth Cady Stanton, he left his entire estate to his mother. And for a month after his death, she dreamed he walked on the porch at Tenafly.

Briefly she considered a new direction for Henry, her marriage, and her children. Excited by the beauty of the West, the opportunities for solitude on the Kansas prairies, the cheapness of the land, and the possibilities in middle age for a new beginning, Cady Stanton joined thousands of Americans in a fantasy. As she wrote her husband in a rare letter: "This is the country for us to move to . . . We could build a house for $3,000. You would feel like a new man. You could be a leader here . . . There is no one who can give a speech like you," she concluded, harking back to the days of their courtship when Henry Stanton had been a respected antislavery speaker and she had loved him for that. But moving to the West proved wishful thinking of the kind in which she seldom engaged.[64]

By the 1870s Elizabeth Cady Stanton and Susan B. Anthony had lost their struggle to include women in the national postwar settlement of Reconstruction. For the first time in American history the word *male* was inserted into the U.S. Constitution through the second section of the Fourteenth Amendment. The Fifteenth Amendment, which had seemed to suffragists an opportunity for constitutional rights, gave the vote to blacks. But only males were entitled. Cady Stanton bitterly inquired of the reformer Wendell Phillips who spoke so righteously about voting rights for the freed slaves if he believed "the African race was entirely composed of males." The answer was that women—black and white—were still invisible even to reformers and sympathizers like Phillips.[65]

The loss of these political battles liberated Stanton from the careful diplomacy that was the hallmark of Susan B. Anthony. She had always opposed women's wasting their time in any organization run by men for men, whether a charitable association or a political party where they "made bed quilts for agricultural fairs or slippers for bishops or sang paeans to politicians." With escalating zeal, Cady Stanton now addressed a panoply of related women's issues—divorce, a concern of hers since 1860, changes in marriage codes in order to protect women from abuse and legal marriage at twelve years of age, women's control over their bodies through voluntary motherhood, and eventually the Bible, which she considered the greatest obstacle to women's equality.[66]

She struck up public associations with controversial supporters such as the race-baiting George Train who briefly financed *The Revo-*

lution. "We are speaking for the cause of Woman, Mr. Train is doing the same. We are satisfied he is a pure minded noble man who neither smokes chews drinks gambols lies steals or swears . . . He lays his talents & wealth at our feet . . ." She would, she said, accept the devil if he supported the enfranchisement of women. Unchaperoned, she rode across the Kansas prairies with Gov. George Robinson during their unsuccessful campaign for women's suffrage in that state. She befriended Hester Vaughan, a victim of rape and sexual exploitation, sentenced to be hung for infanticide but in Stanton's view, a victim seduced and convicted by men. If Vaughan were put to death, she wrote in *The Revolution,* male society would be her murderer.[67]

The acquittal of Daniel McFarlane, who had murdered his former wife's new husband, Albert Richardson, mobilized Cady Stanton as well. McFarlane had been declared innocent on the basis of the unwritten tradition that gave husbands (even former ones) ownership of their wives' bodies under a strained extension of the doctrine of coverture. Such a murder, the argument went, was no more than shooting a burglar in one's home. With the instincts of a propagandist Stanton sensed how a single court case dramatically summarized women's inferior position. To a mass meeting held in New York's Apollo Hall in May 1870, she noted that Abby McFarlane Richardson, who for years had been abused by her drunken first husband, had not even been called to testify. Had she, her testimony "would have changed the opinions of the jury, but as neither women nor slaves can testify against their supposed masters . . . they excluded her testimony from the case." Comparing the McFarlane verdict to the infamous Dred Scott decision of 1857, which had declared blacks—slave and free—without any rights, Cady Stanton anticipated a precedent. Just as the Dred Scott decision had precipitated the Civil War and the end of slavery, so reasonable Americans might be so outraged by the McFarlane acquittal that they would accept reforms for women.[68]

Cady Stanton's positions on divorce, marriage, and what she labeled the "bugaboos" of her time were more nuanced than her opponents allowed in their personal attacks. Accused of free love, she responded that she had lived thirty years with one man and expected to live with him "to the end." Nor did she advocate "easy divorce . . . What I have always insisted on is, that the laws of marriage and divorce, whatever they are, shall bear equally on man and woman which will never be the case until woman has an equal voice in their enactment and administration." In fact Elizabeth Cady Stanton lived a life of bourgeois respectability; it was her theories, her rhetoric, and her associations that separated her from most Americans, particularly the suffragists of Lucy Stone's organization, and at times even members of her own NAWSA.[69]

Most outrageously to her competitor Lucy Stone, she befriended the flamboyant spiritualist Victoria Woodhull, who had moved to New York in 1868. Some called Woodhull a tramp; others believed her a bigamist. But her beauty, intelligence, and seductive personality proved irresistible to powerful men like Massachusetts congressman Benjamin Butler and Commodore Cornelius Vanderbilt, the owner of the New York Central Railroad who set her up in the investment business. In a pamphlet on *The Principles of Social Freedom* Woodhull proclaimed her "inalienable, constitutional, and natural right to love whom I may, to love as long or as short a period as I can; to change that love every day if I please and with that right neither you nor any law you can frame have any right to interfere . . ." Such views as well as her support of suffrage and her prominence brought Woodhull to the attention of Stanton and Anthony, who invited her to speak to the National Woman Suffrage Association convention in New York in 1871.[70]

Victoria Woodhull had already addressed the Judiciary Committee of the U.S. Senate, at the invitation of Benjamin Butler. There she made the case that Susan B. Anthony tried to enact in 1872. Native-born and naturalized women were already citizens under the first article of the Fourteenth Amendment; as citizens American women were entitled to vote. At the suffrage convention, seated between Lucretia Mott and Stanton, Woodhull said: "I have asked for equality, nothing more. Sexual freedom means the abolition of prostitution both in and out of marriage, means the emancipation of woman from sexual slavery and her coming into ownership and control of her own body, means the end of her pecuniary dependence on man, means the abrogation of forced pregnancy, of antenatal murder of undesired children, and the birth of love children only . . . Rise and declare yourself free." Along with a thousand other women, Elizabeth

Cady Stanton rose, waved her handkerchief in the suffrage salute, and applauded views that she had long supported.[71]

But Woodhull, who had begun her public career selling cigars in a tent show and knew as well how to sell herself, intended more than casual appearances before NWSA. By 1872 she had decided to form a political party and run for president. There was no better forum for an official nomination than women collected in convention, especially since Cady Stanton supported her Equal Rights or People's Party, even going so far as to sign Susan B. Anthony's name to a resolution to form this new political party "whose principles shall meet the issues of the hour and represent equal rights for all." Furious at her inclusion in this distraction from suffrage, Susan B. Anthony, on a lecture tour in the West, rushed back to New York, berated Cady Stanton for her support of Woodhull, and after one of those fierce storms that rolled across the friendship of these two women, presided over the National Woman Suffrage Association meeting in May 1872 after a peeved Stanton refused to do so. When an uninvited Woodhull appeared on the platform to turn the meeting into her nominating convention, Anthony ordered the janitor to turn off the gaslights. With Woodhull standing on a dark platform, Anthony instructed her that she was out of order, while the rank-and-file suffragists stumbled toward unlit exits.[72]

Through her friendship with Woodhull, Elizabeth Cady Stanton became entangled in a scandal that reinforced her views about clerical hypocrisy and the manipulation of women by married men. The triangle involved Henry Ward Beecher, the nationally admired rector of the Plymouth Congregational Church in Brooklyn; Elizabeth Tilton, a Sunday school teacher and parishioner in his church; and her husband, Theodore Tilton, the editor of the well-known magazine The Independent, all close friends of both Stanton and Susan B. Anthony.[73]

Stanton first heard about Beecher's affair with Elizabeth Tilton from her husband Theodore, while Anthony heard the story from Elizabeth Tilton, who was the head of a suffrage group in New York. For weeks Beecher had been attacking Woodhull as a depraved sex radical, and Woodhull responded by exposing the affair in the November 2, 1872, edition of her newspaper. She included arch suggestions that free love was natural for Henry Ward Beecher, a man whose strong "amative impulses" derived from the same part of his brain as his preaching talents. To establish her reliability, Woodhull offered as one of her sources Elizabeth Cady Stanton, who promptly announced that she had been misquoted, although eventually Stanton went public with the scandal as she knew it from both Tiltons. The affair was first denied by all the participants, then admitted by the Tiltons, but forever denied by Beecher. He retained his pulpit after a church investigation by members he appointed. And in 1875 he was acquitted in the civil action over adultery and alienation of affections brought by Theodore Tilton.[74]

For Stanton the Beecher-Tilton affair summarized several issues relating to women. There were the iniquities and hypocrisy of a double sex standard and the need for more reasonable divorce procedures. There was the matter of the position of women within the court system and before the world, for it was Elizabeth Tilton who, not able to testify in the civil trial, ended up disgraced, impoverished, and childless. While her husband, an admitted adulterer, was fired as the editor of *The Independent*, he was later offered an editorial position at the *Golden Age*, a new magazine funded by Beecher who intended to buy his silence. And in the added lesson about the punishment of unruly women who challenged male prerogatives, as a result of her coverage of the Beecher-Tilton affair Victoria Woodhull was arrested for sending obscene matter through the mails, under a never before applied post-office statute. In Stanton's view, the moral of this shabby tale was that male adulterers went free, while female reformers were jailed—in this case in New York's oppressive dungeon, the Ludlow Street jail, popularly known as the Tombs. There Victoria Woodhull was incarcerated for weeks.[75]

The Beecher-Tilton affair also opened the door on a chapter of Cady Stanton's private history. For years she had kept silent about a temptation of her own—to elope before her marriage with her brother-in-law Edward Bayard, Tryphena's husband. On a quiet midnight walk she had told the story to her friend Isabella Beecher Hooker, a stanch suffragist and Henry Ward Beecher's half-sister, who believed her brother guilty of adultery. The retelling of the story had a purpose: to illustrate the possibilities of reconciliation for the estranged Tiltons. In Stanton's view the story of her ancient flirtation with her brother-in-law demonstrated the willpower that had become part of her maturing identity—what she promoted for all women as the sovereignty of self. For it had been Bayard—that "son of Adam"—who in 1838 had tempted her, proposing and urging that they run away, and it had been a daughter of Eve—twenty-three-year-old Elizabeth—who had refused.[76]

Final Years

The most important result of the Reverend Beecher–Mrs. Tilton imbroglio was its reinforcement of Cady Stanton's festering anticlericalism. For years she had loathed the "superstitions of the Christian religion," by which she meant the grim Puritan doctrines of original sin. Later she gave strict gender scrutiny to all human institutions and found all tilted against women, but none more destructively than the church and its ministers who, like Henry Ward Beecher, claimed special privilege over women as God's human translators of Christianity. At the 1848 Seneca Falls Convention Elizabeth Cady Stanton was ready with three indictments against the clergy—those *men* of the cloth who placed women in a subordinate position, excluded them from participation in the affairs of the church, and developed a different code of morals for men than women, claiming "apostolic authority" for these insults. Throughout the 1850s and 1860s Christian perfectionists like Theodore Parker helped shape her alternative religion based on free will, not literal scripture, on the humanity, but not divinity, of Christ, and on the presence of God in each person as best developed by that individual male or female. By the 1870s, as she wrote Henry Blackwell, Stanton found "our greatest enemies entrenched in the church."[77]

Early in her life Elizabeth Cady Stanton had rejected her family's practice of "Old Scottish Presbyterianism," which opposed music in church and threatened eternal damnation for sinners. While living in Seneca Falls and New York, Elizabeth went to church only to hear the music in the Episcopal churches, where she had discovered superior organs. Henry occasionally attended the Presbyterian church, but none of the children was ever required to go. Although she shed the grim doctrines of the Presbyterians, for many years she still identified herself as a Christian, adopting America's nondenominational civic religion and appealing to "a professedly republican, Christian people" to right the wrongs of women. But by the time she was in her seventies, Elizabeth was ready to embarrass the women's movement with a devastating critique of the Bible and orthodox Christianity.[78]

In the 1880s she had more time to study, meditate, and write. She had retired from her travels on the lecture circuit. The physical energy of her childhood that had taken her on foot and horseback across the Mohawk Valley in competitive races with boys had drained away, eroded by arthritis. Now she lived a sedentary existence and lost her battle with obesity. Admitting to cravings for sugar, cream, butter, and occasionally chocolate for breakfast, she was the opposite of the abstemious Anthony. In the late 1880s after having to sit ignominiously on a hay scale in order to be weighed, she reported her weight as 240 pounds, stuffed into a body frame of five feet five inches. She looked even heavier, for after giving up bloomer dress in the 1850s, she had never worn the girdles and tight lacing of high fashion. Still the "humiliation and sorrow" of her weight led to six unsuccessful weeks in an upper-state New York sanatorium where after "rubbings, pinchings, steamings, Swedish movements, dieting, massage and electricity," she lost only five pounds and still could not walk more than a hundred feet without puffing.[79]

Henry's sudden death in 1887 from pneumonia released her from the necessity of keeping a home for his weekend visits. Her diary entry on the day she learned of Henry's death evinced not love but aloof regret for what had not transpired during her forty-seven-year marriage. "Ah! If we could only remember in life to be gentle and forbearing with each other, and to strive to serve nobly instead of exacting service, our memory of the past would be more pleasant and profitable."[80]

Finally she was alone. Now she had time for her crusade against the Bible—"a book which teaches that women brought sin and death into the world and shames women." During earlier decades of reform work Stanton had addressed family and civic concerns, and while these were never abandoned, now she focused on a root oppression.

Initially, for this was a vast undertaking and she had no expertise in languages or biblical exegesis, she tried to recruit friends from the suffrage movement. Most, including Susan B. Anthony, declined. The pragmatic Anthony was chagrined that her friend would take on such a toxic issue, and just as the suffrage cause was gaining power in Western states. "I believe it is the weakest production she has ever made," complained Anthony. But Elizabeth Cady Stanton persisted, mostly alone, but sometimes aided by a "revising" committee of twenty-five women.[81]

"We do not propose a new translation," she informed William Lloyd Garrison, Jr. "We simply comment on what men say in plain English. They tell us in one breath that woman owes all she is and has to the Bible and in the next breath they say the Bible is opposed to the claims for larger liberties that women are demanding today. A book that curries women in her maternity, degrades her in marriage, makes her the author of sin and a mere after thought in creation and baptizes all this as the word of God cannot be said to be a great blessing to our sex. Our object is to lift women out of their reverence for it as the word of God." Her suffrage associate Mary Livermore understood the project, more conservatively, to "select and collate the passages in the Bible relating to women and to learn the circumstances, customs and state of society when they were written." But for Stanton the purpose of *The Woman's Bible* was to release women from centuries of intimidation through texts accepted as the word of God. "How can woman's position be changed from that of a subordinate to an equal without opposition, without the broadest discussion of all the questions involved in her present degradation?" she wondered.[82]

Although biblical criticism was an expanding field at the end of the nineteenth century, especially in Germany, no one had scrutinized the testaments from the point of view of women. Few scholars entertained the idea that the Bible was the result of historical interpretations filtered through place- and time-bound prejudice. Cady Stanton saw otherwise. Emboldened by her conviction that the Bible was the work of men writing "during a barbaric age" and that its analysis rested with men who were the misogynist prisoners of their own age, Stanton reviewed it as a collection of often contradictory stories, legends, and proverbs.

She noted the invisibility and namelessness of women save as the mothers of men and even then, as with Moses, without name. She called attention to the contributions of women that passed unmentioned in the sermons of orthodox ministers; she discussed Sarah, Rebecca, Rachel, Miriam, and even Balaam's female ass who saw the Lord before her abusive master in the Book of Numbers. She noted that the first book of Genesis testified to the simultaneous creation of man and woman "with equal title to this green earth." When she moved on to the New Testament, where the letters of Paul condemned women to submission in marriage and silence in church, she commented that Paul's statements were time-bound, had no divine sanction, and were probably directed to unruly women in one community who were asking too many questions. And ever scandalous, she interpreted the virgin birth as a slur on natural motherhood and the Virgin Mary as "appealing in a sexual way to male worshippers and for women the love of Jesus is sexual."[83]

Ahead of her time, in this and other pursuits and perceptions, she concluded that science with its evolutionary principles was on a collision course with the story of God's creation. On this point her reading of Charles Darwin's *Descent of Man* and Herbert Spencer's *First Principles* with their ideas on evolutionary progress encouraged a reinterpretation of what she considered the most damning book of all—Genesis, where there were contradictory versions of the story of creation. "Admit Darwin's theory of evolution," she wrote her cousin Libby Miller, "and the whole orthodox system topples to the ground. If there was no Fall, there was no need of a savior and the atonement, regeneration, and salvation have no significance whatsoever." The narrative of Christianity made women the carrier of evil in the Old Testament in order to establish the need for redemption in the New Testament.[84]

Two weeks after a spectacular eightieth birthday party on November 12, 1895, with eight thousand guests in attendance at New York's Metropolitan Opera House, an event organized by Susan B. Anthony and Stanton's son Theodore, the first volume of *The Woman's Bible* appeared. Celebrating its publication along with that of her autobiography *Eighty Years and More*, she was as much relieved as if "I had given birth to twins."[85]

Public reaction was swift and brutal. Along with the expected opposition and ministerial ridicule as "a work of women and the devil," her suffrage friends deserted. By a margin of fifty-three to forty-one, over Anthony's objections, NAWSA condemned the "so-called *Woman's Bible*" and maintained their organization's "non-sectarianism." Stanton, who had long defended Lucy Stone from her friend Susan B. Anthony's harsh personal attacks, had learned that Alice Stone Blackwell and her father had organized the repudiation, and Anthony's own claque of "girls" believed Stanton's book so damaging to the suffrage movement that it must be disavowed.[86]

Elizabeth Cady Stanton had hoped that the suffrage organization she had founded would find in *The Woman's Bible* "the culminating work of my life—my crowning achievement," a nexus for all women's issues. Instead the stinging rebuke of a censure at the annual convention furthered her distance from the organization she had founded and now largely abandoned. By this time her self-taught autonomy had led her far "outside of all connection with women's organizations. I have not sails to trim to catch the favor of men or women." To her son Theodore she wryly noted that both *The Woman's Bible* and her autobiography *Eighty Years* were selling well. "Whenever there is a lull in the sale of *The Woman's Bible*, some convention denounces it or some library throws it out, then there is immediately fresh demand for it. So the bigots promote the sale every time . . ." And before the end of the year *The Woman's Bible* was a best seller, with twenty thousand copies in print in England and the United States.[87]

Four years after the publication of her second volume of *The Woman's Bible* in 1898, eighty-seven-year-old Elizabeth Cady Stanton died of heart failure. Nearly blind with cataracts and mostly bedridden, she had nevertheless maintained her lifelong optimism, intellectual energy, and self-direction. "So far," she wrote in an article on the benefits of old age two months before she died, "my evening has had no gloom worth speaking of—life is very sweet to me." While she could no longer walk or read, she could still write, and to those who asked she quoted Henry Wadsworth Longfellow's lines: "For age is opportunity no less / From youth itself, though in a different dress."

At a time when fewer than 4 percent of all Americans lived to be sixty-five, during the week before her death, Elizabeth Cady Stanton engaged the Republican president Theodore Roosevelt in a dispute over his equivocation about women's suffrage. (He was much more interested in women as mothers than as voters.) She wrote a letter to Harvard's president Charles Eliot as well. In the spirit of the contemporary crusade of eugenics, Eliot had complained that graduates of Harvard produced only two children. To which Cady Stanton replied with characteristic irreverence that two was enough for Harvard men, given their poor performance as fathers.[88]

A few hours before her death on October 26, 1902, Elizabeth Cady Stanton insisted on standing, with her hands resting on a table. She stood mute for six or seven minutes. Her daughter Harriot believed her to be mentally making a last address. Perhaps this speech was on suffrage, or the need to change divorce laws, or on the proper way to raise "our boys and girls." Possibly she was silently reiterating her lifelong challenge to herself and to other women to live "that solitude which each and every one of us has always carried with them" and to make wifehood and motherhood incidents, not the primal fact of their lives. Then she sat down, was lifted to her bed, and slipped away "peacefully in a few minutes."

Like her friends Lucy Stone and Susan B. Anthony, Elizabeth Cady Stanton was cremated—"roses will grow out of her ashes," said one of her admirers. In a private service in her apartment, with Susan B. Anthony sitting in the armchair where her best friend had spent so many of her last days, the reformer Moncure Conway spoke of Cady Stanton's wit and humanity and her tremendous impact on public opinion, with only words, for she had neither sword nor vote. Then at her interment Lucy Stone's sister-in law Rev. Nette Brown Blackwell eulogized the leader of the nineteenth-century women's movement, and the Rev. Phebe Hanaford commended her spirit to an androgynous God.[89]

4

Mothering America:
The Feminist Ambitions of Frances Willard

Sometime in 1840, Josiah Willard, a prosperous thirty-seven-year-old farmer in Churchville, New York, decided to become a minister. The choice was not entirely his; God had directed it. Like thousands of other Congregationalists, Universalists, and Methodists in northern New York, Willard had experienced a life-changing epiphany, modeled on that of the early Christian organizer Saint Paul. Willard's future and that of his wife and children were forever changed by a call from heaven to repent and serve the Lord. Willard was not alone. It was the time of the Second Great Awakening when itinerant preachers called sinners to convert and pledge themselves to God in public conversions witnessed by their friends and neighbors. Josiah Willard lived in the midst of this search for holiness in "the burned-over district," an area in upstate New York where the fires raged in the individual souls of sinners. Along with as many as one hundred thousand New Englanders and New Yorkers, Willard sought renewed sanctification.

Even before the evangelical minister Charles Finney, who had so terrified young Elizabeth Cady, had come to preach in nearby Rochester, Willard had been a faithful Christian. His family tree included several Baptist and Congregationalist ministers; he had already had one conversion experience in which the Holy Spirit had descended to him as he prayed. As a young boy Willard had left Vermont in a family migration for better farming prospects in New York, and once arrived in Churchville, he had helped build the stone church where his family worshipped in the tiny, eponymous village.

Now after Finney's preaching and a second religious experience, Willard could not simply remain on his farm. His version of Christianity depended on sacrifice, a lesser propitiation, of course, but one that nonetheless paralleled the crucifixion of Jesus undertaken for the salvation of Christians. Although he already knew his Bible and rigorously observed the Sabbath, he needed to study Hebrew and Greek as well as rhetoric and theology. Unless he lived to save others, he could never save himself. So Willard sold his large farm, gave up his other business interests, and moved his wife, Mary, and their two children, seven-year-old Oliver and two-year-old Frances, to Oberlin where Finney had become a professor of religion. There he studied for four years.

It was a sad leave-taking. The Willards had married in Churchville and had buried two children there, one at birth and one who had died of a childhood disease that may have been the family affliction of tuberculosis. In a testament to this family's literary interests, their daughter Frances's first name honored the poets Frances Burney and Frances Osgood, though the austere Josiah Willard always felt Frances "too fancy" a name for his eldest surviving daughter. Her mother, Mary Hill Willard, constantly reminded Frances of what she knew to be the case. Born in 1839, the year after the death of Elizabeth, she was a "welcomed child, a vision of delight" in an age when constant unplanned arrivals sometimes made another baby less than a desired addition. Mary and Josiah Willard also left behind brothers, sisters, and cousins in New York and Vermont. But inspired to become a disciple of Finney's, in the spring of 1841 Josiah hitched up the horses, and following his star, the family traveled (but never on Sundays) in their white-hooded prairie schooner the nearly three hundred miles to Oberlin, Ohio.[1]

Their new home was a pleasant setting for this religiously striving, intellectually engaged family. During the same years that Lucy Stone attended the unique biracial and coeducational Oberlin Institute, the Willards rented a house on Main Street. Mary Willard attended courses in the women's division on how to raise children as well as how better to serve the Lord, and in 1843 gave birth to the couple's youngest child, a daughter named Mary. After four years but before Josiah had finished his studies and been officially ordained, he began coughing up blood. It was an early sign of the tuberculosis that infected so many Willards. Again they must move, according to this era's therapy, to a place with better air and less atmospheric pressure where Josiah could work outside. They chose a remote frontier community in southern Wisconsin where the family resided for the next thirteen years. From 1846 to 1859, Frances Willard spent her childhood and adolescence on an isolated 360-acre farm (later increased to over a thousand acres), bordered by a thick forest along the Rock River, outside of newly settled Janesville, more than two miles from the closest neighbor.

Here she developed a relationship with her mother that became the most influential of her life and that served as the model for the applied motherhood she adopted in her public life. A year after her mother died in 1892, Frances Willard, by this time a national celebrity as the overworked head of the 150,000-member National Woman's Christian Temperance Union (WCTU) as well as the president of the newly formed National Council of Women and a leader of the International Woman's Christian Temperance Union, found time to write a three-hundred-page hagiography entitled *A Great Mother: Sketches of Madame Willard.* "Saint Mary," or as she was sometimes called by her daughter and the women of the union, "Saint Courageous," had a special genius for motherhood. Calm and resolute, kind and faithful to her family, according to her daughter she provided not just religious inspiration, but a lifetime's emotional sanctuary for her famous offspring. Mother Willard became the human incarnation of her daughter's belief in God and Jesus as spiritual providers. "Her talent for motherhood amounted to positive genius," wrote Willard. "She maintained the standards of her own life at its highest to lead the way."[2]

It was only later in the nineteenth and early twentieth century that motherhood became an idealized category, celebrated with its own holiday and the expectation of motherhood as self-sacrificing benevolence. Frances Willard was partly responsible for bringing national veneration to what was previously a natural, unconscious role. Never a mother herself, she relied for her leadership on certain behaviors she assigned to motherhood. These were educating and comforting, in her case, the members of the WCTU and sacrificing herself to their interests, even as they honored and obeyed her. Later Frances Willard's version of virtual maternalism emerged in the specifics of her reform agenda—training mothers in family hygiene and running households, educating children about the evils of drink, and providing state-funded kindergartens.[3] She learned how to reform America from her mother.

Raising three children, nursing an often ill, absent, and authoritarian husband, along with the responsibilities of creating and running a "refined" home in the wilderness, while simultaneously infusing the values of religion and education in her children, demanded patience, ingenuity, and hard work. As travelers attested, American families on the frontier often surrendered their cultural habits of education and religious observance to more pressing tasks of survival. Not Mother Willard. To entertain and teach the children, she organized Fort City, an elaborate make-believe playhouse city that kept the children occupied for years and that featured, as the young Willards' utopia, a peaceful society with a written constitution and foreign policy, but no billiard halls or saloons. In an area that lacked a district school in its early years, Mary Willard homeschooled her daughters, recalling the techniques she had used as a schoolteacher in Churchville before her marriage to Josiah. She was a woman, according to one friend, with a mind "stored with much of the best English prose and verse."[4]

Painstakingly she transferred this literature to her children. Throughout a hectic life filled with frequent speeches and public appearances, Frances Willard could always depend on quotations and paraphrases from Shakespeare, Emerson, the Bible, and the English romantic poets, all memorized at her mother's knee. They came easily to mind in her most harried moments. With few toys, Mother Willard crafted an enchanting life-size doll, and encouraged her children to have live animals as their playmates. She insisted that Oliver, Frances, and Mary keep journals, a useful activity for empty hours in the wilderness and one that her daughters maintained for years. Among other concerns, "my mother had much care about our manners, for we saw nothing of society and she knew we were missing real

advantages." Yet where her father sought to set "bounds to my ambitions," Frances's mother "was less dominating and therefore more
influential."[5]

When her mother returned from a rare absence to visit relatives in
Churchville, Frances Willard recalled the "return of the one divinity—mother." Kneeling with her father, brother, and younger sister to
give thanks for her mother's safe return, Willard conflated adoration
of her mother with Christian values. As she wrote in her autobiography, ". . . that deep motherly heart carried to the Heart [Christ] that
mothers all the world, its love, its trust and adoration." In time the
principles of Christ's life—charity, sacrifice, and unconditional love—
became for Willard the hallmarks of motherhood, itself the most important relationship on earth.[6]

Raised as Congregationalists, the Willards became Methodists in
Wisconsin. Not only was the nearest church outside of Janesville a
Methodist one, but with its culture of evangelism and camp meetings,
that denomination was especially compatible with the family's isolation. Methodism was a frontier faith that encouraged home-churching
and fashioned rituals of family worship useful for those who could not
get to services every Sunday. The denomination emphasized the
Christian home circle with the pious wife and mother as its center. Indeed maternal love with its responsibilities to direct children into
Christian ways was specifically likened to God's power to shape human nature. But Methodists also believed that their religion was a
fighting one, ready to contest with the devil such sinful behaviors as
drinking and among its Southern celebrants, slavery.[7]

While her younger sister, Mary, dutifully learned the traditional
household tasks of cooking and cleaning from her mother, Frances
was a tomboy. She climbed fences, fired guns, shot arrows, played
with stilts, and tried to ride a cow because only her brother, Oliver,
was allowed to ride Jack, the family horse. Throughout her life she
preferred the nickname "Frank." With the common sense that her
daughter treasured, her mother never insisted that she spend time on
the traditional inside-the-house feminine tasks of housekeeping—
those of "needle and dishcloth"—which separated the woman's domestic sphere from the public sphere of farmers like Josiah who
worked outside with his son and the hired help. Frances Willard

loathed the routinized chores that filled most American girls' lives as they became apprentices to domesticity and prepared for marriage. "Mother did not talk to us as girls, but simply as human beings." Under such a regimen Willard grew independent, nonconformist, and ambitious.[8]

"I never knew what it was not to aspire, and not believe myself capable of heroism," she later wrote in an astonishing reversal of the expected values for women. "I always wanted to react upon the world about me to my utmost ounce of power, to be widely known and loved and believed in—the more widely the better." This was no recovered memory emerging after she had become a celebrity. Even as a child she asked her brother and sister if they wondered, as she often did, whether "we shall ever go anywhere or see anybody or be anything." As she grew older, she complained in her journal of what she called her "captivity." The possibility of anonymity preoccupied a girl who meant to be famous, as she refused the call to humility demanded in the familiar hymn the Willards sang during their daily home devotions: "Make me little and unknown / Loved and prized by God alone."[9]

Despite her mother's tolerance, lessons in the differences between parental expectations for boys and girls soon intruded. Her brother, Oliver, crossing a previously invisible line of sibling similarity, was allowed to go to school in Janesville, and when he was fourteen he briefly attended Oberlin and then finished college in nearby Beloit, Wisconsin. Frequently her father was away on public business, either successfully campaigning for a seat in the state legislature in 1848, the year that Wisconsin became a state, or appearing at the state fairs where as an officer of the State Agricultural Society he delivered papers on the best way to raise sheep. But her mother rarely left home. In young Frances Willard's journal her father appears as a distant figure described by Willard as interested in the present, while her mother was concerned with the past and future: "Father in forenoon writing, in afternoon at town."[10]

When father and son set out to vote for the Republican candidate John Frémont in the 1856 presidential election, mother and the girls—all three of whom perceived the discrimination—stayed at home. Thirty years later with her memory no doubt sharpened by her advocacy of women's suffrage, Willard remembered the scene as propaganda in a book entitled *How to Win: A Book for Girls.* She had turned to her younger sister and asked, "Wouldn't you like to vote as well as Oliver? Don't you and I love the country just as well as he and doesn't the country need our votes?"[11]

In 1855 Frank celebrated her sixteenth birthday, and her "romping days" ended. She called it the date of her "martyrdom" and wrote so at the time, describing a new hairdo, insisted on by her mother, in which her hair was done "up in woman-fashion, twisted up like a corkscrew." For almost the first time in her life Frances wore a long skirt and discovered that she could barely walk, much less run races and climb into her tree house. She was choked with ribbons, a veritable "Samson shorn of my strength."[12]

Even in her days as a tomboy, Frances Willard felt a "mighty unrest" and wished for schoolmates and what she called through some special insight, for she knew little beyond the simple life she led and only under duress did her father permit the reading of novels when she was sixteen, "advantages like other people." "I long for school to begin," she wrote in 1856 after a school was organized in Janesville, "to relieve the tedious unendurable monotony." Preoccupied with the future, she worried that ". . . I might write [my autobiography] in advance, what I do for it is the same unvarying round—my life, my young life . . . is enough to dry the fountains of hope and ambition—it is terrible—but school is going to begin on Monday." With education a lever of liberation, loneliness became a habitual companion, especially on the empty Sundays when by their father's command, the Willards could neither play, nor write in their journals, nor read anything but the Bible.[13]

After her mother's early tutoring and even during her limited formal schooling, Frances Willard taught herself, and she would continue this process of self-education throughout her life. Her journal displays the astonishing range of her reading as she quoted and paraphrased Shakespeare, Thackeray, Emerson, and a number of poets, historians, philosophers, and essayists. Immersed in the religious environment her parents created, she knew the Old and New Testament better than many preachers. With only four years of intermittent formal schooling and two of these in college when she was twenty,

Willard remained an autodidact with all the characteristics of that group—independence of mind, intellectual curiosity, and a nonconformist's ability to reach beyond the normal perimeters of orthodox schooling, traits left unchanged by her two years at the Milwaukee Female College.

The latter was a legacy of Catharine Beecher. One of the revivalist preacher Lyman Beecher's thirteen children, Beecher was the foremost exponent of women's education in the United States. She had founded her first school when she was in her twenties, and by the 1840s was well known for writings that included the popular *Treatise on Domestic Economy*, a helpful compendium of information on how to run a home. In fact the *Treatise* was one of the few books Mary Willard had carried from Oberlin to the frontier. In the 1850s many town fathers came to appreciate the necessity of educating their daughters beyond district schools and female institutes, if only so that as wives they could create a proper home and provide interesting companions for their husbands. For the same reasons, women organized educational associations, raised money, and sought to create and thereafter shape the higher education of their daughters.

Beecher argued for more rigorous female education, not as practiced in the coeducational setting of radical Oberlin but rather for middle-class girls whose fathers could not resist her conservative, domesticated version of a potentially radicalizing process. She fused into one educational system the new role of women as schoolteachers and the traditional one of women as homemakers. The future of the latter rested in understanding the efficient organization of the tasks of homemaking, husband serving, and child raising; the future of the former depended on running the classrooms across America where women, paid less and more likely to stay longer, were rapidly replacing men. The result was a mixed curriculum, usually consisting of a so-called "normal" department for future teachers, a department of domestic economy for future wives and mothers, and for both a literary department where the graces of the drawing room were learned. Turning to the West, Beecher raised money to improve several female institutes with the purpose of training teachers for Western schools. The Milwaukee Normal Institute, soon to change its name, was one.

Frances and Mary Willard stayed only one term at the Milwaukee

Female College, but it was enough time to captivate Frances. Returned home, she waged a persistent campaign against her father to go back to college. She employed the same vehemence in her contest with him during the Civil War when she wanted to become a nurse or work for the Sanitary Commission, the precursor to the Red Cross. In both instances her father prevailed. Then, surprisingly and for unknown reasons, Josiah Willard leased the farm in Wisconsin and moved his family to Evanston, Illinois. He took a job in a banking firm in Chicago, part of a wave of American men who were selling their farms and taking up commercial positions in towns and cities. As a result, his two daughters could now enter the local Methodist-run North Western Female College, while their brother, Oliver, enacting the hopes of his father, studied for the Methodist ministry at the Garrett Biblical Institute.[14]

Finding the Way

In 1859 Frances graduated from college, and for the next nine years she pursued the only approved occupation for women. She taught school in mostly one-room classrooms in Illinois, New York, and Pennsylvania. Willard described these years as "thirteen separate seasons of teaching, eleven separate institutions, and six separate towns," though she made clear that she had been invited back by all but one of the schools. It was her restless spirit that compelled her to move. Displaying singular organizational capacity, she also served as an administrator and head, what the nineteenth century called a preceptress or female principal, in several of these female academies. But the fires of ambition never quieted. "Stir yourself—be determined to write—books if you please, why not?"[15]

For twenty-year-old Frances Willard the next nine years began a period of self-conscious, introspective searching for who she was, what she should be as a good Christian, and what she might become as an ambitious woman. She described herself as "not good looking, no sunny locks and a resolute expression . . . five-feet, two and a quarter inches and 95 lbs with freckles and a poor plain face." Having earlier come to terms with her unremarkable features and her resolute, prominent Willard jaw, she was less perplexed by what she looked like and far more concerned with what she might do and become.[16]

Modern psychologists call this period in adolescent lives "an identity crisis," and it is less obvious, or at least less often documented, among young women who find the resolution of their dilemmas in marriage and childbearing than among young men. Willard was different. In her early twenties, she faced three personal crises, which had to be settled before she could establish a career and follow the stars of her ambition. First she must undergo the requisite conversion experience expected of all Methodists. Then she must transcend the numbing grief and turmoil over her sister Mary's death in 1862, her father's death in 1868, and her brother's deepening alcoholism. Finally, and perhaps most intensely agonizing, she must determine her sexuality and love interests at a time when she was engaged to Charles Fowler, a Methodist minister, but loved more Mary Bannister, the woman who became her brother's wife. Only when these conflicts were decided did Frances Willard find the occupation that both served the Lord and satisfied her ambition "to be widely known, loved and believed in, the more widely the better."[17]

During the spring of 1859 Frances Willard was honored as the valedictorian of her class at the North Western Female College. For the occasion she wrote a schoolgirlish address entitled "Horizons." It was a paean to the hard work she held as one of her highest ideals and her aspirations to be somebody. She knew that her college diploma was not the final destination of learning that it was for most of her classmates. It represented only a beginning, as she wrote in her journal, "of the Beautiful Search after Truth & Right & Peace. [The diploma] only started—only opened the door."[18]

Several days before graduation Frances Willard fell dangerously ill from typhoid fever and could not deliver her speech. Her illness turned her toward religion, and she promised, in the classic human-to-deity bargain, that if she lived she would give herself to God, that is, she would repent, submit, and through prayer make room for the Holy Ghost to enter her soul. In a word she would undergo a conversion experience. But such life-changing episodes did not come by human command. Even after her recovery Frances Willard understood herself to be, if not a sinner, at least not a good Christian.

"Don't think much of God or Heaven or Eternity," she acknowledged in July 1860, "not half as much as when I came here first. I am alarmed at myself." Somehow the required sense of submission and self-abnegation did not come to this ambitious young woman. Months after Willard publicly confessed her determination to forsake her sins, she had not had the "change of heart that Christ has promised to those who ask Him rightly." "I acknowledge [my sinful condition] intellectually, but I don't feel it."[19]

Like Benjamin Franklin, she made lists of her transgressions, with ambition, temper, and lack of piety near the top. She prayed, and she sought her mother's counsel. Then unexpectedly Willard found "that Active Peace which accompanies conversion" and marched alone to the altar of the Evanston Methodist Church. "I have commenced! O Lord! I am trying to redeem the solemn promise I have made to Thee. I have publicly declared my determination to forsake my sins—to seek forgiveness for the past and help for the future; to live a good, true, valuable life—a life that shall glorify God and be a blessing to my fellow toilers and sufferers on the earth." No longer did ambition conflict with God's service as personal hubris; rather through "a valuable life" she could serve the Lord.[20]

By 1861 Willard faced another dilemma. She had fallen in love with Mary Bannister, an Evanston neighbor whose father was a Methodist minister. "I have always loved Mary Bannister—I knew it was my destiny when I saw her first . . . I care for her so much . . ." Later, as Willard tried to distinguish her love for her mother from that for Mary Bannister, she wrote, "My heart toward [my mother] is like the Jungfrau or Mont Blanc—toward you [Mary] it is Vesuvius or Etna," a distinction suggesting the erotic nature of her feelings. So began a painful love affair that was more than a schoolgirl's crush and that was elevated to an even more titillating and intense status by the interruptions caused by both young women's out-of-town teaching commitments. "She is gone," wrote Frances in her journal in September 1860. "I said Goodbye & pressed my lips to her for an instant . . . my heart is desolate." And a year later as lovers often do, she heightened the uniqueness of her affair. "Ours is such a Love as no two women ever had for each other, before. It is wild and passionate and all-pervading . . ." The romance of Mary and Frances involved exchanging pictures and journals, calling each other by endearments usually reserved for men such as "my darling, my beloved," kissing on the lips, caressing, and spending the night together. Possibly genitally chaste, the mutual affection of Mary Bannister and Frances Willard nevertheless established for all time Willard's sexual identity.[21]

But if Frances Willard loved Mary too much and even acknowledged her feelings as different and "abnormal," Mary Bannister loved Willard's brother, Oliver, more. "Mary walking beside me, feeling very badly [because she would soon marry Oliver], but not so terribly as I, for she has two sources of comfort—I have none. She went away, leaning on Oliver's arm. He could comfort her . . ." In the spring of 1862 this love triangle ended. Mary Bannister married Oliver Willard and moved with him to Colorado, leaving Frances to wonder how she could exchange her amorous feelings toward a former lover for those more tepid ones toward a sister-in-law. "It is Mary that I want, only Mary . . ."[22]

Meanwhile Frances had her own boyfriend, an entirely suitable one who was a classmate of Oliver's in the Biblical Institute and was soon to become, like Oliver, a Methodist minister. Charles Fowler proposed to, and was accepted by, Frances Willard in the summer of 1861. Doubts and hesitation soon emerged. Frances continued to feel "a deep, thrilling, all-sacrificing love" for Mary Bannister, while Fowler's "caresses were irksome, always—they never aroused an emotion in me. His presence gave me no pleasure, except as I felt him to be a companion . . ." Nor did his absence ever bother her, while she pined for Mary Bannister when they were apart. A few months before an agreed-upon date for their marriage and to her parents' chagrin, Frances Willard broke her engagement, finding herself "tormented with the abnormal love & longing of a woman for a woman . . ." She also discovered herself "open to ridicule from this, to censure from the other side."[23]

During a time when homosexuality was not unknown as a behavior but was not defined as a personal characteristic, a named category, and a conscious state, Frances Willard searched for a title and some precedent for her feelings. Often Mary Bannister stood emotionally as a sister to her, but never did that set of sentiments properly identify her feelings of sexual amorousness. "I feel," she wrote in her journal, "toward Mary as a husband." Sometimes she thought of Mary as a daughter and called her that. Occasionally reversing their roles, Mary, who was two years younger, served as a mother to Frances, offering calm advice and solace about the challenges of their mutual endeavor of teaching. For the rest of her life this unnamed love of women, collectively and individually, defined Willard's emotional existence. Always the depth of her friendships for women surpassed those for men, just as her feelings for Mary Bannister Willard proved far more compelling than those for Charles Fowler. After Mary's betrayal there were other love affairs with women. In these, Willard believed, "I was the one relied on, the one who fights the battles . . ." But given her chosen work she was not always the one who was the breadwinner.[24]

Today we would call Frances Willard a lesbian, although she never established a long-term relationship with one woman. Instead her affiliations were seriatim. Quoting Shakespeare's *A Midsummer Night's Dream*, like Susan B. Anthony she described her life as one of "single-blessedness." To be sure women remained her principal constituents, colleagues, associates, friends, and love objects, although there was never any gossip about Willard's relationships with other women. Like her mother she was not physically affectionate, and for generations her rectitude and probity deflected any consideration of her lesbianism. But after Mary Bannister became her sister-in-law, Willard discovered homoerotic love with Kate Jackson, a fellow schoolteacher who was the daughter of a wealthy New Jersey locomotive manufacturer. From 1868 to 1870 the two women, financed by Jackson's father, traveled together through Europe and the Middle East. But though Jackson and Willard had promised to live together "all our days," Jackson proved a difficult, jealous lover and Willard moved on to others.

In the midseventies Frances Willard found love again with Anna Gordon, "my other self—my little Nan" who, fourteen years younger, became her personal secretary, amanuensis, and chief of staff. For years the two women slept together in Pullman cars when they traveled and when they were home in Willard's Evanston bedroom. Somehow, while they were alive, this relationship with Gordon expanded to accommodate Willard's final intimate friendship.

In her fifties Frances Willard fell in love again, this time with Lady

Henry Somerset, a rich English aristocrat and temperance leader. The daughter of an earl and briefly the wife of a lord who scandalized England with his homosexual philandering, Somerset, "my beloved Cossie," had made "a sorry marriage." But at forty Somerset found Willard—" a woman she could love & trust after a life of loneliness. She was for me a blessed consummation." An unusual ménage à trois—Nan, Conk (Willard's nickname), and Cossie—lived and loved together on Somerset's estate Reigate and in Willard's home in Evanston. Wherever they were, there was always room for "my Little Nan the true & tried, faithful, loving & beloved [who] nestles always in my heart and always will just the same."[25]

Among the crises of Willard's early adulthood was the death of her sister, Mary. As sisters on the lonely prairie these two opposites in temperament and interests had developed a close affection. Frances was bold, ambitious, and plain; Mary was dutiful, conventional, and beautiful. Frances found in the transcendentalist Margaret Fuller's injunction "to grow as an intellect to discern, [and] as a soul to live freely and unimpeded" an expectation for her public future, while Mary read the Bible, played the role of a New Testament Martha, and was her father's favorite. But by the spring of 1862, shortly after Frances had broken her engagement to Charles Fowler, Mary was dangerously ill, coughing, groaning, and gasping at every breath. By June Mary was dead, the victim of the airborne tubercular bacteria that her father carried and to which his wife, son, and eldest daughter were evidently immune after suffering low-grade infections.[26]

Then in 1868 Josiah Willard died, suffering the same agonies from terminal tuberculosis. According to Frances in a scene much anticipated by religious families, at the moment of his death her father talked "most Christianly" about the future, thereby giving to his observant family the consoling sign of the promised resurrection. Of all Protestant denominations Methodists were most concerned with a "happy" death as proof of a good life. Like her father, Mary had died well, crying out as she expired, "I've got Christ—he's right here. Take me quick, God . . ."[27]

The deaths of Frances Willard's sister and her father were accompanied by the loss of her beloved brother to alcoholism. Oliver Willard had begun his professional life as a star in the Methodist

Lucy Stone, in her forties, at the beginning of her campaign for suffrage. Her father once described her face as "like a black smith's leather apron keeping off the sparks." She angrily responded that she wished the mole on her face were an inch long. (Courtesy of the Library of Congress)

A reunion in 1886 of antislavery and women's-rights reformers at the Boston home of the Stone-Blackwells. As she habitually did, Lucy Stone, seated in the back row, is looking off into the distance, perhaps envisioning a better future for women. Her husband, Henry Blackwell, is standing on the right side of the photograph, in the front row, with a trimmed white beard. (Courtesy of the Sophia Smith Collection, Smith College)

In a photograph taken in 1890, the year when her struggling American Woman Suffrage Association merged with the Anthony-Stanton–led National Woman Suffrage Association, Lucy Stone, in her mid-seventies, wears an elegant rose-point lace veil. (Courtesy of the Library of Congress)

ABOVE: Surrounded by photographs of her sisters in the battle for women's civil rights, Susan B. Anthony, in her mid-seventies, works at her desk in Rochester, where she wrote thousands of letters. She was seldom photographed at leisure. (Courtesy of the Library of Congress)

In a photograph taken in Rochester during Stanton's visit to Anthony in 1891, the two women pose in a staged representation of their long-lived friendship and collaboration. Here they are conferring over a speech, a petition, or a call to a convention during the 1890s. (Courtesy of the Library of Congress)

This wood engraving of the young Stanton, appearing in several newspapers, depicts her in the revolutionary bloomer outfit she wore in the early 1850s. She gave it up when she came to believe that it deflected attention from the other, more important commitments of the women's movement. (Courtesy of the Library of Congress)

A complete nineteenth-century feminist, Elizabeth Cady Stanton reveled in her large family of seven children. Here, with a satisfied smile, she cradles her second daughter, Harriot, who was born in 1856. (Courtesy of the Library of Congress)

Three generations of Stanton women—Elizabeth Cady; Harriot; and grand-daughter Nora, named after the heroine of Henrik Ibsen's play *The Doll House*—pose in the 1890s. (Courtesy of the Library of Congress)

Helen Farnsworth Mears's marble representation of Frances Willard shows an erect Willard, the first woman to have her statue placed in the Capitol's Statuary Hall. This was a familiar pose for the head of the WCTU: one hand on a podium and a temperance petition for Home Protection held in her other hand for her followers to sign. (Courtesy of the Library of Congress)

Mother Mary Hill Willard, whom Frances adored; Frances (standing); and Anna Gordon, Willard's secretary, pose in somber clothes in Rest Cottage in 1885. The two younger women are wearing the identifying symbol of the WCTU, a white ribbon. (Courtesy of the Library of Congress)

In a satiric cartoon by the suffragist Henrietta Briggs-Wall, a dignified and intelligent but non-voting Willard is contrasted with her political peers—an idiot, a criminal, a tramp, and a Native American, all of whom could vote, under certain conditions. (Courtesy of the Library of Congress)

A wistful but determined Alice Paul sits for a portrait in 1906 after receiving her Master of Arts degree from the University of Pennsylvania. Her dissertation focused on the legal inequality of women in the United States.
(Courtesy of the Library of Congress)

A photograph taken from a building on Pennsylvania Avenue depicts a crowd surrounding suffragists and impeding their progress along their parade route in March 1913. Note the banner and the two women on horseback at right. (Courtesy of the Library of Congress)

Women carrying these and similar messages picketed the White House beginning in January 1917. Organized by Alice Paul, the pickets were chosen to represent working women, the professions, and, as pictured here, college and university women. (Courtesy of the Library of Congress)

Following the ratification of the suffrage amendment in August 1920, Alice Paul points to the NWP's suffrage flag, with its thirty-six stars, in a photograph taken after the Tennessee legislature voted to accept women's suffrage. She holds a tiny representation of one of the cauldrons used by the women to burn President Wilson's speeches. (Courtesy of the Library of Congress)

church, carrying with him, as Frances put it, "the hopes of Father's old age." At twenty-seven he was a minister in Denver and as the youngest presiding elder in American Methodism not only ran his church, but proselytized throughout eastern Colorado. Three years later he had resigned from the ministry and become an insurance agent in Wisconsin. Chronically in debt and a drain on his father's money, he later became the editor of the *Chicago Evening Mail* before his death, aged forty-two, in 1878. Meanwhile Mary Bannister, a loyal follower of the WCTU, and her four children lived in the other wing of the Willard house as the entire family struggled to reform her two delinquent sons.[28]

Only slowly did Frances Willard come to understand, though rarely to name, the cause of Oliver's decline—that "noble, gifted boy who really is in great jeopardy, in many ways." Her sister, Mary, in the Christian conviction of the Willards, was safe with God. On the other hand Oliver with "his terrible red and swollen face" suffered, "tugged with fortune, and weary with disaster," wrote Frances. Only after her mother's death did she acknowledge that he was "the most gifted child mother had; his native wit and love of letters were always uppermost, but for tobacco and alcohol he would have become the chief pulpit." By that time Oliver's failing was the principal focus of Willard's life.[29]

Gradually Frances recovered from her losses. She canonized Mary Willard in a sentimental, grief-assuaging memoir entitled *Nineteen Beautiful Years or Sketches of a Girl's Life*. In the process she learned that she was a proficient, publishable writer. No longer able to tolerate living in a place where Mary had died, the Willards bought another home in Evanston. Named Rest Cottage, the Greek Revival house with its two wings separated by a front hall became Frances and her mother's home for the rest of their lives, shared with her brother's family. But her nephew Josiah, a self-proclaimed hobo, found the place so feminine that it got on his nerves.

Following the loss of her father, Frances Willard came to understand herself, necessarily, as the head of the family, a strong and effective person who must become its breadwinner. Mary had been expected to maintain a home for their widowed mother. Now Frances must. In Oliver's alcoholism—along with the delinquencies of his two sons, both of whom spent time in reformatories—she found a cause. Still, until the 1870s Frances lacerated herself in her journal with constant reminders that she must change her ways. ". . . do you plan to go on teaching ad infinitum . . . why do you content yourself with such a hedged up life—with acquiring money so slowly with such an obscure life?"[30]

In the fall of 1870 Willard returned to her mother and Evanston, after over two years traveling with Kate Jackson through Europe and the Middle East. She was now far more interested in women's rights than she had been when she left. Yet even as a child, Willard had been alerted through her mother's progressivism and her family's religion, as well as her own girlish rebellions, to the discriminations against women. Advanced by her mother's nurture and her homosexual nature to a precocious consciousness of her secondary status, as a teenager Willard had considered writing a novel on American girlhood with the bold title *Women's Rights*. And, as an adult, following her trip to Europe she believed in "the *Woman Question* more and more." Still, she was no suffragist, complaining when Lucy Stone gave a speech in Evanston in 1859 that she disagreed with Stone's views and her refusal to be called Mrs. Blackwell. But as one ambitious woman recognizing another, Frances Willard admired Lucy Stone's courage.[31]

In Germany she observed women raised only to marry and bear children. In Egypt she saw young girls beaten by male overseers, sold into marriage as children, and thereby delivered to their husbands as virtual slaves to be abused with impunity. In Paris, introduced by the American journalist Anna Blackwell, Lucy Stone's sister-in-law, she met Julie Daubie, a French feminist who at the time was challenging the exclusion of women from French colleges and universities. Over tea the two women discussed John Stuart Mill's recent prosuffrage speech in Parliament. Most horrifying for this sheltered thirty-year-old American of self-proclaimed Puritan ancestry was the prostitution practiced by high-priced mistresses in the Jardin Mabille. She fumed in her journal about "the permitted public indecency of Paris . . . I brought from this gilded pit, a renewed resolution to *help women* if I can . . . One woman can not do much, but what one can do let me essay."[32]

Returned to the United States, Frances began giving paid lectures to popular audiences while she contemplated her future. Her focus was on women, and her speech "The New Chivalry" showcased her new appreciation of the discriminations practiced against them. Her speeches also brought her to the attention of Evanston, as she called for an end "to the empty husk of flattery," hoping instead for "just criticism" from men. In the past men "drank our health in flowing bumpers; those of the new invite us to sit down beside them." It was a gentle reprimand that both illiberal men and acquiescent women could tolerate at a time when the suffragists Susan B. Anthony and Elizabeth Cady Stanton were far less diplomatic. In what became a lifelong strategy, Willard's message never threatened. Instead, poised between the radicalism of feminist change and a deprecating acceptance of the customary submission of women in American society, her views attracted men and women, sheltered housewives, and educated girls.[33]

In 1871 the trustees of the Evanston Ladies College of Northwestern University invited Frances Willard to become head of an institution that stood, like her views on women, balanced, in this case between autonomy as a separate institution for women and domination by the male-controlled Northwestern University. As Willard told the story, she was tacking down carpets in Rest Cottage when the head of the board of trustees offered her the position. "Frank," said Mrs. Kidder, "let someone else tack down the carpets, and do you take charge of the new college . . . ? I shall be glad to do so," came the immediate, self-assured answer. "I was only waiting to be asked."[34]

For the next three years Frances ran the Ladies College with its 236 students in a coeducational program suspended between an enterprise that boldly joined men and women together in classrooms, but offered the female students a separate boarding environment with stricter parietal rules, as well as special courses suitable for women in the departments of Modern Languages, Fine Arts, Music, Health, and Home Industries. As the head of the college—and as such the first female college president in the United States, which she duly noted in her autobiography—Willard positioned herself as "a mother to girls," and sometimes as "a sister of girls." She created an elaborate system of self-government based on the honor system and gave talks on "Moral

Horticulture," intended to teach character. She visited the young women in their rooms, extending maternal counsel. As well she served as a professor of aesthetics and writing in the Northwestern University program where she was harassed by young men unfamiliar with women professors who came to class late and put mice in her desk. Her approach to women's higher education combined the past and the future. Under her regime the girls did not have to march in a procession to church, and they now participated in male debating societies, walking unchaperoned in the evenings to lectures. On the other hand, the curriculum and rules for the young women of the Ladies College were hardly the same as those for the young men of Northwestern.

It did not take long for a new president of Northwestern to challenge the autonomy of the Ladies College. That president, elected by the trustees in part because of his successful fund-raising after the Chicago fire in 1871, was Charles Fowler, Frances Willard's rejected suitor. Within a year these two were locked in a bitter struggle, a battle that in one way or another, at one time or another, but with largely the same outcome, was fought throughout the United States in those institutions of higher learning with affiliated, satellite women's divisions.

Fowler, at a moment when coeducation was under attack throughout Illinois and the Midwest, insisted on equal treatment for both genders. Such calls for equity in the rules regulating the freedom of male and female students served as a strategy for ending the program. Few middle-class parents would accept the same relative permissiveness granted young men for their daughters. Fowler also challenged Willard's vaunted honor system, which she believed taught young women independence and the high-level refined morality that made them the ethical guardians of their families. Fowler considered the system unworkable and, as it was not the same for both sexes, unfair to male students. When on a trip to Chicago in November 1873, Elizabeth Cady Stanton agreed and condemned Willard's ideas as pampering young women, the noted suffragist initiated two decades of acrimony between these two leaders of the women's movement.[35]

In June 1874, after more power had slipped from her hands into Fowler's, a humiliated Frances Willard resigned. She left "the beautiful college that my heart had loved as other women's hearts love their sweet and sacred homes." She had lost nearly all her authority, and in the process the Ladies College had lost its autonomy. Still there was the solace of her faith. The night of her resignation, sobbing as she walked through the quiet streets of Evanston, Willard recalled that "the peace that passeth understanding settled down upon my soul. God was revealed to me as a great, brooding Motherly Spirit."[36]

Slowly recovering, Frances Willard pondered her future. What, as a respectable woman, could she do? How could she abandon one of the few avenues for achievement permitted women of her generation? Perhaps she should return to supervising schools; an offer for the head position had arrived from an academy in New York. But by this time Willard believed that teaching was overcrowded and afforded no opportunities for greatness. Besides she had already suffered the perils of a system run by men. She could not become a minister, though had the practices of the church permitted, this ambition was her preference. Perhaps she could provide for herself and her mother through her lectures, though as Stone, Stanton, and Anthony had learned, the life of an itinerant speaker was uncertain at best, miserable at worst. Still lecturing was certainly a way to stand out, and her lover Kate Jackson had often told her that she was a good "gospel talker." Perhaps she could support herself as an author. Instead, the next year Frances Willard became a reformer, and the mote that she would remove from the nation's eye was the sin of alcohol.[37]

The Cause

Her timing was perfect, her decision sudden. As an organized movement, temperance had long attracted Americans and was nothing new in the 1870s. During the period after the American Revolution drinking increased in a nation where an abundance of apples and easily distilled surplus grain provided cheap, available whiskey, hard cider, and apple brandy. Most employers included a dram of spirits in their employee's pay, and drinking together on payday emerged as a bond among workingmen. Taverns, previously limited in number, proliferated, and less regulated by local and municipal governments they

became poor men's clubs away from home. By the 1840s the development of distilleries along with improvements in transportation nation-
alized the availability of liquor in what one historian has labeled the
"Alcoholic Republic." But as the whiskey trade grew, so too did its opponents, some of whom argued that drinking was more than an individual failing. It was a threat to the nation.[38]

In 1851 Maine became the first state to force temperance on its
residents when its legislature passed a bill to prohibit the manufacture
and sale of liquor. Seven other states promptly followed. But prohibition was never secure. Some courts ruled such legislation violated individual rights. Several legislatures overturned previous statutes, and
enforcement was lax.[39]

Before the Civil War most temperance societies focused on persuading individual abusers to sign a pledge and thereafter abstain.
They couched their argument in moral, patriotic, and religious terms.
Drinking emerged as an individual's moral and political lapse, preventing good Christians from following in the ways of Jesus and respectable Americans from the self-restraint required of citizens in a
democracy. Even in uninhabited Wisconsin, living in a county with
less than a thousand residents, Josiah Willard discovered, and joined
as an honorary member, one of the best-known of these societies—the
Washington Sons of Temperance.

Founded in the East by reformed alcoholics whose all-male membership solicited drinkers to sign a pledge not to buy, sell, or use alcohol, these sons of temperance approached the problem as one of
individual responsibility to be mastered by self-discipline, not solved
by public policy. In a tactic revived in modern times, they used the
confessional sharing of their dismal stories of drunkenness and the
soul-saving redemption of sobriety as an appeal to fellow drunks.
Frances Willard remembered the society's code of rules, proudly
signed by her father, adorning the walls of her home, and she pasted
the abstinence pledge in the family Bible. Of course the Willard
household had another inducement to support temperance when the
Methodist General Conference, having earlier imposed strict limits
on the use of distilled spirits, tightened its stand and demanded total
abstinence from its congregations in 1832. And when the Willard

family decided to leave Wisconsin, not by chance did they choose Evanston, a community of temperate Methodists with no saloons.

Women had always been members of local temperance societies, for drink was a natural enemy in their homes. Alcoholism destroyed families and homes and fell into the domestic domain of women. But as both Susan B. Anthony and Elizabeth Cady Stanton quickly learned, females were lesser members of most temperance associations. As a schoolteacher in Canajoharie, New York, Anthony had joined the local Daughters of Temperance. It was her first reform activity. Elected as a delegate to a state convention in 1852, she soon discovered, through a radicalizing discrimination, that she could not speak in the organization's meetings. In response she formed a temperance society for not just the male half of the world but for what she proclaimed "the whole world." Meanwhile, Anthony's friend Elizabeth Cady Stanton called for action. Connecting the abuse of alcohol to the miseries of women, she urged women to leave alcoholic husbands. "Let no drunkard be the father of [your] children . . . Let us petition our State governments to modify the laws affecting marriage and the custody of children [so] that the drunkard shall have no claims on either wife or child."[40]

Anthony and Stanton moved on from temperance to women's issues, recognizing the impotence of women to do anything about the evils of drinking when restricted to the insufficient tactic of persuasion. But if women could vote, they could elect temperance candidates and help enact local option laws outlawing liquor sales. Begin with temperance, predicted Henry Blackwell in the *Woman's Journal*, "and you will end with suffrage." Yet for many years religious women found a place in the conservatism of temperance. They did not immediately change their views on the more radical issue of woman's suffrage, at least not until Frances Willard persuaded them. Briefly stifled during the Civil War, these religious temperance women emerged in the postwar period, most dramatically in the Woman's Crusade of 1873–1874.

Originating in Ohio in 1873 and spreading rapidly through the towns of the Midwest and then to Eastern cities like New York and Worcester, Massachusetts, women began an extraordinary war against liquor that lasted for a year and a half. Theirs was a response to the postwar repeal of prohibitory legislation and to the perception that alcohol consumption was rising. In postwar America, a lighter pasteurized beer, manufactured and distributed by national breweries that was both cheaper and more appealing to workers' tastes, was replacing whiskey. The widely shared statistic that there was one beer-selling saloon for every fifty adult males terrified women whose homes were threatened by absent husbands and sons who spent too much time in taverns. Some women, not personally affected, simply intended to improve their communities in a permissible activism that opened doors beyond the confines of their households. Other women sympathized with a friend or neighbor who suffered from the crimes that had neither name nor solution—the physical, emotional, and sexual domestic abuse of women by drunk fathers and husbands.

Spontaneously organized, groups of respectable middle-class ladies took to the streets, in public campaigns against taverns, saloons, and even pharmacies that sold distilled alcohol. Often they marched into saloons, where they knelt before startled saloon keepers on sawdust floors permeated with the smell of liquor. They prayed and sang their hymns "Nearer My God to You" and "Rock of Ages." Occasionally they even found a drunk son, husband, or neighbor inside.

They inveighed the barkeeper and his customers to sign a pledge of abstinence. And when some owners cursed and called the police to throw them out (one tavern owner started undressing to get them out), the temperance women stayed, feeling, as one woman put it, "the blessedness of having been reviled for Christ's sake . . . We suffer for his sake." Most often Methodists and Congregationalists, they believed themselves sacrificial evangels spreading the gospel message. And there was no doubt in their minds that, morally superior to men, they were doing the Lord's work.[41]

The women of the crusade adopted several religious procedures. In their diligence, sacrifice, and humiliation, Willard likened them to "Protestant nuns." They prayed in a group as a family might at home, though on public streets in front of bars; they employed the practices of conversion including self-examination as they called sinners to step forward, consider their failing, publicly repent, and ask for redemption by signing a pledge, though unlike the ministry, the women could grant no absolution. They considered themselves missionaries similar to those in distant lands, and they brought that same sense of do-gooder proselytizing to their mission, though they worked close to their homes and knew many of those whom they would save. They based their message on biblical authority, their personal faith in Christ, and God's offer of salvation through Christ, though they held no special status within their churches. And of course they saw themselves as mothers in a virtual sense—many like Willard were single and childless—saving husbands and sons in their communities through the kind of unselfish love that mothers always delivered to their families. Fittingly in the beginning of the movement, the woman they called "Mother Stewart" was their most important leader.

Before 1874 Frances Willard had never worked for any temperance organization. But having grown up in a conscientiously teetotalling family that sheltered a drunken son and brother, enclosed by a religion that included drinking among the designated sins of mankind, and surrounded in Evanston by nondrinkers, she understood the importance of taming the devil of drink. In fact, during her teaching career at the Ladies College she had assigned essays on temperance topics. In a speech delivered in 1866 to the congregation of Chicago's First Methodist Church, she proclaimed drinking "the greatest evil that now demands the earnest efforts of all true hearts." That same year her brother, Oliver, signed a temperance pledge, and his sister optimistically noted in her journal, "Oliver did what will save him and give us comfort—at last." But her brother's abstinence, like that of so many others, was only temporary.[42]

Willard argued that now slavery had been abolished, temperance stood as the next crusade. She entitled her remarks "Everybody's War," and in a speech laced with lamentations from the Old Testament, she called for an organized national movement, the voluntary signing of pledges by drinkers and nondrinkers as well, and somewhat more radically because it moved temperance into politics, "total abstinence enforced by law."[43]

In 1874 after her resignation from Northwestern, during the period of her uncertainty about her future, Frances Willard traveled east to lecture to members of Sorosis, a woman's club in New York, and to investigate another teaching position. Returning home to Evanston through Pittsburgh, she came upon a group of women on Market Street in front of a saloon whose owner refused them entry. The women had marched two by two in the evening at a time when the bar would be full of human displays of drink's ruination. After arranging themselves on the street, the women of the "Ladies Crusade" knelt, prayed, and sang "Jesus the Water of Life Will Give," while, according to Willard, "men with faces written all over and interlined with the record of their sin," passed by, some even politely lifting their hats in "American manhood's tribute to Christianity and to womanhood."[44]

For Willard, familiar with the sudden conversions accompanying revelations from Christ in the form of the appearance of the Holy Ghost, the episode initiated a transcendent epiphany, as meaningful as that of her father's in Churchville years before. "I was conscious that perhaps never in my life, save besides my sister Mary's dying bed, had I prayed as truly as I did then. This was my crusade baptism . . . the door had opened. My life had hardly known a more exalted moment. I seemed to see the end from the beginning and when one has done that, nothing has power to discourage or daunt it." Within the month she had joined and become the president of the Chicago Temperance Union, and the next year Willard was elected the corresponding secretary of the newly organized National Woman's Christian Temperance Union (WCTU) at its first meeting in Cleveland in November 1874. In another five years—and for the next twenty—she served as the president of the largest, most influential women's association in the nineteenth century.[45]

At its founding meeting the mandate adopted by the committee on resolutions of which Willard was a member established the agenda of the WCTU. The women called it their "confession of faith," and having decried the moral decline in the United States, the assembly of over a hundred held responsible the "men in power whose duty it is to make and administer the laws [and who] are either themselves intemperate or controlled by the liquor power." The means the WCTU would use, after a long debate over whether to include the words *Christian* and *National* and a shorter one over whether men should be accepted as members, was to petition Congress for an inquiry into the liquor traffic; to urge physicians to exercise more "conscientious care in dispensing intoxicating liquor" to their patients; to insist pastors preach temperance from their pulpits; to appeal to Christian women for their membership; and, most expansively, to insist on "a general revival of religion throughout our land, knowing that only through the action of the Holy Spirit on the hearts of the Church and the world will [Americans] be warmed to a vital interest in the temperance cause."[46]

Using the Christian model of conversion, women who joined the WCTU came forward and signed a pledge of abstinence and that, along with their annual dues of fifty cents, constituted their membership. The means were feeble, Willard knew, but the solidarity established among women was real and permanent. Certainly the end was comprehensive. As Willard indicated in a preview of her eventual strategy, "everything" was not in temperance but temperance and the WCTU entered into everything from the public chambers of politics to the private rooms of the home.

In her autobiography, Willard described her commitment to the WCTU in sacrificial terms. "Instead of peace I was to participate in war; instead of the sweetness of home, never more dearly loved than I had loved it, I was to become a wanderer on the face of the earth. Instead of libraries I was to frequent public halls and railway cars. Instead of scholarly and cultured men I was to see the dregs of saloon and gambling house and haunt of shame." She also surrendered the assurance of a teacher's annual pay for a reformer's financial insecurity. A frugal ascetic who gave up drinking even tea and coffee, became a vegetarian, and never was much interested in money, Willard depended on personal gifts of wealthy supporters. Rest Cottage was largely furnished from these presents. She was, after all, doing the Lord's work in the manner of a religious mendicant. Only after months, despite her full-time work and her need to support her mother, did the Chicago Temperance Society offer her a month's salary of $120, and not until the 1880s did the WCTU establish her pay as twenty-four hundred dollars plus expenses with another eight hundred dollars for Anna Gordon.[47]

If Willard gave up a great deal to become a reformer, she replaced it with the warm devotion of a community of women whom she loved and whom she tended in her self-assigned role of a mother educating and guiding her children. The WCTU became her extended family, and she shared with its members her private life, including, in her presidential addresses, commentary on the health of her mother, the story of her sister Mary's death, and lavish praise of her friend Lady Somerset, whose picture she once held up and described "as a gift of the Lord to our organization." To her "beloved sisters," she even acknowledged "the master passion" of her life: as she admitted in her presidential address in 1889, "ambition . . . softened to aspiration in my vocabulary has been the most impelling force of my personality." And then as if this expression of her personal pride must be dampened, she ended with a promise to dedicate herself "soul, body and spirit to Christ" through her work in the Union.[48]

Such a style defused opposition. For the most part her comrades responded as obedient children to one of the most successful leaders in American history, with only a few rebellious dissenters the exception. Willard conveyed her purposes as necessity. She had been called. God had determined her life's work. It was this sense of certainty packaged in a Christian model of Pauline apostleship that attracted thousands of women to Willard's WCTU.[49]

Shaping the WCTU

To be sure, Frances Willard never intended to be merely a foot soldier in the crusade, but in the beginning there were better-known, more popular commanders. From 1874 to 1879 Willard engaged in a polite, but intense, battle with Annie Wittenmyer, the WCTU's first president. It was a struggle over personal power and leadership, but it was also a battle over policy between two women who represented the past and the future of American feminism. At first the ambitious Willard cloaked her intentions and obediently followed the older, more established Wittenmyer, the Ohio-born veteran of the Woman's Crusade who had worked with the Sanitary Commission during the Civil War and who was well known as the editor of the popular magazine *Christian Woman*. "I want you to deal with me with the utmost plainness," wrote Willard to Wittenmyer. "I know I speak 'right out' and often it is not for the best, but He can make me discreet as well as gentle."[50]

As the elected corresponding secretary, Willard held the most influential office in the organization. Biding her time, at first she sought no public confrontation over the presidency. Instead she quietly moved to control the union's rapidly increasing membership. No letter of concern about the WCTU plans or procedures was too unimportant to answer, no request too frivolous to pursue, as Willard's correspondence expanded to prodigious proportions. All the while, she was establishing a coterie of supporters. These followers, as the WCTU increased from a few thousand in 1874 to 13,000 by 1876, to 150,000 by 1883, and by the 1890s claims of 500,000 dues-paying members, including young affiliates. But for a time, despite her popularity, Willard declined to challenge the incumbent.[51]

Meanwhile, as its most rapidly rising star, Willard brought to the union, besides her assiduous attention to local concerns, her celebrity status. By the mid-1870s she was one of the best-known women in the United States, admired especially for her performances on the podium. Graceful, feminine, and unremittingly diplomatic, she conveyed no discomfort to any audience, whether it was all-male or in the language of the day, a "promiscuous" one made up of men and women. She spoke at Chautauqua, the famous religious meeting place in New York state where the ruling fathers disliked women speakers but thought Willard, in the words of one promoter, a "magnificent exception." In 1877 she became the only woman speaker in Dwight Moody's revival campaign in Boston.

The spellbinding Moody had modernized the old-fashioned conversion meetings of Charles Finney, adapting them to large urban tabernacles where guilt-ridden listeners prayed and sang hymns. They listened to his graphic gospel preaching about the oppositional states of sin and virtue, bad deeds and good works, heaven and hell, repentance and resurrection, the timbre of Moody's voice modulating when he turned from the wickedness of the past to the goodness of a redeemed future. Moody recognized in Willard similar talents to sway large audiences.

But unlike Willard and the WCTU, Moody disparaged the signing of temperance pledges. Instead he required personal testimony through public conversion as the only way to save a man from drink. For a time Willard followed his directions. But, as had been the case with Lucy Stone and the antislavery movement, when Willard began speaking too often about temperance as a woman's issue and when Moody ordered her not to permit Mary Livermore, a Unitarian who did not accept the Trinity, on her platform, the association ended. Livermore was too important a temperance leader to insult. Still Willard's well-paid lectures for Moody increased her visibility and dispensed, though she needed little enough of this, more self-confidence.

By 1876 Willard had discovered the controversial issue that separated her from Wittenmyer and the latter's older followers. It was women's suffrage. Willard did not directly call for votes for women, as Anthony, Stone, and Stanton were doing in their endless cross-country campaigns that proposed suffrage as a natural right of women on the grounds that they were adult human beings and American citizens. Willard's explanation was different. On a lecture tour in Ohio, during the centennial celebration of the United States, Willard employed the religious identifications that always ratified her positions. As she explained her conversion to suffrage: "Upon my knees there was borne in upon my mind from loftier regions, the declaration, you are to speak for woman's ballot as a weapon of protection to her home." The revelation came with "a complete line of argument and illustration," which Willard employed in various emanations in the coming years.

First, according to her argument, "the rum power" was growing and must be confronted. A new source of authority—that of Christian virtue—was necessary to combat it. Willard found that power in "the instinct of a mother's love, a wife's devotion, a sister's faithfulness, a daughter's loyalty . . . When you can center all this power in that small bit of white paper, the rum power will be doomed as was the slave power when you gave the ballot to the slaves." It was an indirect approach to suffrage made on the religious grounds of protecting the home, but it linked the two most powerful women's reform movements in the United States.[52]

Suffrage, a universal entitlement required in the minds of Anthony and Stanton on the grounds of natural rights, was a tool for Willard, who found the inconsistencies of the federal system useful, just as the suffragists found the divisions of constitutional authority between state and federal government frustrating. For Willard enfranchised women might vote in local option elections, deciding whether their town or municipality would be dry as was her hometown of Evanston. In some communities female voters would constitute a sufficient bloc of voters to prohibit liquor entirely. In others they might vote for stringent licensing requirements and thereby stanch, if not prohibit, the availability of demon rum in public places. With suffrage an instrument and not a natural right, votes for women might not even be permitted in presidential or congressional elections. Women might be given ballots in municipal elections, but not national ones where issues such as the tariff and currency were only distantly related to home protection. Or states might agree to universal suffrage in their capacity to determine voting credentials by statute or constitutional changes. But even in this vague form as a contingent privilege, suffrage was not initially popular among temperance women.

Wittenmyer opposed suffrage as an embarrassing, controversial distraction from the temperance cause, even when couched in the Trojan horse of domesticity. She forbade Willard from discussing the matter in the temperance newspaper *The Union Signal*. Cognizant of her growing power in the organization, at the annual WCTU convention in 1876 a stubborn Willard nevertheless repeated a suffrage plan that argued for votes in order to protect the home—a home protection ballot, as she labeled it in a tactical appeal to domestic women. An angry Wittenmyer dismissed the younger woman: "You might have been a leader, but now you'll only be a scout."[53]

A year later the WCTU's annual convention took place in Chicago's Farwell Hall, and Willard welcomed the delegates. Instinctively charismatic but also properly feminine in her tidy, high-collared dark dress with a rose point lace collar, the cameo pin of her mother's profile pinned at her throat, and her pince-nez glasses magnifying her blue eyes, she mesmerized the convention with an address full of the stylistic devices that delighted her listeners. She greeted the two hundred delegates in a conversational style different from that of more nervous women who, with neck and eyes bent to their text, woodenly mumbled undecipherable comments.

She spoke as if her speech was an impromptu one, though in fact she always had a text that revealed her skillful application of a number of oratorical techniques. She compared intemperance to a raging fire that must be extinguished, conjuring up associations among her listeners with the Chicago fire of 1871. She used antithesis and artful repetitions around the staccato "we speak about." Boldly she hinted at the need for women's suffrage, ending with the religious call to arms adapted from an old Scotch song: "The Christians are coming, Thank God! Thank God!" Even before the speech ended the audience had begun waving their handkerchiefs in the traditional salute ladies reserved for special presentations.[54]

In 1879, after five years of restless apprenticeship, a defeat in 1878, and the persistent currying of the favor of delegates, Willard was elected president of the WCTU with twice as many votes as Wittenmyer. Once installed, she remained president until her death in 1898, annually reelected by overwhelming margins as she avoided the internecine battles that disrupted many organizations and that certainly harmed the suffrage movement. In her victory speech in 1879 Willard asked for God's aid, and she promised the delegates faithful and honest leadership. She would "seek the help promised us by Christ in his words." It was a powerful message for thousands of pious, religiously observant women who found in temperance a conservative enough cause to justify their public activity, and yet a progressive enough one to sanction their limited transgression of domesticity. Temperance, an intended protection of their homes, was not radical enough to place them in what seemed, to many, the extremist camp of suffragism inhabited by harridans like Susan B. Anthony and Elizabeth Cady Stanton.[55]

In the forty-year-old Willard, members of the WCTU found a beloved "Mother Frances," soon sanctified as a saint. Indeed Willard depended on an evangelical style of leadership, shaping herself into a Christian prophet and messenger, in the style of an Old Testament Miriam or Deborah. "Temperance," she told the convention in 1881, "must go forth to the encounter or fail to exhibit David's faith in the presence of Goliath." Ever calm, serene, ladylike, and maternal, ever publicly tolerant of her opponents even as she used her levers of power to retain her authority, Willard easily defused the greatest challenge to her presidency when a group of pro–Republican Party temperance supporters angrily opposed Willard's affiliation with the Prohibition Party. For Willard, WCTU support of a political party that had as its stated purpose in 1884 "the repeal of all laws that permitted drinking and the legal suppression of the baneful liquor traffic" seemed natural. But temperance and women's reform associations had been traditionally nonpartisan, and many conservative women still abhorred any political entanglements.[56]

Playing the role of a mother whose hopes for the future would be carried out by her offspring, Willard argued for support of a political party as a position that Christian women could accept. Then she changed the subject. She reminded members that the motto of their organization was "God and Home and Native Land"—a program that in its amorphousness offered individual choice. She noted the importance of understanding the vote as a means of protecting Christian homes from the disruption of drinking. Under her constant urging, sustained by *The Union Signal* as well as her speeches and pamphlets, the WCTU convention in 1884 passed a resolution deploring the "disenfranchisement of 12 million people who are citizens." Such treatment was "out of harmony with the idea of Christian cooperation." To connect voting to religion was the first of Willard's policy triumphs.[57]

Immediately after her election Willard initiated transformations in the WCTU through her accommodating, religiously grounded appeals. Followers might disagree with her calls for suffrage, but she gave them permission to do so by introducing her inspired strategy of "Doing Everything." In 1881 she authored a controversial resolution in the annual convention that "wisdom dictates the Do-Everything policy." Willard meant by that the application of all the means for social change available to women—petitioning, lobbying, and moral persuasion for temperance along with the vote. But as she sought more radical goals, so her concept of doing everything expanded. At first a means, it came to include broader goals. It even justified her calls for a transformation in American capitalism. From its first enunciation, doing everything joined the home protection ballot as one of Willard's adroit methods of satisfying a membership that was several steps behind her in its approach to change.[58]

In 1882, as a symbolic gesture, Willard invited Susan B. Anthony to the WCTU convention. And there, on the platform, the aging warrior of suffrage sat, despite the belief among some temperance women that Anthony at best did not have proper Christian credentials and at worst was an atheist. But in the diversified accommodation offered by Willard's version of the WCTU, suffrage, just like working for more community water fountains and against prostitution, or laboring for the temperance press and speaking before state legislatures, was part of doing everything.[59]

For several years Anthony, who refused to join the WCTU but admired Willard's organizational talents and certainly wanted her support, had been wooing the temperance leader. In 1876 Anthony congratulated Willard on "breaking the spell" by supporting suffrage. In her best biblical style, Anthony praised Willard's "go[ing] forward—now the Red Sea opens to pass you through . . . for Temperance & Virtue's sake—for Woman's sake." But Willard's commitment to suffrage was never as forthright as the leaders of NWSA wished. Both women knew why. Earlier Anthony had rejected efforts to merge the WCTU and the NWSA on the grounds that "though we are ready to join them . . . they are not ready to join us . . . those who are—like Miss Willard & Mrs. Wallace would not go with us if it were likely to divide their Temp. Society . . ." With a sure sense of the limits of her followers, Willard never compromised the union's unanimity, although she privately wished her members "more keener-minded than they are" about politics.[60]

Twice Anthony asked Willard to postpone or move WCTU conventions from states where suffrage proposals were on the ballot. Too much talk of temperance only increased the backlash from the powerful liquor associations and brewers societies who correctly believed, using Willard's own argument, that women would vote against demon rum. In 1896, optimistic about the chances of a successful referendum in California, Anthony implored Willard to move the scheduled WCTU convention from San Francisco to some other state. "Susan is set," a resigned Willard wrote in her diary, and moved the convention to St. Louis.[61]

Opposition in the WCTU did not deter Willard's policy. And after several years of lobbying, WCTU members resolved in 1881 "that wisdom dictates the Do-Everything policy: Constitutional amendment where the way is open for it; Home protection where Home protection is the strongest rallying cry; equal franchise where the votes of women joined to those of men can alone give stability to temperance legislation."[62]

Eventually Willard's Do-Everything policy, so similar in its diversity to a mother's work in the home, so similar to the individually tailored child-raising methods Mother Willard had employed to raise two very different daughters, included thirty-nine departments, each coordinated by a national supervisor. By 1885 the women of the state temperance organizations and their 1,654 auxiliaries sponsored projects determined by local women that included alcohol education in schools, improving prisons, setting up teahouses and temperance hotels, lobbying for signatures on petitions, working for a national amendment to outlaw drinking, and assisting, as Anthony hoped, the Department of Equal Franchise. After the founding of the World Woman's Christian Temperance Union in 1891, Willard demanded that members must do something—whatever it was to get them out of "their hammocks," and into the struggle for the betterment of home, community, nation, and world.

In lesser hands such decentralization might have led to local autonomy and institutional confusion. To be sure, there was always concern about what some called "the scatteration" of the president's mandates. But Willard stifled disagreement with her compelling rhetoric, her countless visits to locals, and her control over the union's press. Steadfastly, she retained the central mission of the WCTU—to end drinking—working to offset the defused focus imposed by her own support of numerous means to accomplish a multiplicity of ends. As a result, what had been a praying society became a structurally sophisticated, modern organization of women, an association that through its system of locals went beyond particular towns and communities to bind women together into a national federation.

As president of the WCTU, Willard revised the basis of representation in the critically important annual convention from congressional districts to the more realistic dues-paying members. Next she created a powerful executive committee of her supporters, and made state chairs into vice presidents with the same limited authority as that officer held in the national government. She used the increasing contributions from members to finance the *The Union Signal*, the WCTU's newspaper, whose circulation was over thirty-five thousand by the 1880s and whose editorial columns were always available to Willard. Alert to the importance of public opinion, she organized the Temperance Publishing Company and by 1887 the company annually dispensed millions of pages of temperance advocacy along with praise for its president. Willard also understood the importance of symbols, encouraging the building of a twelve-story temperance "temple" in downtown Chicago, which, during the depression of 1893, nearly bankrupted the WCTU.

For this generation of American women there were no precedents among their female forebears for public activity. So Willard provided them first with an instructional manual to use when they organized their locals. She followed this with a similar manual for young boys and girls, who were a primary target for temperance propaganda. Her advice emerged from her understanding that many American women could not hear the call to temperance work because of their belief that participation in public affairs somehow would damage their femininity. Accordingly the president of the WCTU delivered practical advice about how to set up local meetings, provide special seats for pastors, decorate meeting halls with flowers, use religious music, pass the collection late (immediately after the main address), and in one of her secrets, "premeditate the impromptus."[63]

In a few years Willard had transformed the yearly convention from a stolid business meeting into a four-day celebration that brought local leaders from throughout the United States to an ever-increasing number of convention cities chosen to enhance the visibility of the WCTU. Of course she was the star. She fostered rituals such as the wearing of the small white ribbon that made temperance advocates visible to each other at a time when respectable women were just beginning to travel alone. She commissioned a temperance flag, pennants, a motto, a hymn, and a prayer. And always she was the traveling mother prophet called to testify for temperance. In one year she visited every state and territory in the nation, and in ten years, according to a subordinate, "she had left unvisited no town of 10,000 save six and but a few of 5,000."[64]

Willard's speeches became the high point of the convention, and they were acknowledged as such by outsiders with little interest in the movement. Edward Everett Hale found them better reading than most presidential state-of-the-union addresses, though some years they were much longer. In her speech to the 1887 convention, as she was moving toward more progressive causes, Willard obscured the radical nature of her calls for nationalizing industries with religious rhetoric and quotations from the Bible in a preview of what became known as the Social Gospel Movement. "Temperance feeds and clothes the poor, does industrial training, supports better wages, shorter hours of work, and cooperation and arbitration—all these modern modes of blessing will claim for those who work to bring them, the holy declaration from the lips of the carpenter's son; 'Ye did it unto me.'" Under Willard, nothing seemed radical, and if it was deemed so, as suffrage initially was, more squeamish members might focus on something else.[65]

Along with the spiritual tone of her messages, she applied the new methods of the social sciences to the WCTU. Members and their contributions were counted and published. Every year the seven-hundred-page annual report included, along with a list of accomplishments, a careful grid sheet of the WCTU's various activities broken down by the president into evangelistic, social, legal, extending our organization, preventive, and, a final category, of whatever was "instigated and inspired by our local unions." This ever-expanding latter category included the sponsorship of public fountains, free bathing houses and gymnasiums for women, and the introduction of a temperance curriculum that placed WCTU literature in the public schools, a program whose generational dividends became obvious with the rapid and mostly uncontested passage and ratification of the Prohibition Amendment in 1919. If Willard was ever discouraged by the slow progress of her causes, she never informed the membership. Besides, there was always some successful local crusade to describe to members; her optimism, she claimed, was the public legacy of an uncomplaining mother "who had never shed tears about what she had given up."[66]

Between annual conventions, Willard traveled on a schedule that left only a few weeks a year free to spend with her mother in Rest Cottage. There in the den, while her mother pasted news reports of her famous daughter into the eighty scrapbooks that became a mother's legacy and the movement's archive, Frances Willard attended to union business, employing two secretaries and a stenographer to attend to her correspondence. She tried to find time for her writing. She had always wanted to write books, a conventional way for women to distinguish themselves. So she memorialized motherhood and her mother in one book, her dead sister in another, and herself in a seven-hundred-page autobiography entitled *Glimpses: The Autobiography of an American Woman*, published in 1889. It was unusual for nineteenth-century women to consider their lives worth chronicling at all, and at fifty Willard was still relatively young. Yet her celebrity status and self-conscious ambitiousness made her well aware of the significance of her story for supporters, though with a lady's proper humility, she advised in her introduction that the book had been solicited by her followers in the WCTU. Published by the Temperance Publishing Association and promoted by over a hundred temperance agents, *Glimpses* sold fifty thousand copies in three months.

Most controversial of Willard's books was *Woman in the Pulpit*, an effort to persuade Christian denominations, especially her own Methodists, to ordain women. She made her case on biblical grounds, demonstrating her knowledge of the Scriptures as she argued with male clerics adamantly opposed to women clergy. Besides citing instances of women preaching in the testaments, Willard offered women's motherly instincts and values as desirable criteria for the pastoral work of the ministry. The argument failed. Even in the lesser role of elected lay delegate to the Methodist Episcopal General Conference in 1888, Willard and four other women, among some five hundred mostly ordained pastors, were denied seats. *The New York Times*, describing the conference as "made up of elderly men with bald heads and white hair," reported now-Bishop Charles Fowler as jubilant.[67]

Five times during her presidency Willard traveled to the Confederate South, positioning support of temperance as a unifying bridge for all Americans after the divisiveness of the Civil War. As the national process of reconstructing the South into a biracial society faltered, in white communities that still did not accept women as lecturers and activists, Willard never challenged racial segregation. Instead she established a separate Department of Colored Temperance women within the WCTU. Black women did, however, sit with white delegates at WCTU conventions, and Willard favored New Hampshire senator Henry Blair's bill for federal aid to black schools.

In the 1890s Willard's limited commitment to racial equality foundered on the lynching issue. She opposed the terrorist, extrajudicial process of lynching black men in vigilante actions in the South. On the other hand she refused to join the campaign of Ida Wells, a young black journalist and activist who worked to arouse sympathy for black victims by making the case that they were innocent. In the battle for public opinion Willard could be a powerful ally in Wells's antilynching crusade. But when Wells sought her support, Willard balked. While lynching was wrong, she argued, so too "were the unspeakable outrages [of black rape of white women] which have so often provoked such lawlessness." Like other founding sisters, Willard's aspirations never had room for the divisive issue of race, and for that she provoked the anger of not just Wells but reformers like Frederick Douglass, William Lloyd Garrison, and Julia Ward Howe.[68]

In 1888, nearly ten years after becoming president of the WCTU, Frances Willard attended the first meeting of the Woman's Council of the United States and its companion association, the International Council of Women, held under the auspices of the National Woman Suffrage Association. The brainchild of Elizabeth Cady Stanton, this new federation of women's groups intended to celebrate the fortieth anniversary of the Seneca Falls Convention. Stanton and Anthony had as well the larger agenda of providing a permanent organizational clearinghouse—a uniting link—for all the diverse nineteenth-century organizations of women, from literary clubs to labor leagues to educational and industrial associations, both in the United States and in Europe. For a younger generation the council might play the same role in the feminist struggle for equality and collaboration as Seneca Falls had for women like Stanton, Anthony, and Stone.

In their preamble to a formal constitution delegates resolved that "we women of the United States . . . for greater unity of thought, sym-

pathy and purpose and as an organized movement that will best con-
serve the highest good of the family and the State do hereby band ourselves together in a confederation of workers committed to the
overthrow of all forms of ignorance and injustice and to the application of the Golden Rule to society, custom and law . . ." The mild
statement was vague enough for delegates from fifty-three American
organizations and forty-nine foreign nations to accept.[69]

Every founding feminist in the United States attended the week-
long sessions at Albaugh's Opera House in Washington, D.C., during
the last week of March. Lucy Stone and Henry Blackwell were there,
still warring with the NWSA and snubbing Anthony and Stanton.
Nette Blackwell, Anna Howard Shaw (who had moved from temperance to suffrage), Julia Ward Howe, Clara Barton of the Red Cross,
and Mary Livermore all mixed in the lobby along with delegates from
Paris and Denmark. Pandita Ramabai, the Hindu widow investigating
girls' education in the United States and a new recruit to Christianity
and the WCTU, represented the ambitious internationalism of the
nineteenth-century women's movement. Of course Frances Willard
was there, an unavoidable presence, though both Anthony and Stanton had suspicions about her feminism. Stanton, who considered the
organized church the greatest barrier to attaining women's rights, believed Willard's religiosity foolish and her commitment to temperance
a distracting impossibility.[70]

Yet by this time Willard was far too popular to overlook. Presented
to the delegates as "needing no introduction," Frances Willard spoke
more often and longer than anyone else, save Stanton and Anthony.
Willard had somehow negotiated an unusual half hour (most delegates spoke for fifteen minutes) for her remarks on temperance, which
she described as "the enthronement of Christ's spirit in the world in
its customs, habits, and its legislation." Temperance was Christianity
applied; her leadership was motherhood installed. Again on Thursday,
twice on Friday, and once on Saturday—this time on religion—the
diminutive leader of the WCTU addressed delegates on such diverse
topics as organization and politics. Her versatile do-everything program furnished her with a voice beyond simply one cause, and Anthony recognized that her reputation as a "sweet conciliator" who
muted conflict made her an ideal spokesperson for a new organization

full of prickly egos and competing motives. If Willard needed any convincing, this meeting verified her lifelong ambition to be someone. Indeed she had become the leading reformer in the United States, dubbed in the press the "uncrowned queen of American democracy," a combination of Mother Mary and Queen Elizabeth.

Among her topics during the meeting was that of social purity, a new cultural crusade in the 1880s. The WCTU had already established a Department of Social Purity, a Department of White Cross (the latter the name used by a British organization fighting for a single sexual standard), and a Department to Suppress Impure Literature. When no one could be found to head the social purity division, Willard signaled its importance by briefly serving herself. She made purity concerns one of her principal issues, speaking to the council on the need to end the notorious dens in lumbering camps where young girls were imprisoned as sex slaves, to stop prostitution, not just regulate it, and to raise the age of consent, the age at which a girl could legally agree to "carnal relations with the other sex."

As an indication of her growing prestige and expanding aspirations beyond the WCTU, Willard believed herself the leader of an emerging Anglo-American mass movement involving sexual purity. She brought "[my] mother's heart" to a heralded crisis of promiscuous sexuality, lascivious dressing, and pornography. "What the world most needs is mothering, and most of all the spirit's home, the church." She warned her listeners of the national decline in moral standards — women in cigar stores and saloons, women smoking and dancing "round dances" in the great Babylon that America's Gilded Age had become. She repeated her warnings against "the insanity of [female] fashion," the world of high-heeled shoes and low-cut dresses that she had already disparaged in *How to Win*, her popular advice book for young women. Now she admonished the international meeting: "Let us have self-respect. Let us be clothed with a raiment of purity that ought to guard the virgin, the mother and the wife."[71]

A natural extension of temperance work in that it combined the collective cleansing of communities along with the protection of individual homes, social purity became Willard's most significant and practical contribution to women's rights. Her other causes — prohibiting drinking and getting the vote for women — gained acceptance only a quarter century after her death, and then primarily through the activism of other organizations such as the Anti-Saloon League and Alice Paul's National Woman's Party. But Willard's campaigns for purity, while they earned her a reputation as a priggish censor, achieved immediate results. With some success, the WCTU lobbied Congress and state legislatures to raise the female age of marital consent during a period in which most states allowed girls to marry at ten years of age, Delaware at seven. A decade later only five states (all in the South) retained the ten-year age of consent. Willard also furthered the campaign for sex education in schools and especially at home—"the recital of the creative mysteries from a mother's lips imparted to the child's mind."[72]

"Are our girls," she asked with palpable irony in her 1891 presidential address, "to be as free to please themselves by indulging in the lawless gratification of every instinct and passion as our boys?" The answer was no, but only by increasing the authority of women, through voting and public activism, could men be forced to behave with sexual temperance before their marriages, monogamously thereafter, and to surrender for a lifetime those villainies of philandering, tobacco, and alcohol.[73]

Last Years

By any measure Willard had achieved her childhood ambition to be somebody. Even those who considered temperance a crank's crusade admired this fifty-year-old woman who combined a nonthreatening femininity with an increasingly radical program. Even suffragists appreciated the power of the WCTU, which now, with over three hundred thousand adult members, had become the largest dues-paying organization in the United States. Even Southern women, suspicious of any females in public roles and opposed to equal participation by black women, listened to Frances Willard and accepted the nonsegregated seating in the WCTU conventions. Finally, even those members of the WCTU who grumbled at the undeniably autocratic control of their president accepted her leadership. In 1890, in her eleventh year as president, of 384 votes cast for the election of a WCTU president, 380 were for Willard.

Still energetic and ambitious after nearly two decades in the temperance movement, Willard now pursued causes beyond the WCTU. In the early 1890s she attempted her most audacious activism—the creation of a national reform coalition made up of trade unions like Terence Powderly's Knights of Labor, of the Prohibition Party, of which she was a member of the central committee, of farmers' alliances and the newly emerging Populist Party under James Weaver, and of course of all women, but especially members of her white-ribbon crusade. She lacked the basic democratic entitlement of even her own vote, much less the power to bring her organization's members to the polls. But inspired by Edward Bellamy's *Looking Backward: 2000–1887* with its futurist vision of an egalitarian society achieved by the intervention of the state, Willard hoped to include male members of Bellamy's popular nationalist clubs in a new political party.

For several years Willard had been mobilizing her white ribboners to support government intervention in the economy. Because women, like men, were the victims of capitalism—"the rich idlers amusing themselves in Newport while poor workers bury themselves in coal mines," she now placed transformations in general society within the domain of "woman's mighty realm of philanthropy." No longer did Willard believe that drinking caused poverty, any more than she thought signing a temperance pledge would lead to an abstinent America. Instead she reversed the sequence. Poverty, so palpable in the hard times of the 1890s, encouraged drinking, and only public policies could stop the sources of drinking through solutions such as higher wages, an eight-hour day, government control of trusts, and, of course, a prohibition amendment undertaken by a benevolent "Mother State."[74]

To be effective, members of her proposed coalition must first agree on a position paper. With the presidential election approaching, in the spring of 1892 Willard extended invitations to the most important reform leaders in the United States. Forty-eight men and five women met in Chicago and accepted proposals for nationalizing transportation, communication, and the coining of currency, ending speculation in land, supporting antitrust legislation and municipal suffrage for women, and suppressing the "pernicious influence of the saloon." But when the resolutions were presented to the Populist Party at its first national convention a few months later in St. Louis, Willard's fragile coalition shattered, over even limited expressions of support for prohibition and women's suffrage. Southern delegates voted against suffrage; urban and Western delegates opposed prohibition.[75]

Making the best of a humiliating defeat, Willard remained publicly optimistic about the fusion of progressive groups and the "massing" of the reform vote. Although her efforts had failed, she explained to reporters that individuals could continue to embrace "united action among labor reformers and temperance reformers." Intrepidly, given the power of the two established parties, she challenged both. "The Democrats and Republicans are like boulders in the path; the Prohibition and People's parties must combine." But too many issues and personalities barred the way. Still, even in failure, Willard had been responsible for the most sweeping politically progressive endeavor ever undertaken by an American woman. She had pushed her movement of Christian women interested in closing saloons to the point of merger with workers, farmers, and socialists in an ambitious, nondenominational partisan effort. It was the high-water mark of her feminist ambitions.[76]

Four months later Mary Willard—the woman who cautioned her enterprising daughter that "we were born not to reign but to wrestle"—died. Saint Courageous had been in failing health for over a year, and at eighty-seven had lived well beyond the life span of most women of hers or any generation. As she became weaker, she tried to comfort her daughter with the resignation of a good Methodist who anticipated resurrection—going across the river to a better place. Like her daughter Mary and her husband, Josiah, Mother Willard died a good death. It was "a great sunset," declared her daughter. Later Willard acknowledged that the eternal world had always been the real one for her mother, the present one "its vestibule." But as often as she had heard her mother's motto of submission—"my bark is wafted to the strand / By breath divine / And on the helm there rests a hand / Other than mine," nothing consoled. Willard descended into a profound, long-lasting, and incapacitating grief.[77]

Perhaps Frances Willard felt guilty about her absences from Rest Cottage. Perhaps it was the disappearance of the home and the company of her mother—the private sanctuary from the meetings, travel, and speeches of public life provided by a woman who was always able to soothe and calm her daughter. Perhaps it was the loss of what Willard's friend Lady Isabel Somerset called "the embodied fate" mothers transferred to their daughters. Certainly Willard had tried to model her leadership of the WCTU on the characteristics her mother had displayed—orderliness, courage, self-abnegation, service, and charity.[78]

Months after her mother's death Willard acknowledged "this is the first New Year in which no Mother called out her cheery greeting or wrote to her absent child." Willard's New Year's resolutions to forget herself, to believe that others are trying to do right, and to have faith in God never dispelled her enormous loss. Nor did her sentimental deification of her mother, *A Great Mother: Sketches of Madame Willard*. Even in 1895, she still despaired: "Where is Mother? That is the most frequent question. Why is there never sign or token?"[79]

Frances Willard lived for less than six years after her mother's death, and she spent most of these in England, as a guest of her friend Lady Isabel Somerset (Cossie). In 1891, at their first meeting, these two women felt an instant attraction to each other. Somerset, the ambitious newly elected president of the British Women's Temperance Association, had come to America to observe the WCTU's organizational methods, and she stayed long enough to visit Rest Cottage. Thereafter Willard and Somerset were nearly inseparable as Willard became a physical and emotional expatriate living on Somerset's lavish twenty-five-thousand-acre estate in Herefordshire, and on two occasions when she was ill, sending Somerset to the United States to read her annual address to an ever more restive WCTU.

By the 1890s Willard was suffering not just from despondency over her mother's death, but from pernicious anemia, caused by an inability to absorb vitamin B_{12} from the stomach and intestine. Easily treated today by the injection of vitamins, but subject in the 1890s to contradictory and unhelpful therapies of rest and exercise, the deficiency of red blood cells rendered the previously indefatigable Willard intermittently exhausted. She lost her appetite, and a characteristic feature of the disease—sores in her mouth and tongue—made it nearly impossible to lecture. The episodic nature of pernicious anemia led to bursts of energy in a woman who wanted to remain active, always followed by periods of lassitude and fatigue.

When one of Somerset's doctors recommended exercise, Willard, dutifully and awkwardly, began learning how to ride a bicycle. The process became a parable of life with its failures, hard work, and ultimate successes. She fell often, hampered no doubt by a long skirt and boots, and when she finally succeeded, Willard used her experiment as a teaching opportunity for women who needed, in her judgment, to get more exercise. At a time when bicycle riding was still controversial for women, *Wheels Within Wheels, or How I Learned to Ride the Bicycle* carried the imprimatur of the best-known woman in the United States along with some homilies: "An ounce of practice is worth a ton of theory." "There is no terror in the universe for God is always at the center of everything." And her special message for women: "She who succeeds in gaining mastery of the bicycle will gain the mastery of life."[80]

In February 1898, after an appearance at the WCTU convention, Willard died in a New York hotel, en route to England and her beloved Cossie. As had her family before her, Willard died a good death. Anna Gordon remembered her last words as "how beautiful it is to be with God."[81]

Frances Willard's funeral reached epic, near-Lincolnian proportions with a large service attended by two thousand admirers at the Broadway Tabernacle in New York. Afterward a special railroad car carried her body to Chicago, stopping at Churchville, the place of her birth, and slowing in other places where some stations were lined with those wanting to pay their respects to America's greatest woman. "No woman in America was better known, none was more universally loved—as the champion of the cause of women she was foremost in the world," eulogized a Chicago paper in a representative statement. In Chicago Willard's body lay in state in Willard Hall in the Temperance Temple, the physical expression of Willard's ambitions. Finally there were services in the First Methodist Church in Evanston, with the city in official mourning, where ministers and members of the union stretched their vocabularies to pay tribute. After her cremation, her ashes were deposited in her mother's casket.[82]

The apotheosis of Willard began with Anna Gordon's *The Life of Frances E. Willard*, and it proceeded in WCTU-sponsored monuments of drinking fountains and more grandly a statue in the Illinois state Capitol Building and eventually one in the U.S. Capitol Statuary Hall, where Willard remained the only woman to be so honored until the arrival of the controversial statue of Mott, Anthony, and Stanton. Throughout the United States bridges and streets, hospitals and schools bore her name. But led by less effective women, her other legacy—the WCTU—retreated to its original intention of ending the curse of drunkenness and soon ceded primacy in the field to the Anti-Saloon League.

In the process of deification much of Willard's radicalism and social progressivism disappeared. Those women of the union whose sole goal was the eradication of liquor had never approved of Willard's aspirations for women or for the United States. Twentieth-century women whose mothers joined the WCTU as a respectable organization now moved into the more palatable and effective NAWSA. And after the repeal of the prohibition amendment in 1933 temperance lost credibility as only local governments—and few of these save in the South—cared much about stopping the sale of liquor. Believing in drink as a galvanizing villain, Willard never addressed the issue of infringing on the personal liberties of citizens to engage in what for most was merely a recreation, not an addiction. Accordingly the reputation of the most famous feminist of the nineteenth century dissolved into that of a scold, more often ridiculed for calling on churches to give up using wine in their communion services and housewives hard cider in their mince pies than for calling for a fusion of reform groups.[83]

This process of historical bowdlerization has diminished Frances Willard into a minor figure in the history of suffrage and American feminism. Of course she is credited with the creation of the largest women's organization of her time. Sometimes her introduction of conservative women into the associational activities that taught women how to be Americans with public responsibilities is observed. But her social purity crusade emerges as an unfortunate effort at censorship,

symbolized by her friendship with the grim, anti-birth-control advocate Anthony Comstock. Moreover her sentimental religiosity makes
her an archaic figure in the twenty-first century, and her appeals to
bring "a mother heart" into society seem hopelessly dated. On the
other hand her oft-stated desire that women must be, as she undeniably was, ambitious and aspiring is more in tune with contemporary
intentions, but that element of her personality has been exorcised in
the process of her sanctification. How indeed can a saint, especially a
female one, be ambitious?

Yet Frances Willard deserves credit for her understanding that
women's rights involved doing everything—whether raising the age of
consent for girls or ending the double sex standard or joining, as a
voteless woman, a political party or supporting arbitration in labor dis-
putes or teaching women how to ride bicycles. She transformed a
Christian organization of conservative women into an international
movement that focused on secular, nondenominational political matters. But suffrage had never been her final answer. And if in the
process of reforming society, it was necessary to compromise, it was
better to get something than nothing.

5

Endgame:
Alice Paul and Woodrow Wilson

On March 2, 1913, a cool, sunny day in the nation's capital, residents of Washington were preparing for the presidential inauguration that would take place the next day. For the first time in nearly a quarter of a century, a Democrat had been elected, and because the capital remained a southern city in its political tastes and consequently sympathetic to the incoming party, the installation of Woodrow Wilson promised to be an especially exciting occasion. Thousands of partisans—some hungry for patronage jobs, others drawn to the patriotic drama of parades and speeches—flooded into the city to celebrate the victory that had given Democrats control of both the House and the Senate as well as the presidency.

That same day in a small basement office in downtown Washington, Alice Paul, a twenty-eight-year-old suffragist, was overseeing the last-minute details of another parade. She expected her procession to catch the attention of those gathered for Wilson's inauguration. She intended as well to embarrass a government that still did not permit women to vote. Certainly her parade would be different from any the capital had ever witnessed. Suffragists from all over the country had been gathering on Capitol Hill since early morning. At precisely two thirty in the afternoon over eight thousand women—led by stately Inez Milholland astride a white horse and arranged in units representing homemakers, colleges and universities, professionals, and states (with a small contingent of male supporters)—moved down the hill from the Capitol for the mile-and-a-half march along Pennsylvania Avenue. Instructed by Paul "to march steadily in a dignified manner," they walked behind a yellow banner emblazoned: We Demand an Amendment to the Constitution of the United States Enfranchising the Women of this Country. By all accounts an impressive spectacle, Alice Paul's parade "from the doors of the National Congress to those of the National Executive" was meant to convey the popularity of the cause as well as the disciplined activism that women would bring to American politics.[1]

The suffragists followed the same route as traditional inaugural parades, although the authorities had unsuccessfully tried to shunt Paul's procession onto what she disdained as "side streets." When the suffragists arrived at the Treasury Building adjacent to the White House, a symbolic spectacle took place: a red, white, and blue robed female representation of Columbia summoned forth, to the strains of "The Star-Spangled Banner," her American companions attired in colors representing Justice, Charity, Liberty, and Peace. The procession and the spectacle, so patently juxtaposed to the national symbols of a presidential inauguration, expressed the message of a new generation of suffrage women—votes for women must come from men in Washington.

Sometime during that same day, 150 miles to the north in a small college town in New Jersey, President-Elect Woodrow Wilson was enjoying a final serenade from the college boys of Princeton as he walked from his home to the local train station. Accompanied by enthusiastic students singing "Old Nassau" and "For He's a Jolly Good Fellow," Wilson, his wife, and three daughters then boarded a special train for Washington and his installation the next day as the twenty-eighth chief executive of the United States. But when the president-elect arrived in Union Station later that afternoon, the capital seemed deserted. "Where," asked Wilson, "are the people?" The answer came back: "Oh, they are out watching the suffrage parade."[2]

In fact many of the male spectators of that parade, who comprised a clear majority of the crowd, were doing a lot more than watching. Some were grabbing and trampling the suffragists' banners, toppling their floats, yelling obscenities, spitting at, pinching, and groping women as the police turned their backs. Cries of "Why don't you go home and cook dinner?" and "Who is minding the babies?" mixed with salacious importuning for sexual favors. Only federal cavalry troops hastily summoned from nearby Fort Myer restored order. Obviously the public places of the capital, available the next day for the bands and army regiments saluting Wilson, remained off-limits to women. In fact, Wilson's inaugural committee had banned all women from participating in the planned four-and-a-half-hour parade to honor the new president.[3]

More intimidating than the behavior of a crowd estimated at 250,000 was the collusion of the police force. Prior to receiving their assignments, Washington's police had been shown an article from *McClure's Magazine* featuring the radical celebrity suffragist Alice Paul, recently returned from jail in England. The point that women who marched in the streets did not deserve protection was not lost on the young policemen. Later the District of Columbia police excused their inability to keep order by noting that the number of women and babies among the spectators restricted their use of billy sticks, though photographs show a mostly male crowd. The planned orderly procession had so quickly deteriorated into a mob scene embarrassing in its violent abuse of civil liberties that the Senate Committee on the District of Columbia immediately undertook an investigation. The result was the suspension of Chief of Police Richard Sylvester.[4]

The next day Woodrow Wilson took the oath of office promising change in his inaugural address. The new president proclaimed: "Some old things with which we had grown familiar and which had begun to creep into the very habit of our thought and of our lives have altered their aspect as we have latterly looked critically upon them with fresh, awakened eyes . . . we have been refreshed by a new insight into our own life . . . This is not a day of triumph; it is a day of dedication."[5]

Though Wilson was dedicating himself to transform American business practices, an optimistic feminist might have reason to anticipate presidential support for suffrage. He was, after all, a progressive who had won the Democratic presidential nomination from more tested party politicians because of his reforms as governor of New Jersey. There he had supported the democratization of the political process and responsible government through primaries along with the new practices of voter initiative, recall, and referendum.

His speeches had been full of lofty rhetoric about invigorating American democracy through citizen participation, and in his acceptance speech in 1912 he had promised that his duty was not just to the Democratic Party, which he nevertheless believed to be the proper instrument of policy reforms, but to all the people. He viewed the separation of powers between Congress and the president as enfeebling the authority of the latter, and he intended to be a strong chief executive. Such a leader might be expected to lead the fight to extend political freedom to half the people.

Alice Paul knew better. She was convinced that American progressives like Wilson used women to work as volunteers for small-bore local reforms—more public bathrooms for women, more playgrounds, and better teachers—all the while withholding the equalizing lever of the vote. She also knew that American politicians, mirroring the opinion of many voters, came in multiple versions: those who adamantly opposed women's suffrage, those who were indifferent, were silent, or trivialized the subject, those who approved in theory but did nothing in practice, and those who came from suffrage states with women voters where opposition from these new voters carried a potential political price tag. A fifth variety—a politician who actually worked for women's suffrage—was rarer than a prohibitionist, a socialist, and even a vegetarian.[6]

In 1913 Wilson was an opponent of suffrage. Four years earlier, in the paternalistic style that marked his comments about women, he had explained that women had no experience in public affairs, therefore did not understand politics, and consequently should not vote. Earlier he had simply dismissed the subject as one for which he had "neither the time nor the stomach." In 1888 when the esteemed British political scientist James Bryce asked then professor Wilson to contribute a chapter on women's suffrage for a forthcoming study of "the government and institutions of the United States," Wilson declined, wondering sarcastically what he had done to deserve that request. Had Bryce, Wilson inquired to a friend, asked him "because I was at Bryn Mawr—to write a chapter on woman suffrage? . . . What had I done to deserve that?" Earlier Wilson had argued that men and women belonged in separate spheres and had different attributes. In contrast to men who based their choices on reason, females "prefer goodness to ability and are apt to be not a little influenced by charm of manner."[7]

Alice Paul intended to make the president, for the first time in American history, the specific target of a political movement. For the next seven years, she pursued, pressured, and pushed Wilson as he grudgingly converted, through a number of transmutations, from first an opponent of suffrage, to an avoidant who professed indifference about an "unimportant" issue, to a lukewarm supporter who must follow his party's position but not direct it and follow it only if suffrage was accomplished by states, and finally to a president who not only supported the Susan B. Anthony federal amendment but took the unusual step of appearing before the U.S. Senate to urge its passage.

Of course Paul was not solely responsible for Wilson's grudging epiphany; in fact some observers believed she retarded it. Nor was her creation—the National Woman's Party—the only group working for the president's conversion. It shared the stage with the NAWSA founded by Stone, Stanton, and Anthony and run in the twentieth century by Anna Howard Shaw and Carrie Chapman Catt. But indubitably Alice Paul was the most implacable, the most single-minded, the most original, the most self-sacrificing, and the most overlooked of twentieth-century feminists. Implementing the doctrine of the British militants—"Deeds, not Words"—she became the necessary culmination of what had begun at Seneca Falls in 1848. The day after her parade, while Washington celebrated the ritual activities of a presidential inauguration (though Wilson had declined an inaugural ball, believing it simply an occasion to show off "feminine clothes"), the indefatigable Alice Paul and a few of her lieutenants were already at work organizing the first suffrage delegations to the White House, "deputations" that would plague the president.

The Status of Women's Rights

The battle for women's rights had stalled at the end of the nineteenth century. Without question, the incremental gains achieved made life for women in the United States much better than it had been for Lucy Stone, Susan B. Anthony, and Elizabeth Cady Stanton. The symbols of this emancipation—the high school diploma, the typewriter, the file cabinet, and the sewing machine—meant more women worked in offices and clerical jobs and fewer in the domestic positions that for years had been women's principal labor. On the other hand, the 15 percent of American women who worked outside the home in factories confronted miserable conditions and the hostility of male-controlled unions. Female-controlled unions were rare, but one did exist in New York. With the help of the Woman's Trade Union League and Harriot Stanton Blatch's Women's Political Union, garment workers, four out of five of whom were women, had begun organizing. In what their leaders hoped would be a harbinger of the future, twenty thousand young, mostly Jewish women went out on strike in 1909, protesting low wages and long hours in actions that, though they hardly changed management's views, displayed the growing activism of twentieth-century American women.

By 1900 60 percent of high school graduates were women and 20 percent of the nation's college graduates (of the less than 3 percent of Americans who attended college) were female. Still, no new women's colleges had been founded since Barnard had opened in 1889, and the most prestigious private colleges refused to accept women as undergraduates. Acceptance to graduate programs remained a difficult process, with quota systems for females in force at many universities. Women attending coeducational colleges continued to be second-class students discriminated against in a variety of institutionally sanctioned ways. One female learned a painful lesson about double standards at the University of California at Berkeley when she was told that "girls" were not included in that chapter's Phi Beta Kappa selections, no matter what their merit, because that honor must be reserved for men. As breadwinners who must find good jobs, only men could benefit from the distinction of a Phi Beta Kappa key.[8]

Nor were there many changes in the legal status of women, as Alice Paul discovered when she chose that subject as the topic for both her University of Pennsylvania master's essay entitled "Towards Equality" and her doctoral dissertation "The Legal Position of Women in Pennsylvania." In a third of the states married women still did not control their wages or their inheritances. Divorce laws and guardianship rights favored men in nearly all states, and men retained their primacy in a legal system that did not include women on juries.

As far as votes for women were concerned, the deaths of Lucy Stone in 1893, Elizabeth Cady Stanton in 1902, and Susan B. Anthony in 1906 seemed a depressing end to a movement that had depended on strong, dedicated leaders. After 1896 no more suffrage states were added until 1910. During those fourteen years numerous state referendums organized by the National American Woman Suffrage Association were lost by humiliating two-to-one majorities. The location of NAWSA's headquarters in out-of-the-way, small-town Warren, Ohio, the home of its treasurer, Harriet Taylor Upton, signaled how out of touch the organization was with the realities of twentieth-century politics. NAWSA had run out of ideas.

While NAWSA gave lip service to a national amendment, it mostly worked for suffrage at the state level. But amending state constitutions was exceptionally difficult. In some states the process began with the passage of an initial suffrage resolution in the legislature or with a referendum. Then a constitutional convention was called, followed by the approval of the amendment by two-thirds of the customarily hostile male electorate. Defeat was a probability, bordering on a certainty. To Alice Paul calls for enfranchising women through state action were no more than hypocritical delaying tactics on the part of men, and on the part of women, the error of political neophytes. Under such circumstances states could forever avoid giving women the vote, and Paul calculated that as many as twenty-five, notably those in the South, might forever do so. As radical suffragists understood, without a federal amendment black males would still be trying to get the vote in most states.

Year after year the largest suffrage organization lethargically employed the tactics of Stone, Stanton, and Anthony. Significant in their day, they were now routine—the holding of yearly conventions, the development of arguments to sway public opinion, the lobbying once a year before the inattentive Senate and House Judiciary Committees where many legislators yawned, cleaned their nails, turned their backs, and otherwise displayed their silent contempt for the women, the speechmaking at women's clubs throughout the United States, and the organizing of losing state campaigns. With only five thousand dues-paying members in 1900 and its president, Anna Howard Shaw, more admired for her lofty rhetoric than her organizational talents, NAWSA, and with it the suffrage movement, was in the doldrums.[9]

Politicians found no reason to take a stand on the issue. Paul's predecessor in charge of lobbying Congress for NAWSA operated on an annual budget of ten dollars, reporting as the highlights of 1912 her appearance before the Senate Judiciary Committee and a suffrage tea for the wives of senators and representatives. The federal amendment remained buried in the Senate and House Judiciary Committees, and only in 1914 did Congress begin debating the issue and intermittently voting on it. Susan B. Anthony had named her addition to the U.S. Constitution the Sixteenth Amendment. But in a demonstration of just how low a priority suffrage was to this generation, three other amendments—the income tax, direct election of senators, and prohibition—had taken precedence.

Supporters of women's right to vote had settled back into the defeatist conviction that sometime and someplace suffrage would come, if not in their lifetime, then at least in their daughters'—or perhaps their granddaughters'. A play by the suffragist Alice Duer Miller, *Impressions of a Canvasser*, satirized male attitudes:

> It's time you disappeared and let the public utterly forget
> That there are women who wish to vote
> Then at some future time, remote
> In twenty years or twenty five
> If you should chance to be alive?[10]

By 1911 there was even an organized national opposition, besides the liquor lobby and the Catholic Church. The National Association Opposed to Woman Suffrage, led by white middle-class women, provided evidence for a compelling objection to suffrage—women did not want the vote. As the wife of a Princeton friend wrote Wilson, "women in politics [are] dangerous, treacherous and vengeful . . . The sooner her political activity is curbed, the better. If men will stand fast and protect us," there was no reason for women ever to vote.[11]

Alice Paul intended to end this quiescent period. Bold tactics would move suffrage from a trivial matter of little concern to an inescapable issue. In Paul's view, Wilson, in control of his party as it was of the House and Senate and increasingly a force in shaping public opinion, was the key. Alice Paul's preinaugural procession in 1913 was the shot across the bow. So began the confrontation between Wilson, who avoided suffrage as long and as nimbly as he could, and Alice Paul, who knew all about American politics and had as her essential reading the president's own books and speeches, including *The New Freedom*. Although she believed him duplicitous and autocratic, Paul eventually professed admiration for Wilson, calling him a "great leader." Yet as a political tactician, she believed him "a nice kind of man to be dealing with because you could be sure what he would do in a certain situation."[12] For his part the president thought Paul a lunatic.

Beginnings

Born in 1885 in Mount Laurel, New Jersey, a small town across the Delaware River from Philadelphia, Alice Paul was the empowered eldest child in an affluent Quaker family. Alice was recognized by both her parents as the smartest and most competent among their offspring of two girls and two boys. This founding sister never suffered from the parental favoritism for sons that had fired Lucy Stone's and Elizabeth Cady Stanton's egalitarian sentiments. In her father William Paul's comment, "If you want something hard and disagreeable done, I bank on Alice to do it."[13]

Like many eldest children, Alice Paul embraced the values of her parents and was influenced not just by their religion but by the local Quaker community of which her family was a long-standing member. Both her mother, Tacie (whose first name was a familiar Quaker one), and her father, William, traced their ancestors to seventeenth-century dissidents, including William Penn. Both were members of prominent Quaker families in a place where Quakers were in the majority and outsiders heard more of their distinctive plain speaking punctuated by the use of "thee" and "thou" than anywhere in the United States. The ideals of Quakerism, with its commitment to following one's conscience, had long inspired nonconformist rebels. And these same ideals saturated the Pauls' white clapboard home located on a knoll where young Alice listened to stories of Mary Dyer, who was burned at the stake in colonial New England for her heretical Quaker views.

The four young Pauls also went to meeting where their mother took the minutes; during collection, a time when members sat quietly until moved to speak, they heard strong female voices. In fact one of Alice's great-aunts had been a Quaker preacher. They learned as well the spiritual equality that was a given within a church that rejected priestly authority and any notion of gendered souls.

William and Tacie Paul also conveyed to their daughter an understanding of her economic and educational advantages. Though they led a quiet frugal life, their economic circumstances set them apart from others. They had a substantial home and a live-in Irish maid. Hardworking William Paul was the president of the Moorestown Bank and the owner of several working farms in New Jersey; his brothers ran a successful shoe factory in Philadelphia. Her parents could afford the education that Alice sought. And so after finishing the local Friends school, Alice went to Swarthmore College, a nearby Quaker institution and an obvious choice since Tacie's family had been among the founders of this coeducational institution. Tacie herself had attended for two years before her marriage.

Alice Paul was a star at Swarthmore during what was certainly the most frivolous time in her life, though she managed to graduate with a Phi Beta Kappa key in 1905. She delighted in the athletics so new to women's lives. She overslept some classes. She went to football games when Swarthmore played Haverford and to dances with boys. In the playful custom of special girlfriends, she took a wife, in that kind of intimate relationship between adolescent girls that had no necessary sexual connotation. She joined clubs and competed for oratory prizes. And because she knew nothing about the subject, she majored in biology, thus displaying the intellectual curiosity that made formal study one of the themes of her life. And after college, she went to graduate school, eventually receiving a master's and a doctoral degree in sociology from the University of Pennsylvania. And in between these two advanced American degrees, she took graduate courses in economics and politics at the University of Birmingham and the London School of Economics. In her thirties she obtained both a law and doctor of jurisprudence degree from American University's Washington College of Law.[14]

In 1902, when Alice was a sophomore at Swarthmore, her father died suddenly of pneumonia, causing an emotional and financial disruption in the family. Tacie Paul inherited both land and stocks. But knowing nothing about managing money, she worried about supporting four children without her husband, who had always run the household finances. Asked later about the loss of her father, Paul replied that she remembered little about it. "I was too young. Life just went on." But in a revealing aside to the interviewer she continued, "I only talk about these things because you ask me." Clearly the personal life of Alice Paul, to Alice Paul at least, was not significant and was never as important as her work.[15]

During her protracted confrontation with Wilson, Paul, then the head of the National Woman's Party (NWP), had neither a private existence nor friends. "I was so absorbed with the suffrage movement I couldn't keep in touch . . ." Comparing her to Lenin, her followers later acknowledged that "she was the party," and in turn she positioned the membership to become the vanguard of the suffrage movement. Her party was not the largest such organization, but it was unquestionably the most effective. Paul and the National Woman's Party became interchangeable as she submerged herself in the struggle for the suffrage amendment. She was one of those human beings in whom the political is the personal, not the reverse.

She has left few clues to her inner emotions, and it is only in the way in which she led her public life that Paul the person becomes visible. She never married, nor did she maintain the Boston marriage of an enduring relationship with any woman. Nor did she have the kind of passionate brief love affairs with other women as Susan B. Anthony and Frances Willard experienced. For years she had no home and lived in the National Woman's Party Headquarters, wherever it happened to be. Years later in her sixties and seventies she lived alone in isolated communities in Vermont and Connecticut when she was not in residence at party headquarters, the Belmont House in Washington. Considered cold and austere by a generation of women accustomed to effusive female sentimentality (one complained she never said thank you to anyone), Alice Paul was admired by some, loved by a few, removed from most, and intimate with none. Instead she gained a sense of comradeship and emotional support from the many organizations she joined and especially from the NWP. Whether an officer of Swarthmore's Somerset Literary Club or the sorority Pi Gamma Mu or, in later life, the Daughters of the American Revolution and Colonial Dames, she was sustained by group affiliations.[16]

After her father's death and between her graduate studies in sociology, Alice Paul decided to become a social worker. The name and training for this new profession, based on formal academic courses and case studies, developed at a time before state resources provided safety nets for the poor and indigent. Alice entered the New York School of Philanthropy to study, practicing what she learned in her work for the Charity Organization Society on the city's Lower East Side. The next year, in 1907, she signaled her independence from her family by moving to England, first accepting a position in a Quaker settlement house near Birmingham and then a position in London where she worked in· that city's east end slums. When her mother urged her to come home and take an academic job at Wellesley rather than waste her time with impoverished women, Alice replied, "Well I am not doing it for their sakes, but in order to learn about conditions myself."[17]

While she was living in Birmingham in 1908, Paul witnessed a suffrage parade and a tumultuous political meeting interrupted by opponents of suffrage. Both outdoor events had been organized by the radical Women's Social and Political Union (WSPU) led by the Pankhursts: the redoubtable Mrs. Emmeline and her daughters Christabel and Sylvia. Frustrated by the endless promises and delays of politicians, the Pankhursts were applying new tactics to their efforts to achieve votes for women. Holding the Liberal Party, then in power, responsible for the lack of action in Parliament, they focused on its anti-suffrage leader Prime Minister Asquith. When Asquith refused to meet with their delegations and when Parliament delayed bringing a suffrage bill to a vote, the Pankhursts became more confrontational. By 1907—the year that Alice Paul arrived in England—they had begun heckling candidates, shouting at political meetings: "What do you say about Suffrage?" "Why talk about free trade and not free women?"

They disrupted elections and campaign speeches, including Winston Churchill's in Manchester. Forced to end a speech after suffragists began ringing bells, Churchill called the suffragists "she-men" and, in a delaying tactic common to lawmakers on both sides of the Atlantic, he changed his mind several times about the enfranchisement of women.[18]

The Pankhursts and their followers hurled stones through windows, hid in buildings so they could emerge to disrupt meetings, cut telegraph wires, and burned golf courses. Once they followed Asquith, after he had refused to meet with them, onto a golf course where they flung their pamphlets and heckled the prime minister before being dragged away. They marched on Parliament with placards reading "Votes for Women, Chastity for Men." And in time they were beaten up, arrested, and jailed.

By 1909 Alice Paul had found in the WSPU not just a sense of purpose but her life's work. For a time she did no more than watch suffrage parades and listen to feminist speeches in Hyde Park. Academic life still attracted her and she contemplated finishing a degree at the London School of Economics, where she was the only woman and American in several classes. Her professors were impressed; one declared that she was born to be a student and another was surprised that she was able to master the difficult principles of political economy. With such glowing recommendations, Paul applied for several fellowships and hoped to complete a doctoral degree in either London or Berlin. When her mother did not send tuition money, a determined Alice Paul worked in a rubber factory where she had to stand all day for piecework wages amounting to five dollars a week. For a pittance, she boarded in a tiny, damp attic room.

But the mesmerizing Pankhursts soon cast their spell. Paul had always been interested in women's causes. Her academic work at the University of Pennsylvania focused on their position in the legal system; her job as a social worker had centered on poor women. But she had tired of the lack of intellectual challenge in the field as well as its ineffectiveness. As she complained to her mother, "You only help one person at a time," and often, when her client was a baby or a widow, she felt she hardly helped at all. "You spend all your life doing something that you know you couldn't change." In the suffrage movement she would help all women. "I have joined the suffragettes, the militant party of the woman's suffrage question," she proudly informed her mother in March 1908. "The difference between the suffragists and the suffragette militants who have excited so much criticism is that they are the ones who have really brought their question to the fore. They chained themselves to a grill in the parliament and went up in a balloon."[19]

Within months Alice emerged as the boldest of these militants, a group she described to her mother as "the cleverest women in England." She graduated from her apprenticeship selling the WSPU newspaper *Votes for Women* on the streets of London, to heckling at the political meetings of Liberal members of Parliament, to giving speeches, and once dressing as a charwoman to get into and then disrupt a meeting in Scotland. She climbed onto roofs to throw stones at Asquith's window at Number 10 Downing Street. "He sees," she explained to her mother, "deputations of male hooligans and the unemployed and even vivisectionists." But he would not see suffragists. Such treatment shamed her notions of equality, and fueled by a sense of exhilaration and autonomy common among militants, she meant to take her place beside these heroic fighters.[20]

By the fall of 1910 Alice Paul, after refusing the money her mother sent to pay the fine and avoid prison, had been in jail three times. Suffragists did not pay fines. By their logic a legal system that excluded them could not subject them to its punishments. Besides in most cases they had been arrested on frivolous charges. When Paul was denied the status of a political prisoner with its privileges of writing materials, prohibitions on work, and individual cells (as were granted to male Irish dissidents) and was instead treated like a common criminal and ordinary lawbreaker in London's grim Holloway Prison, she, like her comrades, hunger-struck and was force-fed. "Don't worry," she wrote her frantic mother who had unsuccessfully attempted to get the American ambassador Whitelaw Reid, no friend of suffrage, to intervene after reports of Alice screaming and fainting during the force-feedings were printed in the American newspapers. "Other women are doing it. Why should not I? Their parents do not make a fuss about it." And with characteristic stoicism: "Force feeding is simply a policy of passive resistance. As a Quaker thee ought to approve of it."[21]

Still, it was a form of torture, and to her sister Helen she inaccurately predicted that she would never "hunger strike again, I think." In order to prevent the embarrassment of any martyrs dying in police custody, the new Home Secretary Winston Churchill initiated a policy of force-feeding women who refused to eat. Only after she had agreed to come home did Paul describe the process with clinical precision:

> One warden sat upon the knees and held that part of my body quiet. One on the other side held my arms and hands. One doctor stood behind and held my head back until it was parallel to the ground [with] a towel around [my] throat and when I tried to move he drew the towel so tight that it compressed the windpipe and made it almost impossible to breathe. With his other hand he held my chin in a rigid position and put the tube down my nostril . . . Putting the tube down is a rather difficult operation. Usually three quarters of the way through the head he would be unable to push it further. They do it as if trying to drive a stake into the ground. Then they try the other nostril and again and again sometimes on the fifth or sixth into the throat where it causes a spasm of the glottis. Then it is impossible to breathe so doctors draw the tube up until the spasm has passed and then they force the tube into the stomach and pour milk and liquid food into the funnel.[22]

By 1910 militant English suffragists incorrectly imagined that the so-called conciliatory bill enfranchising women householders would pass Parliament. The Pankhursts called a truce and Paul returned home, where she gave suffrage speeches in Philadelphia, finished her dissertation at the University of Pennsylvania, and joined NAWSA. With her American friend Lucy Burns, whom she had first met in a London police station, she reorganized the Congressional Committee of NAWSA, the precursor to the National Woman's Party. She already knew what she must do. Women, according to Paul, must no longer be "comforters of men," but rather must become "a new race whose ideal is strength." In a speech on "The English Situation," she gave members of the NAWSA a preview of her intentions: "The essence of

the campaign of the suffragettes is opposition to the Government . . .
It is not a war of women against men, for the men are helping loyally
but a war of men and women together against the politicians."[23]

The Making of an Antisuffragist

During the years in which Alice Paul was learning the tactics of militant suffragism in England, her future antagonist Woodrow Wilson
was also being educated, in his case in practical politics, first through
his battles with trustees and administration officials at Princeton
University, where he was president from 1902 to 1911, and then as
governor of New Jersey. An unlikely politician—for he lacked its practitioners' instinctive, natural camaraderie—Wilson had grown up in
the South, the son of a minister whose mother was also the daughter
of a southern Presbyterian. With such a heritage Wilson might well
have become a minister himself, for he greatly admired his father. And
he had absorbed at home and in church the Calvinist's sense of duty,
hard work in the pursuit of truth, and the responsibility to use one's
talents for the betterment of mankind. But after graduating from
Princeton in 1879, he studied law at the University of Virginia and
practiced briefly and unhappily in Atlanta, once acknowledging that
he chose the law so he could become a politician. In fact, save for his
presidency at Princeton he might have remained in academic life, for
after the law he turned to scholarship and teaching. He chose one of
the first graduate schools in the country, Johns Hopkins University,
where he concentrated on history and the new discipline of political
science.

In 1885, the year Alice Paul was born, twenty-nine-year-old Woodrow Wilson married Ellen Axson, the daughter of a Presbyterian minister. Needing a job, he accepted his first academic post at the new
woman's college, Bryn Mawr. Even before he took the position, his future wife cautioned that "you would find it very unpleasant to serve, as
it were, under a *woman!* . . . it seems so unnatural, so jarring to one's
sense of the fitness of things, so absurd too." Ellen Axson was right.
Woodrow hated it immediately. In his view, the students were flaccid,
uninteresting, and passive. He hungered "for a class of men." His ulti-

mate compliment to Eleanor, the only one of his daughters who did not go to college, was heartfelt: she "had a mind fit to be a companion with any man's." Few women, he believed, did.

Although Wilson soon became famous for his lectures, he complained that he had "to lift up" these female students on his shoulders. "Lecturing to young women of the present generation is about as appropriate and profitable as would be lecturing to stone masons on the evolution of fashion in dress. Passing through a vacuum your speech generates no heat."[24] The few graduate students at Bryn Mawr were not much better and as for the dean, M. Carey Thomas, Wilson found her impossible. For the most part the women at the college, save for some undergraduates, did not like Professor Wilson either. Fellows like Lucy Salmon, who later became a distinguished historian at Vassar College, found the new professor difficult, patronizing, and given to "extended long-winded monologues."[25]

Wilson's appointment to a woman's college was a mismatch. The Virginian came to Bryn Mawr an enlightened Southerner who was glad the Confederacy had lost the Civil War because it meant progress for the region. But his unreconstructed attitudes toward women had been nurtured by a self-sacrificing Southern mother and wife, and a female culture that viewed its best women as submissive helpmates. As a graduate student at Hopkins, Wilson once attended a meeting of the Women's Congress at the Baltimore YWCA and reported to his future wife that he experienced that "chilled, scandalized feeling that always comes over me when I see and hear women speak in public." He bristled at "talk about 'a woman's right to live her own life' . . . if it means the right of women to live apart from men." Women, he thought, "have mental and moral gifts of a sort and of a perfection that men lack, but they have not the same gifts that men have. Their life must supplement man's life." With such prejudices it was impossible for him to work with professional women as equals, to teach them without bias, or to support any public effort that might help women achieve equality.[26]

In all his pursuits Wilson was ambitious, intending as one of his advisors, Colonel House, once said, to do "big things." It took more than a little hubris to wonder, even as a young man, why "the present age may not write through me its political autobiography."[27] In 1883 he published his first book, *Congressional Government*, a critically acclaimed study of the U.S. Congress in which he characterized that legislative body as the most powerful of the three branches of the American government. His central argument maintained that this was a problem that needed redressing. Interested in leadership and power years before he became president of the United States, Wilson offered remedies to make the executive office more powerful and accountable by seating cabinet officers in Congress and using the political party as a means of diluting the stagnant effect of the separation of powers. He insisted that the presidency was "the vital place of action in the system."[28]

Wilson was on his way to stardom as a political scientist and popular lecturer, but in the world of higher education academic men did not get ahead teaching at women's colleges. And so Wilson moved on, breaking his three-year contract with Bryn Mawr to accept an offer from the coeducational Wesleyan College in Connecticut (though he disapproved of mixing females with males in college), and then finally and happily returning to his beloved alma mater, Princeton, where he became a professor of jurisprudence and political economy in 1890.[29]

At home a self-sacrificing wife and three daughters surrounded Wilson with love and affection and a considerable amount of nursing. He was one of those humans who was often sick with minor intestinal ills, dyspepsia, headaches, and colds and who solicited constant sympathy for his chronic invalidism. He expected to be listened to, and consoled by, the women of his family, even for his minor complaints. But Wilson also suffered from the serious illness of hypertension and cerebral artery disease, which manifested itself in 1896 when he temporarily lost the sight of his left eye from a sudden hemorrhage. Despite the couple's financial worries—for they lived on the meager academic salary of less than three thousand dollars a year supplemented by his modest lecture fees and royalties, and were five thousand dollars in debt (though with fifty thousand dollars worth of investments) when he became president—the family budget always supported his expensive recuperative trips alone to England and Bermuda. His wife encouraged such healthful recreation. After Wilson temporarily lost the use of his right hand and, once again, sight in his left eye in 1906 from an embolus in his carotid artery, he traveled to England and Scotland in 1907 and 1908.

These were the years that Alice Paul, also in England, had begun working with the suffrage movement, and militant acts of civil disobedience were almost unavoidable for tourists. By chance in 1908 Wilson encountered a suffrage meeting in Scotland and described in a letter to Ellen a suffrage advocate who "very effectually if without feminine delicacy" put down the interruptions from poorly mannered men. He went on to observe that "she skipped all the difficult parts of the argument [for suffrage] consciously or unconsciously . . . and made very effective use of the parts which do not require proof."[30]

In 1907, during one of his solitary winter trips to Bermuda, fifty-year-old Woodrow Wilson met forty-four-year-old Mary Ann Hulbert Peck. She was then married to Thomas Peck, a wealthy New England woolen manufacturer. Returning home to Princeton, he began an eight-year correspondence with her of over two hundred letters, although most of Hulbert's letters to Wilson, apparently sufficiently damaging to his reputation, have disappeared. Hulbert represented the liberated upper-class twentieth-century American woman. She was sophisticated and provocative in a way that Wilson's faithful Ellen, whom he adored, was not. In 1910 Wilson praised Hulbert's "wit and charm and vivacious sense." By no means was she the kind of unmarried woman whom Wilson despised as a "sullen virago," like M. Carey Thomas who lived in the deanery at Bryn Mawr College with her lovers Maimie Gwinn and later Mary Garrett. Instead, as Mary Hulbert discussed her desire to end her unhappy marriage, she introduced a parochial Wilson to an important means of female emancipation—divorce.

Hulbert also ushered Wilson into the smart female set in Bermuda and Nantucket who smoked, drank, traveled alone, and even turned to male acquaintances for loans, as she did from Wilson. Probably this relationship was no more than what both parties called it—a platonic friendship—but during a second Bermuda vacation this stern Presbyterian moralist with a wife and three children at home began a letter in shorthand to his new friend, confidante, and constant companion in Bermuda "My precious one, my beloved Mary."[31]

In the White House, one lonely hot night in July 1913 when his wife was away, the president described his love for her as "the fountain of my joy and comfort." But that same night in an equally long letter he took the time to write Hulbert, expressing his pleasure in their friendship and Hulbert's "natural spontaneous force." He proclaimed his female friend "the priestess of Democracy meant for gaiety, light intercourse and the circles where interesting talk is the law of life and of pleasure."[32] In the beginning of their relationship Wilson sent his new friend letters and books, choosing two dry political tomes—Walter Bagehot's *The English Constitution* and his own *Congressional Government*. But in time he gave the woman he obscurely called "Democracy personified " a brooch and lent her seventy-five hundred dollars as well.[33]

Later, the correspondence between the two became a political and personal embarrassment as rumors of efforts by Republicans to buy Mary Hulbert's letters to Wilson spread. When Ellen Wilson died of Bright's disease in August 1914, after imploring her doctor, on her deathbed, "to take care of Woodrow," there were rumors that she died of a broken heart because of her husband's dalliance. Wilson acknowledged that his letters were more ardent than discreet, but he insisted there was nothing unseemly in their relationship, although surely this gay, attractive woman served as a social mistress and an anodyne to Wilson's sense of duty. "It was a passage of folly and gross impertinence," the president acknowledged, and proclaimed himself to be "deeply ashamed and repentant. I did not have the moral right to offer her ardent affection."[34] Hulbert deserves a place in the story of Wilson's life because, as he became entangled with the suffragists, she made him more cognizant of the changed lives and expectations of American women.

So too did his daughters, two of whom attended Goucher College, then the Woman's College of Baltimore, where they became supporters of the suffrage movement. Jessie Wilson was probably one of the ushers at Susan B. Anthony's lecture in Baltimore's Lyric Theater in 1906. At this last public meeting, Anthony left the stage with a salute to college women and a final benediction that the struggle for women's rights and especially their right to vote must never cease. Dutifully the Wilson daughters kept silent about suffrage, merely encouraging Wilson's friend, advisor, and suffrage supporter Col. Edward House to persuade their father. But they never embarrassed their doting father with any public statements.[35]

At no time in his life did Wilson more dramatically express his profound dependence on women than in his rapid remarriage. After an intense courtship of only eight months, Wilson married Edith Galt in December 1915, sixteen months after his first wife died. His mawkish letters, full of the romantic sentiments of a schoolboy, expressed his longing for a woman some found coarse. "If you did not love me, the day's anxieties would be intolerable . . . Good Night, Edith, my precious little girl. How sweet it is to dream that you are actually close against my heart, giving me a long true lover's kiss." By marrying such a short time after his wife's death the president shocked many Americans who believed that anything less than a two-year mourning period for a deceased spouse was disrespectful. But Wilson's need for nurturing female consolation for his ill health and admiring attention for his hard work far outweighed, in his mind, any political consequences. In many ways he had simply replicated his first wife with a woman similar to Ellen Wilson in her superficialities and giddy temperament, her fawning adoration of him, along with the traditional values she held about the proper place of women in American society.[36]

To his first wife, Ellen, Wilson had affirmed his distaste for "a woman's right to live her own life. If it means the right of women to live apart from men, it is untrue to the teachings of history . . . The family relation is at the foundation of society, is the life and soul of society and women who think that marriage destroys identity and is not the essential condition of performance of *proper* duties are the only women whom God intended as old maids."[37] A man with such attitudes was poorly equipped to deal with Alice Paul and her militant suffragists. Still, given the influences of Mary Hulbert, his daughters, and even his belief in the American government as a progressive, evolving organism, such a man was not a reactionary on the matter of women's suffrage. But, for a long time, he was certainly obdurate.

Conflict

After Wilson's inauguration, Alice Paul along with a carefully selected group of suffragists was ready to meet the new president, argue the case for a suffrage amendment, and ask his support in his annual message to Congress. But his prejudice against public women predisposed him to find them distasteful. As the journalist David Lawrence observed, Wilson believed that "the only women interested in woman's suffrage were aggressive and masculine with harsh voices"—not at all like his two Southern-born wives. He must have been surprised, then, at the appearance of their leader—the demure, utterly feminine Alice Paul who greeted him with her soft voice and shook his hand with her dainty, childlike hands.[38]

At five feet, six inches and a hundred pounds, the fragile-looking Alice Paul had luxuriant black hair with auburn highlights swept back in a bun in the Quaker fashion, though she never pulled it as tightly and severely to the back of her head as did Susan B. Anthony. Paul was a handsome woman who rarely looked directly into the camera. Posing side-faced and often with her head down, she might have been a delicate, demure, neurasthenic socialite. At a time when the practical short-haired bob was becoming the style favored by out-of-the-house women, she declined to cut her hair and only did so when she was in her fifties. Her traditional high-necked dresses were long and flowing, and she favored the conservative "female" colors of purple, lavender, gray, and white. Only the dark eyes framed by heavy black brows gave any indication of her intensity, seriousness of purpose, and stubborn determination. Her eyes, one suffragist described, were "like moss-agates . . . orbs" that shone into your soul. Nor, as Wilson expected of all women in the organized suffrage movement, was her voice deep and masculine. In fact, ever sensitive to its feminine lightness, she often turned to others when a public speech was necessary.[39]

When Paul and seven other suffragists arrived at the White House that March day in 1913 shortly after the inauguration, they found a set of chairs arranged in the center of the immense East Room. There they were told to sit, while Wilson, ever chivalrous and faintly amused, stood in front of them as a schoolmaster before his students. Paul, in what proved to be one of only two conversations she ever held with Wilson, began by quoting the president's evocations about democracy from *The New Freedom*, a recently published volume of his campaign speeches. She reminded him of his belief in "the presence of a new organization of society . . . The old political formulas do not fit the present problems." When one woman became too intimidated to speak, the president encouraged her, "Don't be nervous." At first condescendingly polite, Wilson's mood rapidly shifted. When the suffragists lost their initial hesitation and began to make too many arguments and stay too long, he cut them off. The president announced that he had never thought about women's suffrage. It had not, he said duplicitously, been brought to his attention. He did not know what his position might be on this new matter, but he hoped for more information. In the meantime the ladies must try "to concert opinion."[40]

Throughout both of Wilson's administrations, groups of suffragists chosen to indicate the diversity and strength of the movement came to the White House—members of the National Council of Women Voters, a delegation from New Jersey, the College Equal Suffrage League, working women, all appeared before the president or his secretary Joseph Tumulty, to whom he increasingly delegated this chore. When the women could no longer be dismissed on the grounds that the president was not informed about the issue, the president found other explanations. He was too busy, in his first term, prodding Congress to pass his reform agenda of installing the Federal Reserve system, reforming tariff legislation, and establishing a shipping board. He urged patience; such matters, counseled the president, a known authority on the American political system, took time. And when the suffragists informed him they had been struggling for over seventy years, he bristled. "I do not care to enter into a discussion of that." "Much obliged, much obliged," he said, backing out of the room.[41]

By 1914, as more delegations sought "conferences" with the president and he could no longer plead too much work or too little information, Wilson produced another excuse. "I want you ladies, if possible, if I can make it clear to you—to realize what my present situation is . . . I am not a free man. I am under arrest . . . I am not at liberty to urge upon Congress in messages policies which have not had the organic consideration of those for whom I am a spokesman . . . I am by my own principles shut out, in the language of the street, from starting anything."[42] He must follow the party platform, he claimed, which did not support a federal suffrage amendment and which in 1912 had said nothing about votes for women. But when suffragists pointed out that he applied that rule selectively, that he was the leader of his party, that he had reversed the Democratic platform in his support for overturning the American exemption to the Panama toll (the platform explicitly favored it), and that few pieces of legislation passed without his approval, the president left the room, jaw clenched, eyes twitching, Southern gentility swept away by anger.

As his views on leadership and the importance of a strong presidency were turned against him, Wilson retreated to his next-to-final hedge: suffrage was a state matter. When the suffragists pointed to the necessity of a national amendment in order to enfranchise black men and when they asked how many states the president believed would have accepted the federal mandate of the antitrust regulations of the 1914 Clayton Act, Wilson refused any discussion. "I can only say I have tried to answer your questions and I do not think it is proper that I submit to a cross-examination." And as a few women hissed and many refused to shake his hand, he declared the confrontation "a pleasant occasion."[43]

It was apparent to Paul that the president, for personal and political reasons, would forever stall without some reason to do otherwise. Wilson did not want political freedom for women. His supposed passion for local and state authority over suffrage was simply a mask. He put it on for his opposition to women's suffrage, but he took it off when he fought for the federal government's intervention in such matters as an eight-hour workday and the regulation of child labor. He would never use his newly installed direct phone line to Congress, so useful on other matters, to solicit legislative support for a suffrage amendment. And so began Alice Paul's twofold campaign "to concert opinion" until suffrage for women was an inescapable public matter that a majority of Americans supported. She also meant to hold Wilson and his Democratic Party responsible for the failure to get a suffrage amendment passed by Congress.

For two years, first as leader of the Congressional Congress, a committee of NAWSA responsible for lobbying Congress, and then as head of the independent Congressional Union, and finally of the National Woman's Party, Paul and her deputy, Lucy Burns, exercised their talent for arranging spectacular events. They organized a cross-country automobile caravan of suffragists that began in San Francisco, got stuck on muddy roads in Colorado, and ended in Washington, where a petition with a million signatures was delivered to Congress. During Wilson's 1916 State of the Union address when he reached the point where he called for democracy in Puerto Rico, suffragists in the balcony unfurled a yellow banner reading "Mr. Wilson what are you doing for woman's suffrage?" Paul also encouraged pageants and plays about suffrage. And, too, she mastered the commercial culture of the early twentieth century and made sure the NWP employed new forms of advertisement—billboards, badges, pins, and artful window displays.[44]

With a sense of political maneuver informed by the British suffrage struggle, Paul moved her organization's headquarters to Lafayette Square right across from the White House. Now when Wilson looked out the second-floor window of his daughters' bedrooms, he saw the purple, yellow, and white suffrage flag. Adept at raising money, Paul used some of the twenty-eight thousand dollars she raised to start the newspaper *The Suffragist*. She wrote most of the early editorials, sending initially timid women out on the Washington streets to peddle it in the same manner as newsboys. She orchestrated a biographical file on congressmen and senators and brought suffrage lobbying to new levels of sophistication. In 1916 she hired Nina Allender to draw anti-Wilson cartoons ridiculing the president as Hamlet, as a befuddled captain of the ship of state, and once as a drowning man rescued by suffragists.

Members of NWP experienced Paul's implacable forcefulness if they bridled at some request or even if they complained about her rigidly enforced no-smoking policy. But she never raised her voice, pouted, or insulted. She simply listened with her oft-remarked-on stillness until all the objections had been raised and then, with an intensity that few forgot, she "moved them not through affection, but through a naked force, a vital force which is indefinable but of which one simply cannot be unaware." As her awed disciple Doris Stevens noted, ". . . how little we know about this person, and yet how abundantly we feel her power, her will and her compelling leadership."[45]

National Woman's Party

Intent on recruiting foot soldiers and not weak sisters who merely talked suffrage, Paul interviewed all new volunteers, probing their commitment to the cause in her dark office, the single light shining in their eyes. She paid special attention to those who had money, women like Alva Vanderbilt Belmont, and those like Abby Scott Baker with Washington contacts. To Sarah Field, who hesitated to undertake the famous cross-country suffrage auto trip in 1915 because she wanted to write a book, Paul responded, "Well, now you are doing suffrage work. You can get back to the book later." To her friend Mabel Vernon, a fellow Swarthmore graduate who had bested Alice in a college oratory contest years before, she appealed on the basis of their college ties. To Elsie Hill she wrote: "I feel if we put everything aside and work with all our power for a year or two we could end this struggle for good . . . Could you not come be a suffrage organizer? You can teach and make money all your life . . . but there will never come again this great need of helping our movement." Hill came to Washington.[46]

Paul also formed a distinguished all-female national advisory committee that was much too large to interfere with her management. They had been assembled "for ornament rather than use," complained one member. The National Woman's Party, though it had a local executive committee, never operated on democratic principles; it was a dictatorship run by Alice Paul and Lucy Burns. And though its members might shudder at some of Paul's tactics, there was little dissent over Paul's strategy of targeting the president. "We want to convict Wilson of evading us," wrote Paul to Burns. And all the while, the ever calm, serene Paul was challenged by Carrie Catt, the president of NAWSA from 1900 to 1904 and 1916 to 1921.[47]

Catt, newly reinstalled as the president of NAWSA, immediately announced her "Winning Plan," which recognized, as Paul had three years before, the necessity of a national amendment. Yet the lone tactical idea Catt advanced was to insist that NAWSA be nonpartisan. Consequently Paul, with her radical strategy of holding the party in power responsible, was a threat, just as Stanton and Anthony had been to Lucy Stone. "At this time you may connect with a few disgruntled suffragists here and there but you are not likely to command the adherence of the really efficient ones," warned Catt in a letter to Paul in 1915. "For the time and money expended you will garner small results but you may irritate and antagonize to the permanent detriment of your work." To a former member of NAWSA who had joined Paul, Catt angrily exploded, "Has your board lost its senses? Strength lies in unity." And to the Chicago settlement house worker Jane Addams, who thought well enough of Paul to recommend her for the chairmanship of NAWSA's Congressional Committee in 1913, Catt denounced Paul and her organization as "a stupendous stupidity." Within a year NAWSA had expelled Paul and the Congressional Committee on the grounds that their members had heckled President Wilson and had refused to turn money they had raised over to NAWSA's central committee.[48]

Surely Catt had a point. This division in the organized suffrage movement, reflecting a similar one in 1869 between Lucy Stone and the more progressive Susan B. Anthony and Elizabeth Cady Stanton, sustained convenient stereotypes that women could not work with other women. It fostered the perception that in public matters women were unbalanced and lacked the innate reason of men, a view that conveniently overlooked similar male behavior. Nor did it, as schisms sometimes do, clarify differences in purpose and belief, although the argument between the NWP and NAWSA surely highlighted a persistent disagreement over tactics. To be sure, the controversy prevented the possible benefits of harmonious unanimity—the single voice of one suffrage association, which in Catt's view would naturally be NAWSA, with ten times the number of members as the NWP. But it is a certainty that without Paul's constant pressure on Wilson and his eventual support, the passage of the amendment would have been delayed for decades.

The split in the suffrage movement offered immediate short-term advantages for Wilson. Now the president could deal with respectful ladies like Catt and Shaw and thereby position himself as tolerant on an issue to which he was beginning to give lip service. Several times the president asked his secretary, Joseph Tumulty, which group of suffragists wanted to meet with him. Were they the militant "heckling belligerents," whom he would not see, or the pleasant acquiescent ladies of NAWSA, whom he twice asked to lunch? Understanding the difference, Tumulty made Paul a pariah, and left Wilson to deal only with women who even as late as 1916 were willing to accept a minimal Democratic pledge calling for enfranchisement, with the how, when, and where left as vague as it had been in the days of Stanton and Anthony. As early as 1915 the president publicized his conversion, announcing that he would go to New Jersey to vote in favor of a state-sponsored suffrage referendum that, as predicted, failed miserably. His vote earned him the appreciative accolades of Catt and Shaw.[49]

After her expulsion from NAWSA Paul called her tiny band of rebels the Congressional Union, renaming it again in 1916 the National Woman's Party. As her followers—no more than ten thousand in 1918, when there were over a million members of NAWSA—recognized, the fearless, self-confident Paul was "a leader of action, not of thought. She is a general, a supreme tactician not an abstract thinker. Her joy is in the fight itself. " Rarely did Paul indulge in what she considered time-wasting explanations of why women deserved the vote. She believed that earlier founding sisters, especially Anthony, had completed the philosophical stage of the struggle; what she called "suffrage propaganda" wasn't even printed in *The Suffragist*.[50]

On the rare occasions when Paul gave the reasons for her advocacy of women's suffrage, she based her position on the principles of justice and equality. She believed in androgyny: for her the characteristics of men and women were not rigidly assigned. The similarity of the sexes as human beings outweighed their differences and required equal treatment in public policy. She paid little attention to NAWSA's or Frances Willard's claims that women should be given the vote because as mothers they would bring nurturing social agendas to politics. Instead her philosophy was imbedded in her instructive organizational change of surname from an association for women's suffrage to a woman's party.

Paul insisted that her organization welcomed black women. Yet from the time of her refusal to permit an all-black division in her 1913 suffrage parade, she did little to encourage African American participation. She denied any personal prejudice and noted that she was a Northern woman who had never lived in the South: "I belong to a Quaker family which has always taken a stand for the rights of the Negro. The tradition of my family and my home are such as to make me predisposed to side with and not against the Negro in any question of racial difference." This may have been true, but at a time when the Wilson administration was aggressively pursuing its popular policy of segregating black federal employees, the single-minded Paul discouraged any significant black connection to her movement.[51]

The racial issue was a spoiler, and Paul never impaled suffrage on what she considered the extraneous categories of race or class. Her justification was fully stated in 1913 when she was organizing her preinaugural parade: "If we have a large number of Negroes in our suffrage procession the prejudice against them is so strong [that] I believe a large part, if not a majority of our white marchers will refuse to participate if Negroes in any number participate." She later refused to accommodate black women's requests for prime speaking time at a postsuffrage convention in 1921 and would not meet with a group of sixty black women who requested an interview.[52]

Throughout her career Paul consistently dampened the enthusiasm of black women for the NWP, which remained the special preserve of elite, well-educated, mostly wealthy white women. The NWP's national chairman was able to serve as a volunteer because of the check her mother sent every month and when her mother died, her inheritance. Paul saved the party budget a salary such as those it paid less affluent women, and she also donated thousands of dollars to the party. Only later and with embarrassment because she was suspicious of female volunteerism did Paul acknowledge the inherited privilege of being able to work without pay: "it is a great asset to have a little money of your own you can fall back on."[53]

By naming her organization a party (not an association or a society), and a woman's party at that, Paul intended to use electoral politics for the benefit of women. Resolved, she wrote at her party's first convention "that the National Woman's Party, so long as the opposition of the Democratic party continues, pledges itself to use its best efforts in the twelve states where women vote for President to defeat the Democratic candidates for president and Congress." When some women resigned at the audacity of mobilizing four million voting women in Western states into partisans attacking the president on a single issue, Paul was unmoved. "We are right . . . It is better to have a united body of workers than an immense debating society," the latter her description of NAWSA. Parades, as Paul knew, did not change the minds of politicians, nor did the "silent influence" of decorous women.[54]

Off to the cities of California, the wilds of Wyoming, the mountains of Utah, and the granges of Colorado—everywhere where women could vote in the presidential election—went speakers and banners in the summer and fall of 1916. When the Democrats adopted the slogan "He Kept Us Out of War," the women's version became "He Kept Us Out of Suffrage." When the president came to Chicago on a campaign tour in the summer of 1916, members of the Woman's Party were ready with banners reading "Vote Against Wilson and the Democratic Party."

The president was furious, and especially so after Alice Paul and leaders of her party pressured his Republican opponent, Charles Evans Hughes, to go beyond the tepid Republican platform supporting state-by-state adoption of women's suffrage. In early August, after lobbying by Paul and other members of NWP as well as pressure from Republican suffragists, Hughes came out in favor of a national amendment, making the Republican the first presidential candidate of a major party to do so. In response, Wilson announced that he would not "angle for votes." With that condescension he affected in his dealings with political women, the president stated his preference for female respect over female ballots. And besides, as he informed Harriot Stanton Blatch, "a leader must always be abreast of his party and not ahead of it," though everyone knew that he dictated the platform and led the Democratic Party.[55]

Again using NAWSA to diffuse the suffrage issue, Wilson spoke at that organization's convention in September 1916. Playing the professor, he reviewed the history of "this cause . . . for which you can afford a little while to wait. " He noted how *quickly* the movement had grown and concluded that like the tides of the moon "you need not be afraid that it will not come to its flood . . ." Preaching patience, he acknowledged the lack of his own. "I get a little impatient sometimes about the discussion and methods by which it is to prevail," Wilson said in his hour-long speech in which he used the word *women* only five times, never referred to suffrage by name, and never endorsed the federal amendment. But Shaw and Catt were grateful for any attention. Sounding like Wilson, Shaw responded that "democracy is not just a system and form of government. It is a great spiritual force."[56]

As World War I raged in Europe, Wilson was reelected in 1916, with some Western women voting for him because of his neutrality stance and his antiwar pledge; they refused to accept Paul's single-issue approach in a presidential election when so many other matters were contested. Others admired Wilson for the domestic reforms of his "New Freedom," such as the Federal Reserve system and his efforts to break up monopolies, even if they had nothing to do with political freedom for women. Still, some women did vote against him because of his waffling on suffrage. Thus the effectiveness of Paul's strategy of holding the party in power responsible was mixed, although it had established a precedent. The president carried seven of the twelve states in which women voted, compared to nine in 1912. Granted the comparison is inexact: in 1912 there had been four candidates, whereas in 1916 there were only two competitive ones. But in Illinois, where data on the sex of voters was kept, the National Woman's Party celebrated the disproportionate female support for Hughes. Overall the election was close, and Wilson's advisors stayed up all night before it was clear that Wilson had won 277 electoral votes to Hughes's 254. But the presidential coattails were threadbare. The Democrats lost fourteen seats in the House and twelve in the Senate.[57]

Paul spent most of Christmas day 1916 in bed. She had decided not to go home to Paulsdale for the holidays. Instead she chose to rest and contemplate what now must be done, with Wilson in the White House for four more years. Even on a rare day of rest from the incessant daily business of running the NWP, she did not indulge herself in reading a novel. (Paul once acknowledged that she disciplined herself to stay out of bookstores so that she would not waste time on one of her only recreations—reading fiction.) Because the president had overlooked suffrage in his annual message to Congress and had refused to meet with members of her party, she now decided on more radical tactics.

The Struggle Joined

Three weeks later on January 11, 1917, members of the NWP carrying placards—"silent sentinels" as Harriot Stanton Blatch called them; "a perpetual delegation" in Paul's phrase—marched from headquarters and took their stations at the north gates of the White House. "Mr. Wilson, what are you doing for women's suffrage?" read one. "We demand the passage of the Susan B. Anthony amendment." A routine activity today, before 1917 no group of protesters had so defiantly confronted an American president. The ground rules for petitioning were long established, but judicial decisions about picketing as a form of protected symbolic expression lay years in the future. So too did considerations of free speech action and the right to assemble, the latter essential to any group without power. In local communities reactions to political marches were mixed, and some local judges had ruled that even peaceful picketing was by definition illegal. But Paul believed the Clayton Act's provision specifically exempting trade union members from prosecution as "illegal and in restraint of trade" protected members of the NWP from interference.[58]

For over a year, in fact until Wilson finally advised Congress to support the Susan B. Anthony amendment in 1918, members of NWP stood at their stations from ten to five in rain and shine, snow and sleet, every day except Sunday. Immediately they became tourist attractions, inspiring some spectators with their dedication and infuriating others with their challenge to the president. Meanwhile Wilson, as he was driven through the north gates in the presidential Pierce-Arrow for his afternoon outings on the golf course, graciously nodded, tipped his hat, smiled, and waved with ever more strained grace.

Convinced that this was a publicity stunt that would soon end, he encouraged the press to stop their coverage of the pickets. Once on a grim snowy day the president told the head White House steward, Isaac Hoover, to invite the ladies in, an offer that was refused. On Wilson's second inauguration day on March 1917, there was no suffrage parade. Instead on that rainy day, one thousand suffragists ringed the White House. Perched on a stand with his back to the suffrage women, Wilson watched a five-hour parade featuring many more military units than had been the case in 1913.

After the European war began in the summer of 1914, Wilson's attention shifted from domestic matters to the international affairs that he had earlier predicted would be, for him, no more than an ironic diversion. The president's initial response to the war of the Allies —France, Great Britain, and Russia—against the Central Powers— Germany and Austria-Hungary—had been to proclaim neutrality. During the 1916 presidential campaign he stamped American foreign policy with his idealism. The United States, "a special example" for the world, was "too proud to fight," and he appealed to Americans to be what he eventually failed to be, "impartial in thought as well as action" in their attitudes toward the belligerents. But with Great Britain enforcing a blockade, the Germans were employing submarines to destroy merchant shipping supplying England. And submarine commanders did not, as international law required, warn ships before launching torpedoes.

By traveling on English ships, Americans continued to be killed by German submarines; 128 lost their lives on the *Lusitania* in May 1915. Ignoring the advice of his secretary of state, William Jennings Bryan, who argued for strict neutrality and prohibitions on Americans traveling in the war zone, Wilson refused to warn American citizens to avoid travel on belligerent ships. Instead, after Bryan's resignation, the president began to frame the American right to travel as one of the "sacred rights of humanity." By 1917, when the Germans announced a policy of unrestricted submarine warfare, the president was ready to go to war. His message to Congress in April 1917 proclaimed the moral imperative of a war the nation fought to end all wars and to extend American democracy overseas. "We shall fight for the things which we have always carried nearest our hearts—for democracy, for the right of those who submit to authority to have a voice in their own government."[59]

Meanwhile, the women of the NWP refused to suspend their picketing because of the war. As a more compliant NAWSA immediately ended its suffrage efforts and encouraged its members to replace their suffrage activism with war work, the NWP continued to march in front of the White House. Paul had always used Wilson's extravagantly idealistic statements to make the case for women's right to vote, but now the president proved particularly vulnerable. "Mr. Wilson, you say you will make the world safe for democracy. What are you doing for the women in America?" "Mr. Wilson, you say that every people have a right to choose the sovereignty under which they shall live. What about 20 million American women?" In August the NWP banners labeled the president "Kaiser Wilson."

Paul grew ever more audacious. On June 20, when the Russian mission, representing the new provisional government of Kerensky and Lvov that had just enfranchised women, arrived at the White House, the pickets were prepared. As Bakmetief and his delegation drove through the gates of the White House, they were confronted with a large banner reading: "President Wilson and Envoy Root are deceiving Russia. We women of America tell you that America is not a democracy. Twenty million American women are denied the right to vote. President Wilson is the chief opponent of their national enfranchisement. Help us make our government really free. Tell our government that it must liberate its people before it can claim free Russia as an ally." In response, with Wilson proclaiming his innocence, a new presidentially approved White House policy was enforced.[60]

As uniformed police watched and before the mission left the White House grounds, plainclothesmen, most likely from the Secret Service, tore the banner from its supports and destroyed it. They had received, *The New York Times* charged, their orders directly from the president. The women returned with more banners targeting the president, only to be attacked by the crowd. The police merely observed the confrontation. Within hours the District's chief of police appeared at NWP Headquarters to threaten Paul that if the pickets demonstrated again, they would be arrested. "Why?" asked Paul. "Has picketing suddenly become illegal? Our lawyers have assured us all along that picketing was legal. Certainly it is as legal in June as in January." But neither rationality nor legality played any part in the capricious, inhumane treatment of the suffragists that followed.[61]

Paul had declined to use the more aggressive tactics of British militants, though the response of both governments to suffrage protests was the same. Her followers had not hurled stones through the White House windows, or hidden on the grounds. Nor had they followed Wilson on his golf outings or burned trees in Lafayette Park. But for the first time in American history, an organized group of dissidents, not just a single individual like Thoreau, had employed passive resistance and civil disobedience in a direct confrontation with presidential authority.

On June 22 arrests for obstructing traffic began in front of the White House, though these first cases never came to trial. By midsummer suffragists were appearing regularly before a police magistrate who fined them twenty-five dollars or sentenced them to three days of imprisonment. The suffragists chose jail and there confronted abysmal prison conditions. They ate wormy food, slept on blankets on cement floors in unheated cells, wore scratchy prison clothes, and used the same open toilets and water buckets as syphilitic prostitutes. Among the complaints of these middle-class white suffragists who were accustomed to blacks only as servants was the humiliation of having to share their quarters with black women in jails that were racially segregated for common criminals. By the fall their sentences for obstructing traffic had escalated to sixty days in the Occaquan workhouse in Virginia. Several correspondents and political advisors warned the president of the bad publicity of sending the daughters and wives of prominent public officials to the workhouse. When two prominent Democrats whose relatives were in prison asked Wilson how he would like to see his wife sweeping floors in a dirty workhouse next to black prostitutes, the president was shocked and professed his ignorance. But now, said his friend Dudley Field Malone, who resigned his patronage position over Wilson's treatment of the suffragists, "you do know."[62]

In October Alice Paul was arrested for the third time, denied a jury trial, and sentenced to seven months in jail for obstructing traffic. On her way to prison, she explained to a reporter that she and other women of the National Woman's Party were being imprisoned not "because we obstruct traffic, but because we pointed out to the president the fact that he was obstructing the cause of democracy at home, while we are fighting for it abroad." Well known to the authorities, Paul was often targeted by police and by the young servicemen who roamed Pennsylvania Avenue, once fired a gun into headquarters, and frequently harassed the pickets. Like all the suffragists, Paul was denied legal counsel. Demanding political prisoner status, she was treated more harshly than common criminals: Paul was placed in a "punishment" cell, subjected to constant scrutiny by a prison matron who shined a flashlight on her face every three hours, and, most dangerously, taken off to a psychiatric ward.[63]

Such treatment was a common enough method of dealing with unruly women, whose misbehavior was by definition evidence of madness. The intention of the District commissioners and the prison authorities was to remove Paul to nearby St. Elizabeths Hospital where she could be detained indefinitely. At some point Wilson sent a secret emissary, the journalist David Lawrence, to investigate. Paul remembered several strange men entering her cell late at night—for what she did not know, until one began asking questions about her mental state. If an alienist (the contemporary word for psychiatrist) could be persuaded that she displayed the symptoms of paranoia, perhaps taking the form of an obsessive hatred of Wilson, a permanent incarceration would be justified. But Paul was lucky. She was later examined by the enlightened superintendent of St. Elizabeths, Dr. William White, who pronounced her sane, and in fact remarkably well balanced considering her circumstances.[64]

Paul was in the second month of her sentence when on November 17 another group of women was arrested and taken off to the Occaquan workhouse in Virginia. So began what suffragists called the Night of Terror. When these women claimed political prisoner status, refused to give their names, and asked to see their lawyers, guards led by the brutish superintendent Alexander Whitaker, who had previously threatened his prisoners with his walking stick, threw them down stairs, dragged them off to isolation cells by their hair, and threatened sexual assaults and straitjackets. Lucy Burns spent part of the night with her hands handcuffed to the bars above her head. Dorothy Day was pummeled in what she likened to a football scrimmage. Seventy-year-old Mary Nolan was dragged along a damp floor and hurled into a cell. Alice Cosu vomited all night from a concussion. And like Paul, all of them began hunger strikes when they were denied political prisoner status. After three days they joined the growing numbers of women who were being force-fed in what Paul labeled "administration terrorism."[65]

Soon word of the brutality leaked to the press. The fact that long tubes were being forcibly pushed up women's nostrils, down their throats, and into their stomachs not only suggested the vulnerability of women, but also seemed a disgusting sexual invasion of their bodies. Delegations protested to congressmen about such unconstitutional "cruel and unusual treatment." Telegrams and letters poured into the White House, including a form letter that asked Wilson's intervention "in the name of humanity to abolish the terrible treatment by men appointed by you [of those] asking for liberty and democracy for 20 million women." When they could not see the president, mothers converged on Tumulty with their complaints about "the unspeakable brutality." Letters from soldiers overseas worried about their imprisoned sisters and mothers appeared in newspapers. Alice's quiet sister Helen came to Washington and, interviewed by the press, criticized Wilson for risking her sister's life.[66] And among those who were imprisoned, jail proved, as it would for future dissidents, a good training ground for sacrificial service to the cause. For years afterward the imprisoned women referred to each other as "dear cellmate."[67]

Publicly sidestepping the matter of the arrests on the grounds that authority rested with the District commissioners, the president at first announced that he was satisfied with the way things were being handled. When suffragists pointed out that the president appointed the officials who arrested and harassed them, Wilson responded that the authority to issue permits for gatherings and meetings on public streets was not under his jurisdiction. Nor did he have control over the municipal statutes defining obstruction of traffic. Yet privately the president was furious that officers of the government "have indulged these women in their desire for arrest and martyrdom." Press coverage must stop, and there must be no more arrests until he approved them, a condition that made him complicit with the future mistreatment of members of NWP. The fact of the matter was that Wilson had signaled the necessity of stopping the pickets, but had initially delegated the specific means to others.[68]

Certainly, Wilson insisted when asked, there were no political prisoners in the United States. Nor were these women arrested under the new Sedition Act, in part because they quoted Wilson and thereby protected themselves from indictments under the newly passed legislation that made it illegal to criticize U.S. participation in World War I. As Wilson understood, his own words could hardly be deemed treasonous.

Called almost daily to the White House during this period, the District commissioners reported to the president on the status of the jailed suffrage women. Commissioner Louis Brownlow agreed that his frivolous tactic of tempting fasting women with the allure of ham frying in a nearby kitchen had not been successful. William Gardiner, the most mendacious of the commissioners, provided a written report stating that Paul found her cell clean and well ventilated, approved of the food, and did not mind the force-feedings which, in the commissioner's view, were innocuous, though he had previously been informed by the head of the district jail that they could be dangerous. Paul only sought publicity, Gardiner assured the president, and was using the episode as a fund-raising tactic. Intent on trivializing the episode, Wilson was pleased with any information that corroborated his position. And the commissioners encouraged his conviction that these women were unpatriotic lunatics simply making nuisances of themselves. According to the president, their treatment "has been grossly exaggerated and misrepresented."[69]

Then suddenly on November 27—in an action dictated by the uproar over the force-feedings as well as the convening of a Republican Congress a week later—Wilson pardoned the jailed suffragists. Paul was outraged. "We are put out of jail as we were put in it—at the whim of the government. The attempt by the government to terrorize and suppress us has failed." The next day amid her exuberant followers Paul was back at work in her office, making certain that all those who had been arrested provided formal affidavits of their treatment because she intended to ask for a congressional investigation. She also planned a celebration at the Belasco Theater where the freed prisoners received their "jail pins." Within weeks the Suffrage Prison Special left Washington's Union Station on a national tour with suffragists dressed in prison attire the prime exhibits of Wilson's tyranny.[70]

Not every American applauded their release. Some were outraged at women who instead of helping the Red Cross and serving in the Women's National Defense League mocked the president. A few canceled their subscriptions to The Suffragist and resigned from the party.

Others refused to believe the stories of force-feeding. "They must be," wrote Henry Hall to the president, "either traitors or degenerates." In Memphis, Nashville, and Los Angeles, members of the NWP were denied the use of public meeting halls as rumors circulated that they would be prosecuted under the Sedition Act.[71]

Catt and the leaders of NAWSA complimented the president on his "serene and touching" handling of the "so-called" pickets. In turn Wilson insisted that he had not been influenced "by the actions of so small a fraction of the suffrage movement." Yet when Catt pressed for presidential support for an amendment, Wilson noted how busy he and the special session of Congress were with matters of war. An obliging Catt understood. At its annual convention NAWSA agreed to give up its lobbying for the duration.[72]

Other American women, however, found the NWP activism inspiring and volunteered to become pickets. Among them was Katherine Houghton Hepburn. Once a staunch member of the Connecticut branch of NAWSA, Hepburn now found that organization "futile, academic and out of date." She was angry that Shaw, Catt, and other leaders of NAWSA, like the antisuffragists, disparaged the National Woman's Party at a time when unity was required. In her resignation letter to NAWSA Hepburn expressed her admiration for the [NWP's] "honesty, self-forgetfulness and their practical wisdom." Soon she was carrying their banners.[73]

The president again omitted suffrage from his recommendations to Congress in December 1917. It was not a war measure, he said. Nor could he "volunteer" his advice about the matter to Congress. But what the president said at home was diverging from what he claimed abroad. In January 1918 he had laid out his international goals for the self-determination of all nations in his Fourteen Points Address. Here the president included a proposal for what became the League of Nations, and he made clear that all nations had the right to expect "justice and fair dealing as against force and selfish aggression . . . unless justice be done to others it will not be done to us."[74]

But for all his high-minded concern for a new international order, Wilson was also cognizant of the growing popularity of women's suffrage at home. In November 1917 a suffrage referendum passed in New York, after Tammany Hall decided that it was impolitic to alienate women by opposing the amendment. Shortly after Wilson's Fourteen Points Address, the House of Representatives, for only the second time in forty years, was preparing to vote on the suffrage amendment. The afternoon before that vote, a delegation of Democrats arrived at the White House to ascertain the president's position.

A president who had never wanted to be too far ahead of his party was now falling behind. After the meeting Congressman Edward Taylor reported, "the president said that he had always stood on the Democratic platform . . . he still believed the orderly and systematic way of adopting equal suffrage was by state action, but while he had not changed, all the conditions under which we are living have changed and the world is a different place from the world of a few years ago." With such obfuscation and on the basis of women's patriotic service during the war, Wilson encouraged congressmen to vote affirmatively. His influence proved critical. The amendment passed the House 274 to 136, exactly the necessary two-thirds constitutionally required. "We knew all along that Wilson's support and it alone would ensure our success," Paul told a reporter.[75]

Still, the president had no intention of publicizing his support. Displaying the stubborn self-righteousness that would soon wreck his plans for the Senate's approval of the League of Nations, Wilson kept his views secret. Thereby the president limited his influence on a matter he still hoped might disappear—or at least be stalled in the Senate. His position was so confusing that even the complacent Catt complained that "the general opinion prevails that . . . he is not sincere in his advocacy of the federal amendment."[76]

It was a year and a half before the Susan B. Anthony amendment passed both houses of Congress, the Senate finally giving the requisite two-thirds majority on June 4, 1919. In the interim, Paul again pressured the ever-reluctant president. In the summer of 1918 members of NWP returned to their picketing stations outside the White House gates, now burning in a permanent suffrage "watch fire" the president's "beautiful but empty words" and once even a cardboard effigy of Wilson. Alice Paul was imprisoned twice more, but following the British government's famous Cat and Mouse strategy, officials now temporarily released women before force-feeding was necessary, holding them, after they returned to their homes, available for rearrest without any further legal proceedings.[77]

In September 1918 Wilson capitulated. In an address to the Senate, on the eve of the vote in a body that included many Southern senators still opposed to women's suffrage, the president uttered the words Paul had been fighting for five years to hear: neither party, though it was mostly his Democrats, could justify not substituting "the Federal initiative for State initiative." Women's suffrage had become a necessary war measure to show a world looking to "the great, powerful, famous Democracy of the West to lead them to the new day for which they have so long waited," the president proclaimed. "If we reject measures like this, in ignorance or defiance of what a new age has brought forth . . . they will cease to believe in us." And in a utilitarian argument that irritated suffragists who believed that voting was their natural right, Wilson asked, "we have made partners of the women in this war; shall we admit them only to a partnership of suffering and sacrifice and toil and not to a partnership of privilege and right? " Suffrage, he argued, was less a right than a reward.

Having surrendered to a national amendment, the president dismissed Paul and her NWP. "The voices of the foolish and intemperate agitators" had not influenced him at all. Perhaps, but many Republicans insisted that "the pickets got the president" through their politicization of the issue and through their public efforts to display the president's hypocrisy of attachment to democracy overseas, but not at home. The advance had not been obtained through women's service in war organizations, but through their successful public efforts to display the duplicity of the president's democratic vision. So ended the confrontation between Woodrow Wilson and Alice Paul.[78]

Resolution

Three days before the Senate passed the amendment, Alice Paul left Washington to complete her mission of pressuring states with legislatures in session to ratify the amendment. In states where Republican governors hesitated to call special sessions, Paul echoed Susan B. Anthony's threat that no self-respecting woman should work for the success of a party that ignores her sex. Fifteen months later, in June 1920, the Nineteenth Amendment passed the final thirty-sixth state, Tennessee, but only after Wilson, no longer an opponent, urged Gov. Albert Roberts in a telegraph to convene a special session of the legislature. Nina Allender's cartoon for the occasion featured an exhausted suffragist taking a long night's sleep above the caption "Every Good Suffragist the Morning after Ratification."

As Paul's agenda for equal voting moved to completion, Wilson's programs for "peace without victory" stalled in Europe where ancient rivalries made self-determination impossible to achieve. At home Republican senators challenged Wilson's plan to surrender American sovereignty and independence of action to an international body that could make decisions about war and interfere with national designs on Central and South America. In another violation of his oft-stated position to the suffragists that he must never march ahead of the people or his party and that he could express no individual opinion beyond what his party dictated, Wilson began an exhausting national tour in the fall of 1919. He appealed to his "fellow Americans" to support the most controversial part of the treaty he had worked so hard in Paris to obtain—a League of Nations.[79]

With a near-messianic fervor similar to Paul's, the president considered those who opposed him philistines, especially Massachusetts senator Henry Cabot Lodge, who labeled the treaty "an evil thing with a holy name." Wilson responded that he was fighting for a cause greater than the U.S. Senate. But the president did not have Paul's stamina. He was in Denver in September 1919 (three months after the suffrage amendment had passed both houses of Congress) when he suffered a crippling stroke that permanently paralyzed his left side. For the eighteen months that remained in his administration the cabinet that Wilson previously had dominated and the wife whom he had never anticipated would become one of those dreaded "political women," along with his doctor and secretary, ran the U.S. government.

Wilson lost the treaty vote in the Senate in March 1920. Even as an invalid, he had defiantly refused to accept modifications to the treaty suggested by Republicans and even some Democrats. Thereby he squandered his idealistic vision that the United States (and other governments) should no longer act unilaterally in world affairs. Like his struggle with Alice Paul, he had lost another historic opportunity. As president he had also refused to bring political freedom to half the American people by leading the struggle for a national women's suffrage amendment. By his early opposition, later avoidance, and tepid final support on the grounds of expediency, Wilson destroyed any claim on posterity that he had expanded democracy at home or abroad.

Aftermath

Wilson died in 1924, but Alice Paul was only thirty-five years old in 1920 when this long chapter in the struggle for women's rights was completed. For her the end of the suffrage battle proved only the beginning of another campaign—the passage of an equal rights amendment. She never believed that women could achieve equality through the vote. It was at best the beginning of a long journey toward obtaining full citizenship for women. Paul spent a year raising money to pay off the NWP's debt, informing her followers that she would leave to "the women who will have to go on with the work if the organization continues, to decide what they would like to do." But she worked hard to make certain the party continued the struggle for her priority—the battle for equal rights. Exhausted from a campaign that had lasted for over seven years—twice she had been hospitalized for kidney disease and a throat infection—she took a brief sabbatical and stepped down as party chairman. Yet she remained, even as her handpicked choices led the party, an authoritarian vice chairman in an organization whose membership declined precipitously in the 1920s and 1930s until by 1940 there were only four thousand members of the NWP.[80]

Paul had always considered the vote only a stepping stone to the ultimate goal of legal equality for women in everything "the government could touch," and this larger struggle remained the focus of her efforts. Most of her followers had accepted her single-issue approach during the suffrage campaign. But once votes for women had been accomplished, they lacked the energetic commitment and broader feminist vision of their leader. Many felt there was nothing left to do. As Paul said in 1972, "everybody just went back to their respective homes." Lucy Burns, tired of the incessant work of running a national organization, entered graduate school; Sarah Field returned to her suffrage-interrupted poetry and fiction; Dorothy Day traveled, wrote for the *Liberator*, and converted to Catholicism. Others drifted into club work and less demanding, more socially acceptable organizations like the League of Women Voters or the YWCA. A few worked for peace groups such as the Women's International League for Peace and Freedom. And some women retired from public activities forever.[81]

In 1921 the indefatigable Paul began again. This time there was no parade the day before Warren Harding's inauguration. Instead Paul presided over the kind of public ceremony that all the founding sisters had employed to bring attention to their cause and to instill enthusiastic dedication among their followers. On Susan B. Anthony's birthday in February 1921, the NWP presented as a permanent memorial to Congress a seven-ton marble statue of the founders—Lucretia Mott, Elizabeth Cady Stanton, and Susan B. Anthony. Inviting representatives from other women's groups—NAWSA declined, but fifty other groups sent representatives—Paul stayed in the background as speakers celebrated the suffrage victory in the rotunda of Congress. Unimpressed, legislators promptly dubbed the statue "three women in a tub" and buried it in a crypt on the ground level of the Capitol.[82]

During the NWP convention that followed this ceremony, party members debated their future. For an organization previously focused entirely on suffrage, the question was what now to do. In an editorial in *The Suffragist* Paul noted the importance of the vote, but also its insufficiency: "Women still have far to go."[83] For three days members argued about their next steps toward "removing the many remaining forms of woman's subordination." Crystal Eastman argued for a comprehensive public policy agenda involving access to birth control, education, and jobs. Florence Kelley, head of the National Consumer's League since its founding in 1899, spoke for the special protectionist legislation that, in Paul's view, was already hindering working women. Kelley, supporting an eight-hour day for women and children as well as the passage of a minimum-wage law for women, was convinced that "women must be protected whether they demand it for themselves or not." Others suggested that the party transform itself into a political organization focused on electing women to office and getting out the vote. And there was support for the organizations of disarmament and peace such as the Women's International League for Peace and Freedom.[84]

It was Paul who prevailed. As usual she was brief and direct, renaming the demands of the 1848 Seneca Falls Convention as a women's Bill of Rights, a program that would lead to equity for women. But the quickest, surest way to achieve these rights was, just as with suffrage, by means of an amendment to the Constitution. Disdainful of any special legislation that would supposedly improve the circumstances of disadvantaged working women, she argued for the controversial necessity of constitutional equality between the sexes. Paul's opponents in the convention complained that the vague, undefined concept of equality was too abstract to rally women, unlike the more tangible entitlement of the vote. Others argued that twentieth-century women had diverse interests, such as the protective labor reforms important to the increasing numbers of working women and the sexual concerns embraced by a new generation of women who viewed these as the primary source of women's oppression. Paul was never distracted by such claims. In the equal rights amendment she had found the goal that in different ways and places she pursued for the rest of her life, even as the women's movement dwindled away, a victim of depression and war.[85]

First she went to law school so that she could better understand the legal disabilities women faced. Next she focused on restrictions that required American women to give up their citizenship if they married a foreign national, but did not require men to do so. She opposed differences in the marriage age that still permitted girls to marry in some states at twelve. And during the Depression she opposed federal rules that only one partner of a marriage could fill a public job, a regulation that led to the summary firing of many women. Throughout these years she battled women who focused on the protectionist restrictions for the eight million women who worked in industry, a far more popular agenda for working women than any talk of equality. For Paul women would not advance if they relied on specialness and difference as rationales for ending oppression, an argument that had been used intermittently by Stone, Anthony, and Willard.

In Paul's view, protective legislation violated the sameness that, according to her conscience, justice required. She made equality, as she had not made suffrage, an international concern because she believed women more similar in their oppression than in their differences. "Women are the same the world over, no matter what country they live in. They want a worldwide movement like a church, something universal." She organized meetings of women's groups in Latin and South America at Pan American conferences; she worked for equal treaty rights at the League of Nations in Geneva, where she spent much of the 1930s, even though the United States, after Wilson lost his treaty fight, was not a member. And in 1938 she founded the International Woman's Party.[86]

In 1923 Paul presented to Congress her first version of the Equal Rights Amendment, which both the Senate and House promptly buried. Twenty years later during one of her frequent appearances before the Senate Judiciary Committee, she offered a revised version of the ERA: "Equality of rights under the law shall not be denied by the U.S. or any State on account of sex." But congressional support remained as stingy as had been the case with the suffrage amendment. The House Judiciary Committee declined to hold meetings on the ERA until the 1970s when reform winds blowing across the United States, especially in the struggle for civil rights for blacks, uncovered the inequalities in women's status. In 1972 Congress passed the ERA, and twenty-four states immediately approved the amendment.

In her late eighties, a jubilant Alice Paul began her final crusade: lining up the requisite states for ratification. She telephoned congressmen; she wrote letters and editorials. After a period of neglect, she was now hailed for her role in suffrage and was sought out for interviews as the author of the ERA. But by this time the NWP was a feeble pressure group with fewer than five hundred members. Younger feminists, finding Paul to be authoritarian and power-hungry, had drifted off to the National Organization for Women. More telling were the organized efforts of the opponents of the ERA who eventually prevailed as the amendment fell one state short of ratification.

In 1977, at a time when ratification of the ERA seemed a possibility, if not a probability, ninety-two-year-old Paul died of pneumonia in a nursing home in New Jersey. Like so many of the founding sisters, she was blessed with longevity, and also like them, during a lifetime with neither complaint nor diversion, she had used her talents and energies to help achieve rights for women that, in her judgment, must begin with political freedom. Ultimately her efforts for this second national amendment failed, in part because she had been unable to maintain the NWP as an effective militant group, in part because of an organized opposition that returned, in a more modern interpretation, to the ancient doctrine of separate spheres for women, and in part because she had no effective successor as a leader among the thousands of women who supported the ERA.

Like Stone, Anthony, Stanton, and Willard, Paul was a reformer seeking the inclusion of women in American political life. Often she inveighed against "the respectability of uplift [organizations] always ready to serve others and subordinate ourselves. We must have power." She was a radical in the way that she used that power, and it is perhaps for that reason that she has been largely expunged from historical memory. To be sure, the long preoccupation of American women with securing the vote did not lead to full citizenship, in part because it came when voting and political parties were no longer the key to equal rights. Society had moved on. Different issues like marriage and a gender-segregated workforce now demanded attention. For women obtaining rights took so long that these entitlements were often less than relevant when they came. Voting arrived, as historian Joan Hoff has noted, "too little, too late." In the twentieth century legal equality often seemed less than pertinent as social feminists sought different goals. But without the minimalist, retarded deliverance of the vote such reforms would be unthinkable and even more difficult to obtain.[87]

Certainly Paul's efforts at equality represented a new stage of American feminism—a twentieth-century version that ironically led to the passage of ERA statutes in many states as well as women's offhand inclusion in the Civil Rights Acts. In her postsuffrage career Paul had resuscitated feminism in the 1920s and kept the battle for women's rights alive in the 1930s and 1940s when other organizations—such as Catt's League of Women Voters—moved into what Paul considered useless exercises such as getting out the vote. Throughout she made many American women aware of the disparities in their circumstances compared to those of men, and she politicized a battle that required not just asking but demanding, not just waiting but acting.[88]

Afterword

When Alice Paul died in 1977, the lifeline connecting three generations of suffragists ended. Paul had no successor in the battle for
women's equality. The network of sisters whose friendships had sustained Stone, Anthony, Stanton, and Willard as well as their associations dwindled away into a number of separate and often overlapping
organizations. Though Paul habitually looked to the future, she remembered the past in a way that modern feminists who dismissed the
importance of women's suffrage did not. Paul had singled out Susan
B. Anthony, "the mother of us all" and a fellow Quaker and advocate
of "single blessedness," as her hero. But there was no one to venerate
Paul.

For inspiration and support Paul always drew on the lives and ideas
of other feminist predecessors. For example, she derived her rationale
for suffrage from the lofty androgynous philosophy of Stanton and
fiercely rejected the protective legislation that made women separate
and unequal. And having split away from the major suffrage organization NAWSA, Paul understood that she lived in the same divided
world of activists that Stone had inhabited in her Boston-based AWSA
during the period when two national organizations represented the
tiny women's suffrage movement. Just as Stanton and Anthony considered Willard's WCTU an unfortunate diversion from the central
mission of obtaining the vote, so Paul understood groups like the Fed-

eration of Women's Clubs as distractions draining off women who should be fighting for the ERA into meaningless sororital activities. She was dismissive of the League of Women Voters, the successor to NAWSA, because, in her judgment, it acted as no more than an insignificant political schoolhouse that did not even endorse the few women running for office. Yet by the 1930s and 1940s her own National Woman's Party no longer attracted new members. When Paul died, the continuity of the struggle for women's equal rights disappeared into the newly named crusade for women's liberation. Demands for more egalitarian forms of marriage and an end to humiliating portrayals of women in the media, to be accomplished by grassroots egalitarian activism, drowned out Paul's constitutional solution of an equal rights amendment.

As for the study of suffrage, for years it lay, with only a few exceptions, mostly dormant. Implicit in the revival of women's history in the 1980s was the understanding that the study of women's culture—that is, female habits, domesticity, ways of doing things, and life course— was far more significant than investigating the process whereby women got the vote.

In her busy life Paul never found time to write the history of the National Woman's Party she had founded, as Stanton, Anthony, and Willard did for their organizations. Despite her restless desire to be doing rather than talking, Paul's historical sense was, however, sufficiently developed to accommodate a long oral history enabling future generations some access to her own feelings (though she denied she had many) and how her personality influenced her public activism. Having little personal life beyond the movement, Paul was unconscious of how the lives of the women she admired had affected their work. Rarely distracted from the task at hand, save for an occasional bout of stomach trouble, she assumed Stone, Anthony, Stanton, and Willard to be no different than she was. In a word, Paul never appreciated the claim of modern feminists that the personal was the political.

In its comprehensive sense this slogan simply meant that after women got the vote personal, familial, and domestic issues inevitably became public concerns. And so with marvelous promptness they did, the classic examples being the 1921 Sheppard-Towner Act providing federal funds to establish programs in which public health nurses and doctors provided preventive health care to pregnant women and new mothers; the establishment of the Woman's Bureau in the Department of Labor in 1920; the Cable Act in 1922, which gave women equal citizenship with men; and a child-labor amendment sent to the states for ratification in 1924. Without the vote women would never have received such legislative attention from Congress.

Applied to the individuals in the movement, connecting personal lives with public ones helps to explain the course of suffrage history. No virgin birth, the movement was made in the private lives of the women who conceived it. For example, Lucy Stone's miserable childhood and especially the daily humiliation of her mother in service to an angry, heavy-drinking father undergirded a daughter's challenge to a system that condemned women to submission to their husbands and silence in church. Like many rebels, Stone tested her father, wanting his affection or at least his commendation. She also learned from his behavior and her mother's frequent pregnancies to hate sex. When despite his disapproval, she earned her college degree from Oberlin, she became that rare nineteenth-century woman—an autonomous human being who did not have to look, like most American women then and now, into the mirror in order to establish a sense of self-affirmation. Paid for her audacious lectures against slavery, she was her own breadwinner. And so for a time, she resisted Henry Blackwell's ardent courtship.

To be sure, Stone was never entirely liberated from the practices of her day and in fact was far more conventional and conflicted than Anthony and Stanton about matters of sex, marriage, and divorce. She married, but only after Henry agreed that she would not take his name, that she would control her pregnancies, and that she would continue her career. When Henry's affair with a married friend coincided with disagreements among the suffrage women as to whether to accept their exclusion in the Fifteenth Amendment, Stone expeditiously saved her marriage and her leadership by moving to Boston. Distance in ideas as well as geography was enough to justify the formation of her own suffrage organization. Yet only a woman of will and determination could have undertaken such a move, and only a guilty husband who had violated his wedding vows would have agreed to uproot. Now suffrage became a familial enterprise, as the cautious Lucy supported a state strategy for the advancement of woman's suffrage. She left Alice, her only child, as her legacy to accomplish reunification, and to maintain, with Susan B. Anthony's niece Lucy, the sense of continuity that bound the suffrage sisters together.

Through her antislavery, temperance, and women's rights lecturing, Lucy Stone became well known to the second member of the suffrage triumvirate, Susan B. Anthony. As a young woman, Anthony sought close, even romantic friendships with other women in the movement, and on those occasions when the imperious Mrs. Stanton was unavailable for lectures and organization, Lucy became Susan's favorite. The latter's predilection for sisterly love as the central intimacy of her life began early. As a young child with her mother absorbed in the recurring female cycle of pregnancy, birth, and nursing along with constant cooking and housekeeping, Susan turned to her sisters for affection and companionship, while Mary Anthony offered her entire devotion to her beloved older sister throughout both their lives. To be sure, Anthony's Quaker father had schooled a receptive Susan in the inequalities of white to black and rich to poor, so she was primed during her youthful years as an underpaid schoolteacher to see the injustices of men to women.

While Stone's struggle to leave her family and exist independently framed the division of the suffrage movement, Anthony's cherishing of sisterly love suffused the organization she and Stanton founded in 1869 and ran for over twenty-five years. NWSA was her extended family, just as the WCTU was Willard's. By nature Anthony was an organizer, attentive to detail, energetic in promotion, and gifted with the kind of emotional intelligence that made her optimistic for success. If such an approach did not quickly win the vote, it was what allowed the movement to survive. With distaste for the "aristocrats of sex," Anthony suffered personal humiliation whenever her suffrage sisters, and especially Lucy Stone, married. Any sacred oath to love and obey a husband meant a diminished love for her, just as marriage and childbearing inevitably compromised activity for the women's movement. When Anthony emerged as the best known and hardest working of the suffragists, she publicly disdained any interest in finding the husband most women believed essential to their happiness. The legal customs of nineteenth-century marriage—no divorce, ownership of a wife's body, male guardianship of children—were enough for Anthony to dismiss this arrangement of "man-marriage."

From her dependence on female friendships emerged a suffrage association that relied on personal relationships among women to sustain its public activities. But Anthony was not always successful in her demands on other women for the kind of single-minded love and devotion to work she provided for her followers. During her passionate affair with Anna Dickinson, when for one of the few times in her life this sober, dutiful activist fell head over heels in love and was diverted, though only briefly, from her public campaign for votes for women, she could not persuade Dickinson to join the movement. Of course Anthony's most enduring female friendship was the adamantine one she established with Elizabeth Cady Stanton. The match of their strengths—Stanton's ideas and writing with Anthony's promotion and organization—assured that the National Woman Suffrage Association became the most important arm of the suffrage movement in the United States. But that was not saying much given the reluctance of American women to join an organization that most felt threatened their femininity. Although the numbers rose rapidly during the decade before the amendment passed, in 1900 there were only seventeen thousand dues-paying members of NAWSA.

Meanwhile Stanton's commitment to suffrage emerged from her childhood desire to please a father whom she admired and wished to emulate, but who, as his sons died and his daughters flourished, could not bring himself emotionally to replace his lost male children with his living female ones, even the brilliant Elizabeth. Alert to the inequalities she experienced within the household of her birth, Stanton became the family rebel, even marrying a man her father disliked. Her public introduction to what she had originally experienced within her family came at the famous London antislavery meeting when female delegates, including her hero Lucretia Mott, were not seated because they were women. Returned to the United States, Stanton immersed herself in the domestic tasks of raising seven children and running a household. Only in 1848 in the Declaration of Sentiments did she establish herself as the intellectual leader of the first feminist movement in U.S. history. But she never had as much time as Anthony for the organizational work of suffrage.

From a busy life as wife and mother with little time for herself came Stanton's other contribution to the feminist movement. Like the Declaration of Sentiments, it was an intellectual one. Women, she believed, would never be free until they gave up their dependence on men and relied on themselves. In her groundbreaking lecture in 1892, "The Solitude of Self," she demanded that men give up their dominance over the souls, bodies, and minds of women. She called for self-reliance among women who, never encouraged to take care of themselves, must be freed to take responsibility not just for their political lives—that point a justification for the ballot—but for their economic and emotional ones as well. All human beings endured loneliness, in Stanton's view, but women did so in the special events that shaped their existence—their marriages, childbearing and raising, and widowhood. In the private understanding that she struggled to create for herself during her "general dissatisfaction" of managing a household and small children, Stanton argued that women must assert themselves to become individuals, not simply the "spaniel" wives of their husbands or the sacrificial mothers of their children. Then when the moment of solitude came, they would be better prepared to survive and protect themselves. Such an understanding of individual self-sovereignty grew out of her own experiences—her need to salvage some pride before her father's chauvinism, her need to survive her husband's nonchalance about women's causes, her need to pay for her children's tuitions, and most of all, her deeply felt obligation to herself.

It was from Stanton that American feminists came to understand the women's movement as an international one. Influenced by Lucretia Mott, whom she first met overseas, Stanton soon saw the universality of the plight of women who, notwithstanding national, cultural, and religious variations, were all oppressed. By 1853 women's rights conventions reflected the nature of an American feminism that Stanton persistently couched in transnational terms. Conventions during this period always featured activists from Europe in prominent roles. Customarily addresses were sent to leaders in Britain and France seeking their cooperation in the mutual struggle for freedom. It was Stanton who initiated the idea for the international meeting of women in 1888 that brought American women, including Stone, Anthony,

Stanton, and Willard together with delegates from all over the world.

Such a spirit of globalism emerged naturally from Stanton's personal life—her international traveling that had begun on her honeymoon and that, after her daughter Harriot's marriage to an Englishman and subsequent residence in England, continued to the end of her life. To be sure, as the suffragist who provided the ideas for the movement, Stanton traveled vicariously through her reading. More than Stone, Anthony, Willard, and Paul, she was in touch with intellectuals on both sides of the continent, and she appreciated the extent to which American feminism was part of a larger movement. When faraway New Zealand became the first nation to give women the right to vote in 1893, Elizabeth Cady Stanton applauded, using the victory as an argument for American suffrage.

Frances Willard traveled a different path to suffrage and women's rights. The isolation of her early years on a Wisconsin prairie, her disastrous love affair with her future sister-in-law, her continuing romantic attractions to women, along with the humiliating episode that led to her firing as the first female president of a college by her rejected male lover, established her gritty independence, as she came to exemplify the saying "a soft hand in an iron fist." By the time Willard was in her thirties she was sovereign of herself, and just the kind of woman whom Stanton could admire (save for her temperance commitment and religiosity) and Anthony could attract to the suffrage movement. Like many suffrage supporters, Willard was influenced by her encounters with the hierarchy of the movement. She had heard a speech by Anthony in Evanston in 1876; she had listened to both Stanton and Anthony in Philadelphia, and she had visited Stone in her office at the *Woman's Journal*. Convinced of the need for suffrage, Willard used practical arguments to demonstrate its importance, and she pushed her reluctant followers to protect themselves through the ballot.

Throughout, Willard's approach to reform was shaped by her understanding of maternalism, modeled on the role her mother had played in her life. As mothers did in their multifaceted efforts to shape their children, so she took up many reforms from camps for wayward girls to more water fountains to stopping pornography. At the end of her life, in her efforts to mother America, Willard called for state in-

tervention in order to correct the ills of an industrial society, and by
the 1890s she supported progressive changes such as an eight-hour
day and the nationalization of the railroads.

Of the five leaders considered in *Sisters: The Lives of America's Suffragists,* only Alice Paul lived to cast a ballot in a presidential election,
voting for the Republicans who for years had been more sympathetic
than the Democrats to the cause of women's suffrage. Twenty-six million other Americans voted in 1920; over a third were women, although it would be years before the turnouts for men and women
were roughly the same. As Alice Paul learned after the ratification of
the suffrage amendment, women retired from participation in public
life for nearly a half century.

Some observers have taken this retirement as evidence of the ways
in which the movement for suffrage overshadowed demands for more
significant reforms affecting women. In one analogy the single-
minded devotion to the ballot by Stone, Anthony, Stanton, Willard,
and Paul was similar to the behavior of the despised cowbird that takes
over the nests of others in order to lay its egg. Women's suffrage is also
viewed as outside the central experience of women with the battle
over protective legislation a more crucial one. In this argument voting,
ever a blunt instrument to effect change, delivered an individual right
to a group better served by the collective sensibility of consciousness-
raising encouraged by later feminists. Suffrage leaders have also been
rightly criticized (though a double standard may prevail here) for their
failure to support universal voting of blacks and the foreign born. And
in another dismissive view, enfranchisement would have come anyway because of changes in employment, education, and the declining
birth rate.

But more to the point, as the historian Joan Hoff argues, women's
suffrage was so long delayed that an unequal class got the right to vote
when the ballot was no longer the key to equality. During the nineteenth century politics was in the air everywhere. Male participants established themselves as virtuous, civic-minded residents of the new
republic by casting a ballot. But by the twentieth century party politics
was less important. Turnouts were dropping; ambitious young men no
longer used politics as an avenue to prominence. Thus women were
in the position of the proverbial frog who forever jumps half the dis-

tance to her goal and never gets to the end point, in this case of equality. Moreover, according to Hoff, fitting an unequal category of Americans into male standards at such a retarded pace meant that supposed progress, such as obtaining the vote or access to birth control, rarely corresponded to the contemporary needs of women.

Still, without the vote what credibility did women have to achieve other goals? Without the sameness to men as citizens, women would not have achieved access to education and the professions. To underestimate the importance of the vote, an entitlement that until 1950 over half the women in the world did not have, is to overlook the grudging deliverance that suggests just how crucial it was. What was at stake in this seventy-two-year-long struggle was nothing less the civil rights of half of the American population. Voting implies, even if it does not deliver, equal status, which is not to say that women were automatically free after they got the vote. Certainly the leaders of the suffrage movement never saw the ballot as a panacea.

Instead the women whose lives are told here intended to use it for other goals: they saw it as a symbol, a vehicle, a psychological solution and always a natural right promised to all Americans. Specifically Stanton would use it to change legislation about marriage and especially married women's rights insofar as their legal status was concerned. But Stanton noted that the vote would achieve for women no more than it had for men. Anthony would use it to improve the lives of working women and to secure equal pay for equal work; Stone for more access to education; Willard to prohibit drinking; and Paul to install what she considered the ultimate level for equality—an equal rights amendment. In the final analysis a nation that places the stories of other struggles—the American Revolution, the emancipation of slaves, and the civil rights movement of the mid-twentieth century—foremost in its historical imagination, should make room for the tales of women's suffrage. And they are best told by connecting the uncelebrated lives of the suffrage sisters to their public work for freedom and equality.

Notes

1. The Martyr and the Missionary: Lucy Stone and Henry Blackwell

1. Henry Blackwell to Lucy Stone, June 13, 1853, January 22, 1854, Blackwell Family Papers, microfilm edition. (Lucy Stone lost the battle to keep her birth name with archivists. She is listed as Mrs. Henry Blackwell in the study guides to this extensive collection.) Hereafter cited as BFP. Many of these letters are also in Leslie Wheeler, ed., *Loving Warriors: Selected Letters of Lucy Stone and Henry B. Blackwell* (New York: Dial Press, 1981). There is also a collection of Stone letters in the Blackwell Family Papers in the Schlesinger Library, Radcliffe College, Cambridge, Mass.

2. Andrea Kerr, *Lucy Stone: Speaking Out for Equality* (New Brunswick, N.J.: Rutgers University Press, 1992), 73.

3. Lucy Stone to Henry Blackwell, June 21, 1853, ibid.

4. Lucy Stone, "Reminiscences," BFP; Lucy Stone to Hannah Stone, May 26, 1855, ibid.

5. Lucy Stone, "Reminiscences," BFP.

6. Ibid.

7. Sarah Stone to Lucy Stone, August 9, 1845, BFP.

8. Elinor Rice Hays, *Morning Star: A Biography of Lucy Stone, 1818–1893* (New York: Harcourt Brace, 1961), 18, 20.

9. Lucy Stone, "Reminiscences," BFP; Hays, 27.

10. Lucy Stone to Father and Mother, September 11, 1843, BFP.

11. Lucy Stone to Father and Mother, August 16, 1846; Francis Stone to Lucy, January 11, 1845, BFP.

12. G. M. Ditchfield, *The Evangelical Revival*; Barbara Solomon, "The Oberlin Method and Its Impact on Other Colleges," Carol Lasser, ed., *Educating Men and Women in a Changing World* (Urbana: University of Illinois Press, 1987), 81–91.

13. Lucy to Sarah, March 13, 1846, BFP.
14. Carol Lasser and Marlene Merrill, eds., *Friends and Sisters: Letters Between Lucy Stone and Antoinette Brown Blackwell, 1846–1893* (Urbana: University of Illinois Press, 1987), 5.
15. Lucy Stone to Hannah Stone, March 14, 1847, BFP.
16. "Disappointment Lecture" in BFP.
17. Lucy to Mother, March 14, 1847, BFP.
18. Sarah Stone to Lucy Stone, November 11, 28, 1846; March 28, 1847, BFP.
19. P. T. Barnum to G. Trail, February 2, 1854, NAWSA Papers, LC; Alice Stone Blackwell, *Lucy Stone: Pioneer of Women's Rights* (Boston: Little, Brown, 1930), 270, n. 9.
20. Lasser and Merrill, 31.
21. Henry to Lucy, January 3, 1855. For Lucy's attitude that bloomer dress not only was a convenience but improved her health and her stamina, see Lucy Stone to Nette, November 24, 1852, in Lasser and Merrill, 125–26.
22. Henry Blackwell to Lucy Stone, August 24, 1853, BFP.
23. Ibid., October 10, 1854.
24. Lucy Stone to Henry Blackwell, October 8, 1854, ibid.
25. Lucy to Henry, December 30, 1853; Henry to Lucy, July 2, 1853, ibid.
26. Henry to Lucy, July 2, 1853; Lucy to Henry, October 8, 1854; February 1, 1855. Also for a perceptive look at the dynamics of the Blackwells, see Margo Horn, "Family Ties: The Blackwells: A Study in the Dynamics of Family Life in 19th-Century America," Ph.D. Diss. (Tufts University, 1980), 112, note 119.
27. Horn, 22; Wheeler, 135–37; Lucy to Henry, September 10, 1854; February 1, 1855.
28. Elizabeth Cady Stanton, Susan B. Anthony, and Matilda Joslyn Gage, *History of Woman Suffrage* (Rochester, N.Y.: Charles Mann, 1889), 1:261. This version, taken from the newspapers, omits the provision about control over childbearing. Also Wheeler, 135–37.
29. Clipping, Reel 69, BFP; Thomas Higginson, *Letters and Journals of Thomas Higginson 1846–1906* (Boston: Houghton Mifflin, 1921), 60–63.
30. Nancy Cott, *The Bonds of Womanhood* (New Haven, Conn.: Yale University Press, 1977), 80–82; "Reminiscences," 21, 29, 30; Moore, 80. William Bowman Stone to Lucy Stone, February 17, 1846; Luther Stone to Lucy, June 1, 1847, BFP; Henry Clarke Wright, *Marriage and Parentage: On the Reproductive Element in Man as a Means to His Elevation and Happiness* (Boston: Bela Marsh, 1855).
31. Elizabeth Blackwell to Harry, December 27, 1854; February 22, 1855, Lucy Stone to Isabel Hooker, April 1883, BFP; Elizabeth (Blackwell) to Harry, January 11, 1854, BFP.
32. Anna Blackwell to Harry, March 23, 1855, BFP; Hays, *Bright Star*, 111.
33. Lucy Stone to Hannah Stone, May 26, 1855, BFP.
34. Lucy Stone to Nette Dear, March 29, 1855, in Lasser, 143. Hays, *Bright Star*, 130; Moore, 225.
35. Horn, "Family Ties"; Harry to Lucy, September 9, 1853; July 21, 1853, BFP.

36. Horn, 152, 116.
37. Elizabeth Blackwell, *Pioneer Work in Opening the Medical Profession to Women* (London: Longmans Green, 1857), 7.
38. Lucy Stone to Susan B. Anthony, May 30, 1855, BFP.
39. Lucy Stone's "Reminiscences"; Henry Blackwell's "Reminiscences," Reel 68; Fragment in Reel 65, BFP.
40. *History of American Suffrage* 1:703; Andrea Kerr, *Lucy Stone, Speaking Out for Equality* (New Brunswick, N.J.: Rutgers University Press, 1992), 62; *New York Tribune*, May 8, 1853.
41. "To the Friends of the Cause of Women," January 15, 1851, BFP; *Liberator*, October 8, 1851; Lucy Stone to Dear Friends at Home, July 29, 1856, BFP.
42. Lucy Stone to Susan B. Anthony, July 20, 1857, BFP.
43. Ann Gordon, ed., *The Selected Papers of Elizabeth Cady Stanton and Susan B. Anthony: In the School of Anti-Slavery 1840–1866* (New Brunswick, N.J.: Rutgers University Press, 1997), 360.
44. In the summer of 1859 while on an extended trip with Henry and with Alice staying with her aunt Dr. Elizabeth Blackwell, Lucy delivered a stillborn son. See also Nette Blackwell to Susan B. Anthony, January 9, 1855.
45. Lucy Stone to Henry Blackwell, April 19, 1868; Dorothea Moore, "Reclaiming Lucy Stone: A Literary and Historical Appraisal," Ph.D. Diss. (University of Texas at Arlington, 1996), 2: 125–30.
46. Henry Blackwell to Lucy Stone, May 7, 1858, May 26, 1858; Lucy Stone to Henry Blackwell, May 26, 1858, June 13, 1858, BFP.
47. Lucy to Nette, February 20, 1859, in Lasser, 150.
48. Henry Blackwell to Lucy Stone, August 29, September 12, 1855; Lucy Stone to Henry Blackwell, May 21, 1858, BFP; ibid., July 22, 1864.
49. Ibid., July 31, 1864.
50. Marian to Elizabeth, December 3, 1871, BFP, Schlesinger Library.
51. *HWS*, 2:488.
52. Lucy to Susan B. Anthony, July 12, 1864, BFP.
53. For a discussion of suffrage and the Fourteenth Amendment see Ellen DuBois, *Woman Suffrage and Women's Rights* (New York: New York University Press, 1998), 81–113; also Jean H. Baker, "Defining Postwar Republicanism: Congressional Republicans and the Boundaries of Citizenship," in *The Birth of the Grand Old Party*, ed. Robert Engs and Randall Miller (Philadelphia: University of Pennsylvania Press, 2002), 128–48.
54. Lucy Stone to Susan B. Anthony, May 1, 1867; Lucy Stone to Olympia Brown, September 30, 1867, BFP; Wheeler, 213; Henry Blackwell and Lucy Stone to Alice, March 31, 1867, BFP.
55. Kerr, 128.
56. Henry Blackwell, *What the South Can Do: How the Southern States Can Make Themselves Masters of the Situation*, in *HWS*, 2; 929–31.
57. Lucy Stone to Emily Blackwell, April 15, 1870, Henry Blackwell to George Washington Blackwell, April 23, 1866, BFP, Schlesinger Library; Kerr, 106, 116, 144, 270, n. 26. Emily Blackwell to Elizabeth Blackwell, September 14; Octo-

ber 11, 1869; December 1869, March 15, 1870; Elizabeth Blackwell to Emily Blackwell, August 20, 1869, BFP, Schlesinger Library; Moore, "Reclaiming Lucy Stone," 374.

58. Lucy Stone to Henry Blackwell, April 1872, BFP.
59. HWS, 2:383–84.
60. Ibid., 382.
61. Ibid.
62. Alice Stone Blackwell, "Closing Days," BFP; Lucy Stone to Mrs. Field, March 24, 1869, BFP.
63. Henry Blackwell to Lucy Stone, November 1, 1869, BFP; Wheeler, 233–34.
64. Henry Blackwell to George Washington Blackwell, March 9, 1870, BFP; Henry Blackwell to Elizabeth, May 3, 1870, BFP.
65. Alice Stone Blackwell, Lucy Stone: Pioneer of Women's Rights (Boston: Little, Brown, 1930), 238; Agnes Ryan, The Torch Bearer: A Look Forward and Back at the Woman's Journal (W. J. News, 1916).
66. Lucy to Mrs. Margaret Campbell, April 12, 1876, BFP.
67. Stone Blackwell, Lucy Stone: Pioneer; Lucy Stone's "Reminiscences," BFP.
68. Alice Stone Blackwell, Journal, December 15, 21, 1873 BFP; see also Marlene Merrill, Growing Up in Boston's Gilded Age (New Haven: Yale University Press, 1990), 238.
69. Ibid., 40.
70. Growing Up in Boston, 178, 193.
71. Lucy Stone to Alice, September 21, 1877; Lucy Stone to Reverend Warren, August 21, 1878; Lucy Stone to Frances Willard, August 23, 1888, BFP.
72. Growing Up in Boston, 31; Alice Blackwell to Kitty Barry, n.d.; Henry Blackwell to Alice, n.d., 1888; Henry Blackwell to George, November 27, 1892, BFP, Schlesinger Library.
73. Woman's Journal, July 24, 1882.
74. Henry Blackwell to Mrs. Isabel Hooker, December 26, 1869, Isabella Beecher Hooker Papers, Stowe-Day Library, Hartford, Conn.
75. Constitution of the American Suffrage Association, Shattuck-Robinson Papers, microfilm edition.
76. Lucy Stone to Susan B. Anthony, October 19, 1869, BFP.
77. Lucy Stone to Isabel Hooker, April 1883; Lucy to Nette, January 10, 1886, also in Lasser and Merrill, 250; Growing Up in Boston, 216; Susan B. Anthony to Harriet Robinson, December 18, 1881, February 10, 1882, Robinson-Shattuck Papers, microfilm edition; Lucy Stone to Henry Blackwell, January 10, 1886, BFP.
78. Elinor Rice Hays, Those Incredible Blackwells: The Story of a Journey to a Better World (New York: Harcourt Brace, 1967).
79. Moore, 33.
80. Lucy to Susan B. Anthony, November 25, 1866; April 12, 1853, January 11, 1856; Lucy Stone to Margaret Campbell, October 2, 1887, BFP.
81. Lucy Stone to Susan B. Anthony, October 19, 1869, BFP.
82. Lucy Stone to Mr. Foulke, February 15, 1888.
83. Ibid.

84. "Tax Controversy," January 16, 1858; Lucy to Mr. O'Reilly, December 8, 1878, BFP.

85. Sarah Stone Lawrence to Lucy Stone, March 28, 1847; Lucy Stone to the National Woman's Convention, March 6, 1857, BFP.

86. Lucy Stone, "Address to the New Jersey Legislature," August 15, 1867; Stone, "Reminiscences"; Lucy Stone to Alice Blackwell, August 15, 1893; Blackwell, 254.

87. *Woman's Journal*, October 18, 1873.

88. Lucy Stone to Margaret Campbell, September 19, 1886, BFP; Wheeler, 264–69.

89. Henry Blackwell to Dearest Wife and Cub, October 16, 1887, BFP.

90. Henry Blackwell to Lucy Stone, July 31, 1889, BFP.

91. Henry Blackwell to Lucy Stone, July 14, 15, 16, 1889, BFP.

92. Lucy Stone to Henry Blackwell, February 20, 1887, BFP.

93. Ibid., April 30, 1878.

94. Lucy Stone to Henry Blackwell, April 30, 1879; April 6, 1880; April 11, 1877, BFP.

95. Lucy to Mrs. Stanton, August 3, 1876, BFP; *HWS* 1: pref.

96. Lucy Stone to Mrs. Campbell, March 17, 1888; Kerr, 224–26.

97. Lucy Stone, "The Gains of Forty Years," Suffrage pamphlet (February 1891); Clipping in Shattuck-Robinson Scrapbook.

98. Stone, "Reminiscences."

99. Henry Blackwell, "Reminiscences"; Wheeler, 352–54.

2. In the Blessed Company of Faithful Women: Susan B. Anthony and the Sisters

1. Susan B. Anthony to Lucy Stone, February 9, 1854; March 12, 1854, The Papers of Susan B. Anthony and Elizabeth Cady Stanton, microfilm edition. Hereafter cited as SBA-ECS Papers. For the most part I have relied on this edition, but I have also benefited from *The Selected Papers of Elizabeth Cady Stanton and Susan B. Anthony*, edited by Ann D. Gordon.

2. Table Talk, clipping, n.d., Reel 7, SBA-ECS Papers.

3. Lucy Stone to Susan B. Anthony, February 13, 1854; Elizabeth Cady Stanton to Susan B. Anthony, February 19, 1854, ibid.

4. Susan B. Anthony and Elizabeth Cady Stanton to Lucy Stone, February 16, 1854; Susan B. Anthony to Lucy Stone, February 9, 1854; ibid., March 7, 1854; February 12, 1854.

5. Susan B. Anthony to Lucy Stone, June 16, 1857, July 21, 1857, SBA-ECS Papers; Elizabeth Cady Stanton, "Reminiscences," *Woman's Journal*, December 2, 1899.

6. Elizabeth Cady Stanton, *Eighty Years and More: Reminiscences 1815–1897* (New York: Schocken Books, 1971), 163; Ida Husted Harper, *Life and Work of Susan B. Anthony* (Indianapolis: Hollenbeck Press, 1898), 1: 64.

7. *Birmingham News*, January 27, 1895; Susan B. Anthony to Lucy Stone, March 7, 1854, SBA-ECS Papers; Susan B. Anthony Scrapbook, 1, Library of Congress; "Grievances Without Number," *The Selected Papers of Elizabeth Cady Stanton*

and Susan B. Anthony, Ann Gordon, ed. (New Brunswick, N.J.: Rutgers University Press, 1997), 1: 254; Elizabeth Cady Stanton to Isabel Beecher Hooker, July 5, 1876, Isabella Hooker Papers, microfiche edition; also in Gordon, 3: 241–42.

8. Harper, 1: 98–99, 478–79; Gordon, 1: 278–79; *Philadelphia Evening Bulletin*, July 4–6, 1876.

9. Susan B. Anthony to Lucy Read Anthony, October 29, 1848; Daniel Anthony to Susan B. Anthony, July 16, 1848, SBA-ECS Papers.

10. Susan B. Anthony to Lucy Read Anthony, April 1863, ibid.

11. Susan B. Anthony to Lucy Read Anthony, March 7, 1849, ibid.

12. Susan B. Anthony to Harriet Robinson, February 10, 1881, ibid.

13. Harper, 1: 231; Diary, December 2, 1892, Reel 30; Susan B. Anthony to Mary Buttro and Mrs. Emma Buttro Winans, December 14, 1893; Susan B. Anthony to Rachel Foster, May 1880, SBA-ECS Papers.

14. Susan B. Anthony to Aaron Vail, June 15, 1839, Anthony Papers, Schlesinger Library, Radcliffe University, Cambridge, Mass.; Diary, June 10, 1839; Katherine Anthony, *Susan B. Anthony: Her Personal History and Her Era* (New York: Doubleday, 1954), 63–67.

15. Susan B. Anthony to ?, November 1888, Reel 26; *San Francisco Chronicle*, January 28, 1896, in Scrapbooks, 1892, NAWSA Papers, LC.

16. Susan B. Anthony to Sister, June 15, 1839, Anthony Papers, Schlesinger Library; Lee Virginia Chambers-Schiller, *Liberty, A Better Husband: Single Women in America: The Generation of 1780–1840* (New Haven, Conn.: Yale University Press, 1984), 30–32; Susan B. Anthony Diary, July 22, 1898, SBA-ECS Papers.

17. Clipping, September 1896, SBA-ECS Papers.

18. "Homes of Single Women," handwritten copy, 1877, Reel 19, SBA-ECS Papers.

19. Sylvia Hoffert, *When Hens Crow: The Women's Rights Movement in Antebellum America* (Bloomington: Indiana University Press, 1995); Susan B. Anthony to Isabella Hooker, December 28, 1896; *Rochester Democratic Chronicle*, January 5, 1894, SBA-ECS Papers.

20. *New York Sun*, clippings in Scrapbook 1, Library of Congress; Harper, 1: 138, 150, 156; Wendy Venet, *Neither Ballots nor Bullets: Women Abolitionists and the Civil War* (Charlottesville, Va.: University Press of Virginia, 1991), 30, 115.

21. Susan B. Anthony to Aaron Vail, October 22, 1843; Susan B. Anthony to Lucy Stone, March 22, 1858, SBA-ECS Papers.

22. Susan B. Anthony to Lucy Stone, March 7, 1854, SBA-ECS Papers.

23. Susan B. Anthony to Lucy Stone, May 1, 1853, SBA-ECS Papers; Susan Zaeske, *Signatures of Citizenship: Petitioning, Antislavery and Women's Political Identity* (Chapel Hill: University of North Carolina Press, 2003).

24. Susan B. Anthony to Lucy Stone, March 7, 1854; ibid., June 16, August 2, 1857; Nette to Susan B. Anthony, December 10, 1873, SBA-ECS Papers.

25. Elizabeth Cady Stanton to Susan B. Anthony, January 24, 1856; Susan B. Anthony to Nette, September 4, 1858; Nette to Susan, December 10, 1873, SBA-ECS Papers.

26. Susan B. Anthony to Lucy Stone, August 2, 1857; Susan B. Anthony to Elizabeth

Cady Stanton, March 22, 1858; ibid., to Sallie Joy White, June 26, 1881; ibid., to Mrs. Elizabeth G. Mathews, January 11, 1897, SBA-ECS Papers.

27. Norma Basch, *In the Eyes of the Law: Women, Marriage, and Property in Nineteenth-Century New York* (Ithaca, N.Y.: Cornell University Press, 1982), 194–95, 235; Joseph Warren, "Husband's Right to Wife's Services," *Harvard Law Review* 38 (1925), 421–40, 622–49; Carol Shammas, "Re-Assessing the Married Woman's Property Acts," *Journal of Women's History* 1 (Spring 1994): 9–29.

28. *Proceedings of the Tenth National Woman's Convention Held at the Cooper Institute* (Boston: Yerrington and Garrison, 1860), 60–95; Material in SBA-ECS Papers, May 1860.

29. Susan B. Anthony to Elizabeth Cady Stanton, n.d. (January 1861), Vassar Library, Poughkeepsie, N.Y.; also in Gordon, 1: 456–57.

30. David Bogen, "The Innkeeper's Tale: The Legal Development of a Public Calling," *Utah Law Review* 1996, 51–98; Daniel Anthony to Susan B. Anthony, Scrapbooks, 1, 129, LC; Susan B. Anthony to William Lloyd Garrison, January 1861; Susan B. Anthony to Charles Sumner, February 19, 1872; Susan B. Anthony to Daniel Anthony, May 11, 1849; also Gordon, 1: 146.

31. Susan B. Anthony to Clara Colby, May 10, 1898, SBA-ECS Papers.

32. Faye Dudden, "The New York Strategy: The New York Woman's Movement and the Civil War," in *Votes for Women: Suffrage Revisited,* Jean H. Baker, ed. (New York: Oxford University Press, 2002), 56–77; Susan B. Anthony to Lydia Mott (1862?), Reel 10; also Gordon, 1: 474–75.

33. Gordon, 1: 489–93; Venet, 102–4; *Proceedings of the Meeting of the Loyal Women of the Republic* (New York: Phair, 1863).

34. Gordon, 1: 492; Venet, 106–7.

35. Susan B. Anthony to Samuel May, September 21, 1863, SBA-ECS Papers; Gordon, 1: 474.

36. Ibid., May 9, 1863; Susan B. Anthony to Charles Sumner, March 1, 6, 23, 1864, SBA-ECS Papers.

37. Susan B. Anthony to Anna E. Dickinson, October 23, 1866, Reel 11, SBA-ECS Papers; Gordon, 2:111.

38. Susan B. Anthony to Amelia Bloomer, January 7, 1881; ibid., to Harriet Hanson Robinson, August 4, 12, 1879; ibid., December 18–19, 1881, SBA-ECS Papers.

39. Susan B. Anthony to Harriet Hanson Robinson, May 13, 1881, SBA-ECS Papers; Gordon, 2: 272.

40. *New York World,* May 14, 1868; Harper, 1: 300–301; Susan B. Anthony to Olympia Brown, January 1, 1868, SBA-ECS Papers; Gordon, 2: 121.

41. Gordon, 2: 125, xxiii.

42. *The Revolution,* January 8, 1868.

43. Harper, 1: 301–2.

44. Susan B. Anthony to Ellen Wright, January 27, 1875; diary entries for 1873 and 1877 in SBA-ECS Papers.

45. Scrapbook 1, NAWSA Papers, Library of Congress.

46. Susan B. Anthony to Anna Dickinson, April 14, July 1, 1864, Anna Dickinson Papers, LC.

47. Ibid., December 6, 1866, Anna Dickinson Papers, LC; Susan B. Anthony to Darling Anna, May 14, 1866. See also ibid., May 20, June 4, October 23, 1866; February 3, March 18, 31, 1868; June 7, 29, 1872. The Anthony-Dickinson correspondence is in Reels 10–14 of the SBA-ECS Papers and in Reel 6 of the Dickinson Papers.

48. Lillian Faderman, *Surpassing the Love of Men* (New York: Morrow, 1981), 157–77; Carol Smith-Rosenberg, "The Female World of Love and Ritual: Relations between Women in Nineteenth Century America," *Signs* 1 (Autumn 1975): 1–30.

49. Anna Dickinson to Susan B. Anthony (Spring 1869), SBA-ECS, Reel 13; Susan B. Anthony to Anna Dickinson, undated, Reel 6, Dickinson Papers.

50. Faderman, 211; Susan B. Anthony to Anna Dickinson, March 18, 1867, February 2, 1870, Dickinson Papers.

51. Susan B. Anthony to Anna Dickinson, November 5, 1895, Dickinson Papers.

52. Susan B. Anthony to Nette Brown, October 1859, SBA-ECS Papers.

53. Susan B. Anthony to Rachel Foster, April 5, 1882; ibid., April 28, 1881; ibid., December 8, 1880; April 6, 1895, ibid., Also Susan B. Anthony to Rachel Avery, March 15, 1886, in Susan B. Anthony–Rachel Avery Foster Papers, Rochester University, Rochester, New York.

54. *Philadelphia Inquirer*, February 20, 1883. Susan B. Anthony to Rachel, August 12, 1882; May 12, 1882, SBA-ECS Papers.

55. Susan B. Anthony to Sarah Eddy, December 31, 1887, SBA-ECS Papers.

56. Susan B. Anthony to Rachel Foster, February 6, 1882; ibid., to Miriam (Foster), June 24, 1887; Susan B. Anthony to Harriet Upton, March 14, 1892, SBA-ECS Papers.

57. Rachel Avery to Susan B. Anthony, February 3, 1898; Susan B. Anthony diary, January 1898, SBA-ECS Papers.

58. Susan B. Anthony to Helen Louise Mosher, June 7, September 3, 1883; ibid., to Louise and Donnie, October 20, 1877; ibid., to Anna O. Anthony, October 14, 1893; ibid., to Lucy Anthony, August 27, 1883; ibid., to Maude Anthony Koehler, May 5, 28, 1897; ibid., to Sarah Pugh, January 1872, SBA-ECS Papers.

59. HWS, 2: 627–36.

60. Susan B. Anthony to Elizabeth Cady Stanton, November 5, 1872, ibid., to Isabella Beecher Hooker, June 19, 1872, SBA-ECS Papers.

61. Ellen Carol DuBois, *Woman Suffrage and Women's Rights* (New York: New York University Press, 1998), 99–103, 122–26.

62. Elizabeth Cady Stanton to Susan B. Anthony, February 19, 1873, Susan B. Anthony to Isabella Beecher Hooker, March 15, 1871, SBA-ECS Papers.

63. Susan B. Anthony to Martha Coffin Pelham Wright, January 1, 1873, SBA-ECS Papers; interview with the Cincinnati *Observer*, May 1, 1872, Scrapbook 4, SBA-ECS Papers.

64. Susan B. Anthony to Mr. J. Gordon, March 11, 1873, SBA-ECS Papers.

65. *United States v. Susan B. Anthony* 24F.829 (U.S. C.C.N.D.N.Y. 1873); Ellen DuBois, "Taking the Law into Our Own Hands: Bradwell, Minor, and Suffrage

Militance in the 1870s," in *Visible Women*, Nancy Hewitt and Suzanne Lebsock, eds. (Urbana: University of Illinois Press, 1990), 19–41.

66. *An Account of the Proceedings on the Trial of Susan B. Anthony* (New York: Arno Press, 1974); Records of the District Courts of the U.S.; District Court for Northern District, Hearing on the Writ of Habeas Corpus, January 10, 1873, SBA-ECS Papers; also Susan B. Anthony to Isabella Beecher Hooker, July 14, 1873; John Vorhees to Susan B. Anthony, December 18, 1872, SBA-ECS Papers.

67. Susan B. Anthony to E. B. Foote, July 2, 1873, SBA-ECS Papers.

68. *Minor v. Happersett* 88 U.S. 162 (1875); Joan Hoff, *Law, Gender and Injustice* (New York: New York University Press, 1991), 170–74.

69. Allison Sneider, "Woman Suffrage in Congress: American Expansion and the Politics of Federalism, 1870–1890," in *Votes for Women: The Struggle for Suffrage Revisited*, 77–89; "Women's Campaign," 1873, Susan B. Anthony to Mrs. Thompson, August 1881; ibid., to Elizabeth Harbert, November 12, 1876; ibid., to Martha Pelham Wright, January 1, 1873, SBA-ECS Papers.

70. Susan B. Anthony to Ira Taylor, March 28, 1900, SBA-ECS Papers.

71. Susan B. Anthony to Olympia Brown, November 7, 1867; ibid.

72. Interview in the *Leavenworth Times*, May 4, 1894; Harper, 2: 695.

73. *Leavenworth Times*, May 4, 1894; Harper, 2: 695; Susan B. Anthony to Elizabeth Cady Stanton, May 19, 29, 1872; ibid., to Lucy Holloway, June 19, 1872, SBA-ECS Papers.

74. Gordon, 1:321.

75. Stanton, *Eighty Years and More: Reminiscences 1815–1897* (New York: Schocken Books, 1971), 166, 187; Gordon, 1: 321.

76. In a paraphrase from Shakespeare's *Hamlet*, Stanton referred to their friendship as bound with "hooks of steel." Certainly both women agreed that "those friends thou hast and their adoption tried / Grapple them to the soul with hoops of steel."

77. Harper, 2: 525, 913, 919; Susan B. Anthony to Harriet Hanson Robinson (1881), SBA-ECS Papers.

78. ECS Diary, October 28, 1881; Susan B. Anthony to unknown, September 1881, Diary, November 1881; Harper, 2: 537, 539; Susan B. Anthony to Mary Anthony, March 22, 1883, SBA-ECS Papers.

79. Harper, 2: 668, Elizabeth Cady Stanton, "Friendships of Women," February 15, 1890, Reel 27, SBA-ECS Papers.

80. Elizabeth Cady Stanton to Susan B. Anthony, August 1895, June 1870, SBA-ECS Papers; *Eighty Years and More: Reminiscences 1815–1897*, 187; Theodore Stanton and Harriot Stanton Blatch, *Elizabeth Cady Stanton as Revealed in Her Letters, Diary and Reminiscences* (New York: Harpers, 1922), 2: 254; 2: 124–25.

81. *New Orleans Daily Picayune*, January 23, 1895; *Rochester Democrat and Chronicle*, July 28, 1895; also January 8, 1894; Anthony, "How to Keep Young," July 7, 1895; Elizabeth Cady Stanton to Theodore Stanton, March 2, 1886, SBA-ECS Papers.

82. Stanton, et al. on Susan B. Anthony in *Eminent Women of the Age* (Hartford, Conn.: S. M. Betts, 1868), 400.

83. Susan B. Anthony to Elizabeth Cady Stanton, April 2, 1896; ECS to Clara Colby (1896), ECS-SBA Papers; ECS Diary, January 1889, in Theodore Stanton and Harriot Stanton Blatch, eds.; "Educated Suffrage," *The Independent*, February 14, 1895; Susan B. Anthony Diary, September 4, 1897, ECS-SBA Papers; Harper, 2: 856–57.

84. Harper, I: 488–89; Susan B. Anthony to Elizabeth Cady Stanton, December 2, 1898; Harper, 2: 631; *Proceedings of the Twenty-Eighth National American Woman Suffrage Association 1896* (Philadelphia: 1896); ibid., 1890.

85. Susan B. Anthony to Elizabeth Cady Stanton, January 2, 1871; Elizabeth Cady Stanton to Susan B. Anthony, July 26, 1877; ibid., February 19, 1873; ibid., to Martha Coffin Pelham Wright, March 8, 1873; Susan B. Anthony Diary, February 1, 1888; Susan B. Anthony to Olympia Brown, June 1890; ibid., to Mrs. Robinson, April 4, 1882, SBA-ECS Papers; *Chicago Daily Record*, June 29, 1895.

86. Elizabeth Cady Stanton to Susan B. Anthony, n.d.; Elizabeth Cady Stanton to Mrs. Wright, January 2, 1871; Stanton, *Eighty Years*, 160.

87. Susan B. Anthony to Elizabeth Cady Stanton, July 1891, SBA-ECS Papers. For a rare personal comment of Anthony about Stanton, see Susan B. Anthony to Rachel Foster, March 1889, SBA-ECS Papers; Harper, 2: 712–13.

88. *Rochester Democratic Chronicle*, October 28, 1902; Susan B. Anthony to Elizabeth Miller, December 29, 1902; Elizabeth Cady Stanton to Susan B. Anthony, May 1894, ECS-SBA Papers.

89. *Handbook and Proceedings of the National American Woman Suffrage Association*, Harriet Eaton, ed. (Washington: NAWSA Publishing, 1906).

90. Anna Howard Shaw, *The Story of a Pioneer* (New York: Harper, 1915), 233; Harper, 3: 1419.

3. Elizabeth Cady Stanton and The Solitude of Self

1. Elizabeth Cady Stanton, *Eighty Years and More: Reminiscences 1815–1897* (New York: Schocken, 1971), 20.

2. Daniel Cady to Peter Smith, December 2, 1814, ECS-SBA Papers, microfilm edition.

3. Daniel Cady to Peter Smith, October 17, October 20, 1820, ibid.

4. ECS to Clara Colby, n.d. (1896), ibid.

5. Daniel Cady to Peter Smith, December 2, 1814; October 17, 1820, ibid.

6. ECS to John Greenleaf Whittier, July 11, 1840, ECS-SBA Papers; Theodore Tilton, et al., *Eminent Women of the Age* (Hartford, Conn.: Betts, 1868), 335–38.

7. *Eighty Years*, 23.

8. Mrs. A. W. Fairbanks, ed., *Emma Willard and Her Pupils, 1822–1872* (New York: Mrs. Russell Sage, 1898).

9. *Women's Tribune*, April 2, 1892; *Chicago Chronicle*, September 1, 1891; *The Revolution*, January 29, 1868.

10. Whitney Cross, *The Burned Over District* (Ithaca, N.Y.: Cornell University Press, 1950); Paul Johnson, *A Shopkeeper's Millennium: Society and Revivals in Rochester, New York, 1815–1837* (New York: Hill and Wang, 1978), 102–9.

11. *Eighty Years*, 42.
12. Ann Gordon, ed., *The Selected Papers of Elizabeth Cady Stanton and Susan B. Anthony: In the School of Antislavery* (New Brunswick, N.J.: Rutgers University Press, 1997), 1: 5; ECS to Amelia Bloomer, July 25, 1880, ECS-SBA Papers.
13. Elisabeth Griffith, *In Her Own Right: The Life of Elizabeth Cady Stanton* (New York: Oxford University Press, 1984), 10; *Eighty Years*, 36, 441–47.
14. *Eighty Years*, 60.
15. Daniel Cady to Gerrit Smith, December 2, 1814; December 14, 1839, Smith Papers, Syracuse University.
16. Henry Stanton to ECS, January 1, 1840, ECS-SBA Papers; Ellen Rothman, *Hands and Hearts: A History of Courtship in America* (New York: Basic Books, 1984), 57.
17. *Eighty Years*, 71.
18. Gordon, 1: 4; Sarah Grimké to ECS, December 31, 1842, ECS-SBA Papers.
19. Henry Stanton to Gerrit Smith, February 27, 1840, Smith Papers.
20. *Eighty Years*, 71–72.
21. ECS to Lucy Stone, May 8, 1855, in ECS-SBA Papers; ECS to Rebecca Eyster, May 1, 1847, ibid.; Gordon, 1: 471; ECS to Wendell Phillips, August 18, 1860; Susan B. Anthony, Diary, 1878, ECS-SBA Papers; *Woman's Journal*, October 22, 1898.
22. Betty Fladeland, *James Gillespie Birney: Slaveholder to Abolitionist* (Ithaca, N.Y.: Cornell University Press, 1955), 194; John Greenleaf Whittier to Henry Stanton, April 8, 1846; ECS to Elizabeth Neall, January 25, 1841, ECS-SBA Papers; *Eighty Years*, 202; Alma Lutz, *Created Equal: A Biography of Elizabeth Cady Stanton* (New York: John Day, 1940), 68.
23. *Eighty Years*, 79; Lori Ginzberg, *Women and Benevolence: The Work of Benevolence, Morality, Politics and Class in the Nineteenth Century United States* (New Haven, Conn.: Yale University Press, 1990), 89, n. 51.
24. Gordon, 1: 10.
25. *History of Women Suffrage* 1: 131; *Eighty Years*, 82–83.
26. Henry Brewster Stanton, *Random Recollections* (New York: Harper's, 1887), 76, 110, 147; Arthur Rice, "Henry B. Stanton as a Political Abolitionist," Ph.D. diss. (Columbia University, 1968), 223–50.
27. Gordon, 1: 35–37, 48–49; Henry Stanton to ECS, February 23, 1841, Autumn 1843; March 30, 1844; October 1842; ECS-SBA Papers; ECS to Henry, March 16, 1842, February 13, 1851 in *Elizabeth Cady Stanton*, Theodore Stanton and Harriot Stanton Blatch, eds. (New York: Arno Press, 1969), 2: 8, 26–27.
28. Gordon, 1: 254; 396; ECS, *The Woman's Bible*, 1: 11.
29. Janet Farrell Brodie, *Contraception and Abortion in Nineteenth-Century America* (Ithaca, N.Y.: Cornell University Press, 1994), 56–86; Helen Horowitz, *Rereading Sex* (New York: Knopf, 2002), 275–84.
30. Brodie, 310, n. 10; ECS to Abigail Kelley Foster, January 12, 1851, ECS-SBA Papers.

31. ECS to Madge, October 20, 1892: ibid., to Elizabeth Smith Miller, January 24, 1856; ibid., to SBA, June 10, 1856; ibid., April 10, 1859, ECS-SBA Papers.

32. Ibid.; ECS to Elizabeth Smith Miller, December 1, 1858, ECS-SBA Papers. Ellen Carol DuBois, "Outgrowing the Compact of the Fathers: Equal Rights, Woman's Suffrage and the United States Constitution, 1820–1870," *Journal of American History* 74 (December 1987): 856.

33. ECS to SBA February 10, 1851; ibid., to Lucretia Mott, October 22, 1852, ECS-SBA Papers; ECS to Henry, February 2, 1851 in Stanton and Blatch, 2: 26.

34. ECS Diary, version printed in Stanton and Blatch, *Elizabeth Cady Stanton*, 2: 210; *The Lily*, n.d., in Reel 1 of ECS-SBA Papers; ECS to Laura Curtis Bullard, December 28, 1884, ibid.

35. ECS to Henry, March 16, 1842, December 9, 1850, in Stanton and Blatch, 2: 8, 25; *Eighty Years*, 117–26, 146; ECS to Mrs. Moulton, August 30, 1875, ECS-SBA Papers.

36. Donald Ray Kennon, "A Knit of Identity: Marriage and Reform in Mid-Victorian America," Ph.D. diss. (University of Maryland, 1981), 13–17, 29–30.

37. SBA to Antoinette Blackwell, September 4, 1858, ECS-SBA Papers.

38. *Eighty Years*, 142; ECS to SBA, June 10, 1856, ECS-SBA Papers.

39. Ibid., 10–11, "Our Boys," lecture, Reel 1, ECS-SBA Papers.

40. ECS to Martha Wright, March 21, 1871, ibid.

41. E. C. Clarke, *Sex in Education* (Boston: James Osgood, 1872); Peter Gay, *Schnitzel's Century* (New York: W. W. Norton, 2002), 75–78, 82–83; Gordon, 1: 603; "Our Girls," version in ECS-SBA Papers.

42. SBA Diary, May 2, 1873, ECS-SBA Papers.

43. ECS to SBA, June 10, 1856; ECS-SBA Papers; Stanton and Blatch, 2: 42.

44. Betty Friedan, *The Feminine Mystique* (New York: W. W. Norton, 1983), 11–16; Stanton and Blatch, 2: 53; ECS to Paulina Kellogg Davis, December 6, 1852; Gordon, 1: 214.

45. *History of Woman Suffrage*, 1: 68–73; Judith Wellman, "The Seneca Falls Woman's Rights Convention: A Study of Social Networks," *Journal of Woman's History* 3 (Spring 1991): 9–37; Stanton and Blatch, 1: 145.

46. See text of the Declaration of Sentiments in Gordon, 1: 75–83; also the textual notes on ECS's address in Gordon, 1: 94–95.

47. Joan Hoff, *Law, Gender and Injustice: A Legal History of U.S. Women* (New York: New York University Press, 1991), 443, n. 45.

48. ECS to George Cooper, September 11, 1848, ECS-SBA Papers.

49. ECS to SBA, September 10, 1855, in Stanton and Blatch, 2: 60–61; Griffith, 52–57.

50. Alma Lutz, *Created Equal: A Biography of Elizabeth Cady Stanton 1815–1902* (New York: John Day, 1940), 46; SBA to Lucy Stone, February 9, 1854.

51. ECS to SBA, September 10, 1855; SBA to Lucy Stone, February 9, 1854, ECS-SBA Papers; Gordon, 1: 105.

52. Gordon, 1: 95–107; ECS to Lucy Stone, November 1, 1856, ECS-SBA Papers.

53. Elizabeth Cady Stanton, "The Solitude of Self," in *Elizabeth Cady Stanton, Susan B. Anthony: Correspondence, Writing, Speeches*, Ellen Carol DuBois, ed.

(New York: Schocken Books, 1981), passim; also a slightly different version in Reel 1, ECS-SBA Papers.

54. ECS to Neil, October 14, 1851, Reel 1; Ellen Carol DuBois, *Harriot Stanton Blatch and the Winning of Woman Suffrage* (New Haven, Conn.: Yale University Press, 1997), 22–23.

55. Helen Horowitz, *Alma Mater* (New York: Knopf, 1984), 56; Mabel Newcomer, *A Century of Higher Education* (New York: Harpers, 1959), 37, 46.

56. ECS to Gerrit Smith, January 25, 1879, Gerrit Smith Papers, Syracuse University; Alma Lutz, *Challenging Years: The Memoirs of Harriot Stanton Blatch* (New York: Putnam's, 1940), 35.

57. ECS to Gerrit Smith, January 29, 1869, ECS-SBA Papers.

58. ECS to Paulina Davis, August 12, 1869, ibid.

59. ECS to Francis Blair, October 1, 1868, ibid., ECS Papers.

60. Lutz, *Created Equal*, 140; Kathi Kern, *Mrs. Stanton's Bible* (Ithaca, N.Y.: Cornell University Press, 2001), 112–14; *Woman's Journal*, January 5, 1895; *Woman's Tribune*, March, 23, 1889.

61. Lutz, *Created Equal*, 140.

62. Hiram Barney to Abraham Lincoln, January 9, 1864, General Correspondence, Robert Todd Lincoln Collection of Abraham Lincoln Papers, LC; Gordon, 1: 509; Arthur Rice, "Henry B. Stanton as a Political Abolitionist," Ph.D. diss. (New York: Columbia University, 1968), 422–62; U.S. House of Representatives, Reports of Committees, 111, New York Custom House, 43–44.

63. Blatch, 245: ECS to Gerrit Smith, June 2, 1864; ECS Diary, November 12, 1880; March 2, 1891; Stanton and Blatch, 2: 272; Gordon, 1: 509.

64. ECS to Henry, October 9, 1867, ECS-SBA Papers.

65. ECS to Wendell Phillips, May 25, 1865; ibid., December 26, 1865, in Stanton and Blatch, 2: 104–5, 109–10.

66. *Woman's Journal*, February 5, 1898; Gordon, 2: 426.

67. ECS to Edwin Studwell, November 30, 1867, ECS-SBA Papers; *The Revolution*, August 6, 1868.

68. Gordon, 2: 338; Hendrik Hartog, "Lawyering, Husband's Rights, and the Unwritten Law in Nineteenth-Century America," *Journal of American History* 84 (June 1997): 67–96.

69. Gordon, 2: 337, 442; *The Revolution*, August 8, 1868.

70. Gordon, 2: 452; Victoria Woodhull, "The Principles of Social Freedom," in Madeline Stern, *The Victoria Woodhull Reader* (Weston, Mass.: M&S Press, 1974), 15–17.

71. Woodhull, "Secession Speech, 1871," *Woodhull and Claflin's Weekly*, May 27, 1871; Emanie Sachs, *The Terrible Siren: Victoria Woodhull* (New York: Harpers, 1928); Barbara Goldsmith, *Other Powers: The Age of Suffrage, Spiritualism, and the Scandalous Victoria Woodhull* (New York: Knopf, 1998), 272–75; Amanda Frisken, *Victoria Woodhull's Sexual Revolution* (Philadelphia: University of Pennsylvania Press, 2004), 85–111.

72. Ida Harper, *Life and Work of Susan B. Anthony* (North Stratford, N.H.: Ayer Publishing, 1998), 1: 413–14.

73. Susan B. Anthony to Isabella Beecher Hooker, November 16, 1872, ECS-SBA Papers; Richard Fox, *Trials of Intimacy: Love and Loss in the Beecher-Tilton Scandal* (Chicago: University of Chicago, 1999).

74. Goldsmith, 261, 338.

75. *Chicago Tribune*, July 23, August 1, 1874.

76. Lutz, *Challenging Years*, 214: ECS to Isabella Beecher Hooker, November 19, 1872, Griffith, 23–24; Lutz, *Created Equal*, 16–17, 21–23; ECS to Harriot (Stanton Blatch), October 1, 1889, ECS-SBA Papers.

77. *Eighty Years*, 25; ECS to Henry Blackwell, April 27, 1870, Blackwell Family Papers.

78. Gordon, 1: 104.

79. Elizabeth Cady Stanton to Elizabeth Smith Miller, September 9, 1888, ECS-SBA Papers; *Eighty Years*, 419.

80. ECS to Elizabeth Miller, June 30, 1888, ECS-SBA Papers; Stanton and Blatch, 2: 236–37.

81. ECS, *The Woman's Bible* (Boston: Northeastern Press, 1993), 1: 11; Griffith, 210–13; Harper, 2: 845–47.

82. ECS to William Lloyd Garrison, Jr., January 6, 1896; Mary Livermore to ECS, September 1, 1886, ECS-SBA Papers; introduction to *The Woman's Bible*, vii.

83. Ibid., 104, 114, 210; ECS to Harriot, April 17, 1880, ECS-SBA Papers; Mary Pellauer, *Toward a Tradition of Feminist Theology: The Religious and Social Thought of Elizabeth Cady Stanton, Susan B. Anthony, and Anna Howard Shaw* (Brooklyn: Carlson Publishing, 1991), 38, 44; ECS to Mrs. Underwood, March 1889, ECS-SBA Papers.

84. ECS to Elizabeth Smith Miller, March 5, 1887, ECS-SBA Papers; for a modern reading of Cady Stanton's point, see Jack Miles, *Christ: A Crisis in the Life of God* (New York: Knopf, 2001). Stanton, *The Bible and the Church Degrade Women* (Chicago: H. L. Green, 1892).

85. Diary, December 24, 1897, in Stanton and Blatch, 1: 329.

86. Kern, *Mrs. Stanton's Bible*, 173, 189, 213–14; ECS to Clara Colby, January 24, 25, 1896, Colby Papers, State Historical Society of Wisconsin.

87. *New Era*, March 17, 1895; ECS to Theodore Stanton, September, 4, 1895, ECS-SBA Papers.

88. ECS to Mr. Roosevelt, October 22, 1902; ibid., to Kermit Roosevelt, Harriot Blatch to Helen Gardner, n.d., ECS-SBA Papers; Griffith, 216–18; *The Independent*, November 5, 1902; diary entries for October 1902 in Stanton and Blatch, 2: 368–69.

89. Moncure Conway, "Address at ECS Funeral," ECS Papers; miscellaneous material and clippings in Reel 5; *The New York Times*, October 27, 1902; Harper, 3: 1262–64. There was no public mention of her cremation—a radical decision in this period—save in Susan B. Anthony's comments to the press.

4. Mothering America: The Feminist Ambitions of Frances Willard

1. Frances Willard, *Glimpses of Fifty Years* (Chicago: Temperance Publishing Association, 1892), 1–2.
2. Frances Willard, *A Great Mother: Sketches of Madame Willard* (Chicago: Woman's Temperance Association, 1894), 23.
3. Ibid., 31, 101.
4. Anna Gordon, *The Life of Frances E. Willard* (Evanston, Ill.: National Christian Temperance Union, 1921), 180.
5. *Glimpses*, 10; Willard, *A Great Mother*, 136–37.
6. Ibid., 56.
7. A. Gregory Schneider, *The Way of the Cross Leads Home: The Domestication of American Methodism* (Bloomington: Indiana University Press, 1993).
8. *Glimpses*, 25.
9. Amy Rose Slagell, "A Good Woman Speaking Well: The Oratory of Frances Willard," Ph.D. diss. (University of Wisconsin-Madison, 1992), 612; *Glimpses*, 688.
10. Ruth Bordin, *Frances Willard: A Biography* (Chapel Hill: University of North Carolina Press, 1986), 16; Willard, *A Great Mother*.
11. Frances Willard, *How to Win: A Book for Girls* (New York: Funk and Wagnalls, 1886), 16; *Glimpses*, 125.
12. *Glimpses*, 69.
13. Ibid., 81; *Writing Out My Heart*, Carolyn Gifford, ed. (Urbana: University of Illinois Press, 1995), 29.
14. In a complicated set of changes after the North Western Female College was founded in 1855, it was later absorbed into the Evanston College for Ladies, which opened in 1871. Northwestern University had been chartered in 1851 as a Methodist institution for men.
15. *Glimpses*, 133; *Writing Out My Heart*, 194.
16. Ibid., 45–46, 105.
17. *Glimpses*, 687–88.
18. Slagell, "A Good Woman Speaking Well," 89–94; *Writing Out My Heart*, 45.
19. Ibid., 47, 81.
20. Ibid., 33, 53–55.
21. Ibid., 59, 85–86, 97, 134.
22. Ibid., 136, 153.
23. Ibid., 128, 146, 157.
24. *Glimpses*, 149–50; *Writing Out My Heart*, 93. There has been speculation that Willard was attracted to Delavan Scoville, a mathematics teacher at the Genesee Weslyan College. But her most intense affection was to Kate Jackson during this period.
25. *Writing Out My Heart*, 380.
26. *Glimpses*, 54; Margaret Fuller, *Woman in the Nineteenth Century* (New York: Oxford University Press, 1994), 20.
27. *Writing Out My Heart*, 185, 261.
28. Ibid., 249.
29. Ibid., 230, 386.

30. Ibid., 185, 194, 261.
31. *How to Win*, 18; *Writing Out My Heart*, 40, 130, 266.
32. Ibid., 309.
33. The text of "The New Chivalry" is in Slagell, 128–43.
34. *Glimpses*, 206.
35. Mary Earhart, *Frances Willard: From Prayers to Politics* (Chicago: University of Chicago Press, 1944), 118; *Chicago Tribune*, November 25–27, 1873.
36. *Glimpses*, 239.
37. Ibid., 347.
38. W. J. Rorabaugh, *The Alcoholic Republic: An American Tradition* (New York: Oxford University Press, 1979).
39. Samuel Unger, "A History of the National Woman's Christian Temperance Union," Ph.D. diss. (Ohio State University, 1933).
40. Elizabeth Cady Stanton, Susan B. Anthony, et al., *History of Woman Suffrage* (Rochester, N.Y.: Charles Mann, 1889), 1: 476–82, esp. 482.
41. Susan Lee, "Evangelical Domesticity: The Origins of the Woman's National Christian Temperance Union Under Frances Willard," Ph.D. diss. (Northwestern University, 1980), 85.
42. Gifford, 231.
43. Slagell, 110–17.
44. Mrs. Annie Wittenmyer, *History of Woman's Temperance Crusade* (Philadelphia: Office of Christian Women, 1878), 10–16.
45. *Writing Out My Heart*, 339–40.
46. Frances Willard, *Woman and Temperance* (Chicago: Woman's Temperance Publishing Association, 1897), 133.
47. *Glimpses*, 342.
48. Minutes of the 1889 WCTU National Convention, Presidential Address, 163, Reel 3; Minutes of the WCTU National Convention, 1890, Reel 11 in microfilm edition of Prohibition and Temperance Papers, Series III.
49. *Glimpses*, 342.
50. Willard to Wittenmyer, December 12, 1874, Reel 11.
51. Membership figures are notably illusive for the WCTU, which sometimes included in its total membership young members of its junior auxiliaries and inflated its membership beyond its paid members. With over ten thousand local organizations the tabulation was difficult. Willard in *Glimpses* claimed in 1888 a half million members but the paid up membership was 138,527. See Unger, 49.
52. Slagell, 190–91.
53. *Glimpses*, 352.
54. Slagell, 223–26.
55. Christine Bolt, *Sisterhood Questioned* (London: Routledge, 2003).
56. Minutes of the 1881 WCTU Convention, Reel 3.
57. Minutes of the 1890 WCTU Convention, Reel 3.
58. Bordin, 129–31, 146.
59. WCTU members were more likely to be single than the general population, and also more likely to have attended college. See Janet Giele, *Two Paths to Women's*

Equality: Temperance, Suffrage and the Origins of Modern Feminism (New York: Twayne, 1995).

60. *The Selected Papers of Susan B. Anthony and Elizabeth Cady Stanton*, Ann Gordon, ed. (New Brunswick, N.J.: Rutgers University Press, 2003), 3: 474.

61. Bordin, 223; Gordon, 3: 261–62.

62. Minutes, 1881.

63. Frances Willard, *Woman and Temperance*, 632–37.

64. *A Great Mother*, 101.

65. Slagell, 418.

66. Ibid., 30–31.

67. *The New York Times*, April 29, 1888; Minutes of the 1889 WCTU Convention; Frances Willard, *Woman in the Pulpit* (Chicago: WCTU Association, 1897); Bordin, 116, 165.

68. Bordin, 216–17.

69. Anna Garlin Spencer, *The Council Idea* (New Brunswick, N.J.: J. Heidingsfeld, 1930); Mary Wright Sewall, *Genesis of the International Council of Women* (1914); *Report of the International Council of Women* (Washington: Rufus Darby, 1888), 2–3, 450–51.

70. *Pandita Ramabai's American Encounter* (Bloomington: University of Indiana Press, 2003), 36, 40, 246–47.

71. Willard, *How to Win*; *Report of the Council*, 450; *Glimpses*, 467.

72. Minutes of WCTU Convention 1886, 1888, Reel 11; David Pivar, *Purity Crusade: Sexual Purity and Social Control, 1868–1900* (Westport, Conn.: Greenwood Press, 1973), 141–42.

73. Slagell, 357; Report of the WCTU, Presidential Address, 1891, Reel 3.

74. Presidential Address, Minutes of the 1891 WCTU Convention, 93; Slagell, 555.

75. Quoted in Bordin, 183.

76. Willard to Henry Demarest Lloyd, October 22, 1891, quoted in Mary Earhart, *Frances Willard*, 228; Minutes of the WCTU Convention, Reel 3, 71.

77. *A Great Mother*, 61, 122.

78. Ibid., 31, 102.

79. *Writing Out My Heart*, 363, 426–27.

80. Willard, *How to Win*, 72; *A Wheel Within a Wheel or How I Learned to Ride a Bicycle* (New York: F. H. Berrell, 1895).

81. *Writing Out My Heart*, 426–27.

82. *Chicago Record-Herald*, February 19, 1898, in Earhart, 372.

83. Ibid., 1.

5. Endgame: Alice Paul and Woodrow Wilson

1. Official Program of the Woman Suffrage Procession, Box 16, Alice Paul Papers, Schlesinger Library, Radcliffe College, Cambridge, Mass. Hereafter cited as Paul Papers.

2. Inez Haynes Irwin, *The Story of the Woman's Party* (New York: Harcourt Brace, 1921), 30.

3. *Washington Evening Star*, February 12, 1913.

4. *Violence in America; Interference with the Suffrage Procession 63rd Congress, 1st Session*, Special Session of the Senate, Document 1, 1914 (New York: Arno Press, 1971), 537; *McClure's Magazine* (August 1912), 20.

5. *The Papers of Woodrow Wilson*, ed. Arthur Link, et al. (Princeton, N.J.: Princeton University Press, 1978), 27:150–51; hereafter cited as PWW.

6. Alice Paul to Harriet Taylor Upton, June 14, 1914, National Woman's Party (NWP) Papers, microfilm edition, LC; hereafter NWP Papers.

7. *PWW*, 9: 448; 5: 707–9; 4: 316–18; 6: 31; 18: 3–4.

8. Jane Matthews, *The Rise of the New Woman: The Women's Movement in America, 1875–1930* (Chicago: Ivan Dee, 2003), 12.

9. Shaw, the designated successor to Susan B. Anthony, became president of NAWSA in 1892. Catt replaced her from 1900 to 1904. She retired entirely in 1915, when Catt took over again until in 1921 NAWSA became the League of Women Voters.

10. *The History of Woman Suffrage*, Ida Harper, ed. (New York: J. R. Little, 1922), 5: 339. Bettina Friedl, *On to Victory: Propaganda Plays of the Women's Suffrage Movement* (Boston: Northeastern Press, 1987), 370.

11. Mary Wilson Thompson to Wilson, July 30, 1916, PWW, 37: 502–3.

12. Alice Paul, "Woman Suffrage and the Equal Rights Amendment," 1976 interview by Amelia Fry, Bancroft Library Suffragists Oral History Project, University of California at Berkeley, hereafter cited as Paul Interview.

13. Anne Herendon, "What Her Home Town Thinks of Alice Paul," *Everybody's Magazine* 41 (October 1919), 362.

14. Alice Paul, Swarthmore Journal, Box 1, Paul Papers.

15. Paul Interview.

16. Ibid.

17. Alice Paul to Dear Mamma, December 12, 1908, Box 2, Paul Papers; Paul Interview.

18. *Illustrated London News*, May 9, 1908.

19. Alice Paul to Dear Mamma, March 17, 1908, January 14, 1909, Box 2 and undated Box 2, Paul Papers.

20. Ibid., Box 16.

21. Ibid., December 1909; November 10, 1909.

22. Ibid., December 27, 1909, Box 2.

23. *History of Woman Suffrage*, 5: 280–81; Linda Ford, *Iron-Jawed Angels: The Suffrage Militancy of the National Woman's Party* (Lanham, Md.: University Press of America, 1991), 5.

24. *PWW*, 3: 494; 29: 372; 5: 605, 619.

25. John Milton Cooper, *The Warrior and the Priest* (Boston: Harvard University Press, 1983), 373, n. 21; Helen Horowitz, *The Power and Passion of M. Carey Thomas* (New York: Knopf, 1994), 195, 242; *PWW*, 5, 605.

26. *PWW*, 3: 389; 4: 316–18.

27. Ibid., 6: 646.

28. Daniel Stid, *The President as Statesman: Woodrow Wilson and the Constitution* (Lawrence: Kansas University Press, 1998).

29. *PWW*, 3: 494.

30. *PWW*, 18: 410.

31. Frances Saunders, "Love and Guilt: Woodrow Wilson and Mary Hulbert," *American Heritage* (April/May 1979), 71–80.

32. *PWW*, 28: 44–47.

33. *PWW*, 28: 14, 87; Saunders, "Love and Guilt."

34. *PWW*, 34: 496, 497, 506–7.

35. *New York Tribune*, April 29, 1913. "Margaret Wilson Out for Suffrage," Woodrow Wilson Material, Goucher College Archives, Towson, Md.; Ida Husted Harper, *The Life and Work of Susan B. Anthony* (Indianapolis: Hollenbach, 1908), 3: 1389–96; *PWW*, 35: 360.

36. *PWW*, 34: 176–79.

37. *PWW*, 4: 316.

38. David Lawrence, *The True Story of Woodrow Wilson* (New York: Doran, 1924), 135.

39. Irwin, 14, 15.

40. Woodrow Wilson, *The New Freedom* (New York: Doubleday, 1913), 3–4; Irwin, 33; Paul Interview; *HWS*, 5: 375.

41. Irwin, 57–65; Doris Stevens, *Jailed for Freedom: Women Win the Vote* (New York: Boni and Liveright, 1920), 33–45.

42. *HWS*, 5: 375–76; *PWW*, 29: 20–22.

43. *PWW*, 30: 226–28; *The New York Times*, July 1, 1914.

44. Margaret Finnegan, *Selling Suffrage: Consumer Culture and Votes for Women* (New York: Columbia University Press, 1999), 1–13, and passim.

45. Doris Stevens, *Jailed for Freedom*, 10–11.

46. Alice Paul to Elsie Hill, March 10, 1914, Reel 8, NWP Papers; Mabel Vernon, Speaker for Suffrage and Petitioner for Peace, Suffragists Oral History, Berkeley.

47. Alice Paul to Lucy Burns, May 17, 1915, Reel 16; comment on advisory committee, Report of Advisory Committee, Reel 87, NWP Papers.

48. Robert Booth Fowler and Spencer Jones, "Carrie Catt and the Winning Plan," in *Votes for Women*, Jean Baker, ed. (New York: Oxford University Press, 2002), 130–43; Catt to Paul, April 12, 15, 1912, Paul Papers; Catt to Jane Addams, January 4, 1914, Carrie Chapman Catt Papers, Sterling Library, Yale University, New Haven, Conn.

49. *PWW*, 35: 28; 37: 49.

50. Ibid.

51. Ibid., 27: 290–92; 28: 265.

52. Alice Paul to Miss Blackwell, January 15, 1913, Reel 1, NWP Papers.

53. Christine Lunardini, *From Equal Suffrage to Equal Rights* (New York: New York University Press, 1986), 161–62; Freda Kirchwey, "Alice Paul Pulls the Strings," *Nation*, March 2, 1923, 323; Inez Robinson to Alice Paul, February 2, 1917, NWP Papers; Nancy Cott, *The Grounding of Modern Feminism* (New Haven,

Conn.: Yale University Press, 1987), 68–71. Also W.E.B. Du Bois to Paul, March 1913, Reel 3, NWP Papers; *PWW*, 27: 290–92; 28: 265; Paul Interview.

54. Paul to Miss Eunice Oberly, March 6, 1914, Reel 8, NWP Papers; Irwin, 174.
55. Harriot Stanton Blatch, *Challenging Years* (New York: Putnam's, 1940), 268.
56. *PWW*, 38: 161–67; 37: 491.
57. Using an equality mark—that is the number needed to receive a majority of the vote, which would be 25 percent in the 1912 election and 50 percent in 1916— Wilson was 38 percent above equality in 1912 and 10 percent below it in 1916. Of course this assumes a projected equality for the progressives of Theodore Roosevelt, the Republicans of Taft, along with the Socialist and Prohibition Parties. Irwin, 166–83.
58. Linda Lumsden, *Rampant Women: Suffragists and the Right of Assembly* (Knoxville: University of Tennessee, 1997), 114–15.
59. *PWW*, 41: 526–27.
60. For descriptions of June 20 picketing, Irwin, 208–64.
61. Irwin, 210; *The New York Times*, June 22, 1917; Ford, 163.
62. *The New York Times*, July 18, August 13, 1917; Irwin, 239–42; *PWW*; 43: 201–2.
63. Doris Stevens Interview, Berkeley Oral History Project.
64. Ibid.
65. Dorothy Day, *The Long Loneliness: The Autobiography of Dorothy Day* (New York: Harper & Row, 1952), 73; Affidavits of NWP members, Reels 52 and 53, NWP Papers; Stevens, 192.
66. Form Letter, November 20, NWP Papers, Reel 52, Case File 89, *PWW*. None of this material that is available in the microfilm edition of the Wilson papers appears in the sixty-nine-volume edition edited by Arthur Link. And it is still possible to write studies of Wilson's presidency that hardly mention suffrage. See John Thompson, *Woodrow Wilson: Profiles in Power* (New York: Longman's, 2002) for the persistent invisibility of the suffrage issue during Wilson's presidency. Also *The New York Times*, November 9, 1917.
67. *PWW*, 43: 205.
68. *PWW*, 43: 201, 207; Lumsden, 236–37, 132–34.
69. Warden Zinkham to Judge Alexander Mullowney, November 27, 1917, in NWP Papers. *PWW*, 43: 202; for Commissioner Gardiner's report, see Gardiner to Wilson, November 9, 1917, *PWW*, 44: 559–61; Wilson to Tumulty, November 13, 45: 40. Louis Brownlow, *A Passion for Anonymity: The Autobiography of Louis Brownlow, Second Half* (Chicago: University of Chicago Press, 1958), 78–79; *The New York Times*, November 7, 1917.
70. Paul to Anne Martin, November 27, 1917, Reel 52, NWP Papers.
71. *PWW*, 43: 476–77.
72. *PWW*, 43: 284–85; 44: 372, 391. Maude Park to Helen Gardiner, November 24, 1917, *PWW*, 45:121.
73. Katherine Houghton Hepburn to the executive board of CWSA, September 19, 1917; copy in NWP Papers.
74. *PWW*, 45: 536.
75. *PWW*, 46: 80; *The New York Times*, January 10, 1918.

76. *PWW*, 51:158–61, 46: 79, 48: 271.
77. Irwin, 370.
78. *PWW*, 51: 158–61; Irwin, 370.
79. *PWW*, 61: 435–37, 63: 379–80, 45: 536; July 10, 1919, address.
80. Lunardini, 155.
81. Ford, 257.
82. *The New York Times*, August 13, 2003; for material on the ceremony, Reel 85, NWP Papers. In 1997 a new generation of political women persuaded Congress to move it to the more public rotunda.
83. *The Suffragist*, January–February 1921, 339.
84. Ibid.; Convention of the National Woman's Party, February 15–20, 1921, Group 11, National Woman's Party Papers, LC.
85. *The Suffragist*, January–February 1921; Group 2, National Woman's Party Papers, LC.
86. *Equal Rights* 27 (April 1941).
87. Convention, February 1921, NWP Papers; Joan Hoff, *Law, Gender and Injustice: A Legal History of U.S. Women* (New York: New York University Press, 1991).
88. Susan D. Becker, *The Origin of the Equal Rights Amendment* (Westport, Conn.: Greenwood Press, 1981), 279.

Index

"Solitude of Self, The," 236
statue of, 4, 181, 226
Stone and, 34, 35, 52, 208
temperance movement and, 157
Tenafly home of, 120
Willard and, 154, 174, 237
Women's Loyal National League and,
32, 69, 87, 123
writing talents, 116–18
Stanton, Gerrit Smith (son), 105, 119
Stanton, Henry Brewster (husband),
99–105, 111, 130–31, 235
as abolitionist, 99–100, 101, 103–105
career of, 105, 111, 120, 123–24
death of, 131
as father, 105, 111
women's rights and, 101, 104, 115,
116, 236
Stanton, Henry Brewster (son), 105,
118, 119
Stanton, Robert (son), 107, 108, 119,
120
Stanton, Theodore Weld (son), 105,
108, 111, 119, 133, 134
Starr, Ellen, 76
state legislatures, 29, 45, 49, 189
ratification of Nineteenth Amendment and, 11, 22, 223–24
social purity movement and, 176
state power over voting rights, 41–42,
189, 234
limited suffrage, states granting, 9, 44
Minor v. Happersett, 7–8, 85
NAWSA and, 189
referendums, *see* referendums, on
suffrage for women
Willard and temperance movement
and, 165
Wilson's views on, 206, 222
Stevens, Doris, 207
Stone, Francis (father), 14–17, 24, 233
Stone, Hannah (mother), 14–15, 18, 232
Stone, Lucy, 4, 13–53, 174, 187, 236,
239

Anthony and, *see* Anthony, Susan B.,
Stone and
antislavery movement and, 13–14, 233
appearance of, 16, 28, 39–40
AWSA and, 8, 38, 42–43, 49, 50, 53,
71, 231, 233
Blackwell and, *see* Blackwell, Henry,
Stone and
Boston home, 39, 40
childhood of, 14–16, 232
death of, 4, 51–52, 189
dress reform and, 21, 56
education of, 16–17, 232
health of, 18, 25, 30, 45, 48, 49
as lecturer, 13, 19, 20, 21, 28–29, 30,
31, 233
marriage, attitude toward, 14, 20, 65,
102, 233
as martyr, 13, 18, 20, 36, 37, 39, 50
as mother, 29–32, 40, 65, 110
patience of, 44–45
pessimism of, 18–19
sex, attitude toward, 21–22, 24, 31,
35, 41, 233
Stanton and, *see* Stanton, Elizabeth
Cady, Stone and
Willard and, 152
Woman's Journal and, 8, 38, 39,
40, 46
women's suffrage and, 10, 33–53
Stone, Luther (brother), 24
Stone, Rhoda (sister), 14
Stone, Sarah (sister), 14, 15, 16, 19, 47
Stone, William Bowman (brother), 24
Stone Blackwell, Alice (daughter of
Lucy and Henry), 10, 40, 46, 47,
52, 110, 234
Anthony and, 43
appearance of, 40
childhood of, 30, 31, 34, 39, 40, 44
education of, 40–41
merger of AWSA and NAWSA and,
43, 50–51, 80
NAWSA and, 50–51, 53, 134